# MODERNIST FICTION

# MODERNIST FICTION
## *Revised Edition*

### RANDALL STEVENSON
*University of Edinburgh*

An imprint of **Pearson Education**

Harlow, England · London · New York · Reading, Massachusetts · San Francisco
Toronto · Don Mills, Ontario · Sydney · Tokyo · Singapore · Hong Kong · Seoul
Taipei · Cape Town · Madrid · Mexico City · Amsterdam · Munich · Paris · Milan

**Pearson Education Limited**
Edinburgh Gate,
Harlow,
Essex CM20 2JE
England

and Associated Companies throughout the world

*Visit us on the World Wide Web at;*
www.pearsoned.co.uk

First published 1992 by
Harvester Wheatsheaf
This revised edition published 1998 by
Prentice Hall

Typeset in 10/12pt Times
by Dorwyn Ltd, Rowlands Castle, Hants

Produced by Pearson Education Asia Pte Ltd
Printed in Singapore (MPM)

---

Library of Congress Cataloging-in-Publication Data

Stevenson, Randall.
    Modernist fiction / Randall Stevenson. — Rev. ed.
       p.  cm.
    Includes bibliographical references and index.
    ISBN 0–13–837659–X (pbk. : alk. paper)
    1. English fiction—20th century—History and criticism.
    2. Modernism (Literature)—Great Britain.  I. Title.
    PR888.M63S74   1997
    823'.91209112—dc21                  97–27972
                                              CIP

---

British Library Cataloguing in Publication Data

A catalogue record for this book is available from
the British Library

ISBN 0-13-837659-X (pbk)

10  9  8  7  6  5
06  05  04

# CONTENTS

For
Sarah, Andrew, Matthew and Anna

# PREFACE

In a pioneering analysis of modernist fiction published in 1966, *The Turn of the Novel*, Alan Friedman remarks

> The roots of the change in the novel lie tangled deep in the modern experience. Causes in fields other than literature there doubtless were – a confluence of psychological, philosophical, scientific, social, economic, and political causes, analogues, and explanations . . . I think it is probably too soon to evaluate that confluence properly. (pp. xii–xiii)

As Chapter 1 suggests, it may be more appropriate to consider some of the factors Friedman mentions as 'analogues and explanations' for the change in modernist literature, rather than directly *causes* of it. Nevertheless, three decades after his work was published, it is no longer premature to examine modernist fiction in terms of the 'confluence' he outlines. The present age is as distant from *Ulysses* (1922) as *Ulysses* itself was from the fiction of Charles Dickens. In looking back at modernism, it should now be possible to establish the perspective Friedman considered unavailable when he wrote – to place in the context of the twentieth century's history writing which continues to seem its major achievement and a central influence on its literature.

Moreover, some of the tools of literary criticism – of narrative theory particularly – have developed considerably since Friedman wrote. The availability in translation of the ideas of the Soviet theorist Mikhail Bakhtin, and of the narrative analysis of Gérard Genette, assists assessment of how the style and structure of the novel changed early in the twentieth century. *Why* it did so – the other question of principal interest to the present study – is clarified by the criticism of the United States Marxist, Fredric Jameson, as well as by the wide-ranging cultural history Stephen Kern provides in *The Culture of Time and Space 1880–1918* (1983).

While recent critics and theorists have much to offer analysis of modernism, so too do commentators writing from within the modernist period itself. A lengthening historical perspective may offer objectivity: on the other hand, distance may simply make some things harder to see clearly. Proximity contributes useful and occasionally surprising perspectives to the views of contemporary critics. One of the most surprising of them, R.A. Scott-James (further discussed in Chapter 1), emphasizes as follows the particular advantage of their work:

> Is it not a mockery of modesty to assert that we have less right to judge our own contemporaries, being as we are bone of their bone and flesh of their flesh, than a diffident posterity? For the writers of our time are influenced by the prevalent thoughts and feelings which move us, so that though we know nothing of their value for posterity we have the best means of knowing their value for ourselves. (*Modernism and Romance*, p. xi)

As Scott-James remarks, contemporary critics are sometimes in a better position than later ones to recognize what is valuable, new, or unusual in the writing of their age, and to judge how far this is likely to have been affected by 'prevalent thoughts and feelings' which may later be forgotten, or difficult to identify with so much certainty. Throughout, this study often relies on contemporary commentary for this sort of suggestion. Chapter 3 turns in particular to Wyndham Lewis, whose huge volumes assessing the state of contemporary culture make him one of the most substantial, and neglected, of commentators on the 1920s.

Assessed in relation to critics of the time and since, and to a range of roots and analogues in contemporary experience, modernist fiction offers a field too wide to be examined in its entirety in a single volume. Though making an exception of Marcel Proust (for reasons explained in Chapter 1), this study confines itself to fiction written in English, and within this context looks only briefly, where appropriate, at modernist writing in the United States. Though it might seem simplest to state that the focus is therefore on 'British fiction', it would be misleading, even dishonest, to do so. The authors concerned – principally Henry James, Ford Madox Ford, Joseph Conrad, Dorothy Richardson, May Sinclair, D.H. Lawrence, James Joyce, Wyndham Lewis and Virginia Woolf – could be said to belong loosely to a British context, since they each began or spent part of their working lives within it. Yet by no means all of them could be said to be British by nationality. As Chapter 4 explains, complex conditions of national or cultural identity often formed part of the background – even a likely source – for the modernist disposition of their work.

Wherever possible, references to this work are to currently available paperback editions, which are listed in the Select Bibliography. This also contains details of other volumes referred to. Where necessary, further information about the source of quotations is given in footnotes: rarely containing more than publishing details, these need not distract readers from the text. Since a feature of modernist fiction, in the work of Ford Madox Ford and Dorothy Richardson particularly, is its frequent use of a set of dots to represent pauses in characters' thoughts, a convention is required to distinguish such pauses from ellipses indicating omissions in the course of a quotation. Throughout, three narrowly spaced dots (...) reproduce authors' own usage, while three widely spaced ones (. . .) indicate that words or sections have been omitted from a quotation.

Even confined loosely within the British context, modernist fiction and the modern experience provide an exciting but wide and challenging field of study, and I am very grateful for help received in writing about it. Tony Seward and Jackie Jones were patient, encouraging editors of the first edition, the latter instrumental in seeing it through to publication with Harvester Wheatsheaf. I'm also grateful to Christina Wipf Perry of Prentice Hall for suggesting and looking after this second, revised edition, which allows the expansion and updating of several sections of the argument, and the correction of some small errors and omissions which appeared in the first. Ideas and methods of analysis have often been borrowed from friends, or worked out in discussion with them: Brian McHale, Colin Nicholson, Susanne Greenhalgh, John Cartmell, Jane Goldman, John Orr and Roger Savage have all helped in this way. I have also learned a great deal about the material concerned when delivering lectures on it to the Scottish Universities' International Summer School, and in the course of discussion with many groups of students in Edinburgh University's Department of English Literature. My main debt is to those who read, talked over and added their ideas to various chapters in the process of their completion: to Ron Butlin, Sarah Carpenter, Vassiliki Kolocotroni and Olga Taxidou, many many thanks.

# ── *1* ──

# MODERNISM

## AND

# MODERNITY

Just as authority has been undermined in religion and morals, so too in art. The old accepted standards cannot satisfy a changing age . . .

The old fixed canons of taste have lost their validity . . . the novelist ignores the earlier conventions of plot . . . vocabulary, literary structure, and orthodoxy of opinion . . .

When we come to some of the essentially modern novelists we feel that the psychological tendency has gone . . . as far indeed as it can go . . .

The spirit of psychological analysis . . . this is 'modernism' with a vengeance.

(pp. 22–3, 92, 109, 266)

R.A. Scott-James's views in his study *Modernism and Romance* are typical of comments on new, modern or 'modernist' tendencies in contemporary literature which were made in the 1920s. One of several studies of fiction published at that time, Elizabeth Drew's *The Modern Novel: Some Aspects of Contemporary Fiction* (1926), for example, likewise remarks that

the great majority of the present generation of novelists . . . have made psychology, conscious and deliberate psychology, their engrossing interest, and it is natural that such an interest should entail their finding the older technique too clumsy for their new purposes. (p. 248)

Many later critics have followed the kind of thinking outlined by Drew and Scott-James. What has come to be known as modernist fiction – at its strongest in novels published in the 1920s by James Joyce, Virginia Woolf, and D.H. Lawrence – is usually defined on the grounds of its rejection of techniques and conventions apparently inappropriate or 'too clumsy' for new interests at the time. A principal part of these new interests is usually held to have been in the 'psychology' – or heightened concern with individual, subjective consciousness – which Drew and Scott-James identify. The present study traces this interest, and examines the stream-of-consciousness and interior monologue styles developed to reflect it, throughout Chapter 2.

Given how representative of critical thinking in the 1920s and since Scott-James's comments are, one of the most interesting things about them is that they were made as early as 1908, at a time when it is unusual to find the word 'modernism' applied to literature at all. For any study of writing in the early twentieth century, there is a good deal to be learned not only from Scott-James's remarks themselves but from the surprisingly early date of their publication. First, his views emphasize that the disposition for change and transformation in the novel, so obvious to commentators by the 1920s, actually originated much earlier than Joyce's *Ulysses* (1922) and the other modernist fiction of that decade. The roots of transformation in modernist writing need to be considered as reaching back at least to the fiction of Henry James – one of the novelists Scott-James refers to when he talks of 'the spirit of psychoanalysis' (p. 109) – and other authors, Joseph Conrad in particular, working around the turn of the century.

Secondly, Scott-James helps define a division of opinion apparent early in the twentieth century, and widening in the years that followed, about the relative merits of tradition and transformation in the art and life of the times. Scott-James may have used the term 'modernism' early, but he does not use it approvingly. In the passage quoted above he talks darkly of ' "modernism" with a vengeance', and throughout his study the term is most often used in relation to transformations in his age which he considers neither welcome nor worthwhile. He remarks, for example, that

> there are characteristics of modern life in general which can only be summed up, as Mr Thomas Hardy and others have summed them up, by the word *modernism*. The hybrid may not be very pleasant to delicate ears, but perhaps what it expresses is not a very pleasant thing. (p. ix)

Scott-James's views of the indelicacy of the term 'modernism', and of what it signifies, are corroborated by the *Oxford English Dictionary*. This shows that at least until the early twentieth century, 'modernism' was most often used to designate fashionable new-fangledness, the sort of innovation which betrayed the solider values of tradition. Even the terms 'modern' and 'modernity' were certainly not consistently ones of approval.[1] By contrast, among the generation of writers and artists coming into prominence after Scott-James wrote, it was more and more often tradition rather than innovation which was viewed with suspicion. 'Modernism' and 'modernist' are therefore terms appropriately applied – even if they may sound 'hybrid' – to the work of writers sharing the belief that a modernizing of forms and the reshaping or abandonment of tradition were necessary conditions of their art. This belief distinguishes the group of novelists to be assessed in this study from the many others who went on writing, throughout the early decades of the twentieth century, more or less within styles and conventions established in the latter part of the nineteenth.

Arnold Bennett, John Galsworthy and H.G. Wells are the examples of this traditional sort of novelist whom Virginia Woolf singles out for criticism in essays which usefully clarify the new preferences of her time – 'Modern Fiction' (1919) and 'Mr. Bennett and Mrs. Brown' (1924). The 'modern' of her first essay's title is certainly not a term of disapproval, but one which helps define writing able to generate new styles to accommodate the priorities of a new age. For Woolf, the work of Bennett, Wells and Galsworthy – 'the most prominent and successful novelists in the year 1910', as she calls them – remained restricted by limited vision and outmoded fictional conventions. In her opinion, it was essential to recognize instead that 'the proper stuff of fiction is a little other than custom would have us believe it', and to follow the new example of 'young writers' such as James Joyce.[2] Even a few years after she wrote, it was clear that in some areas Woolf's wishes had been thoroughly fulfilled. By the mid-1920s, the example not only of Joyce but of novelists such as D.H. Lawrence, Dorothy Richardson, May Sinclair and Woolf herself, had made 'the stuff of fiction' substantially different from what it had been twenty or thirty years earlier, in ways impossible for commentators at the time to overlook. Thomas Hardy, for example, one of the last successful Victorian novelists, summed up the 'modernism' he saw in contemporary fiction in 1926 by remarking – simply if rather wearily – 'They've changed everything now . . . we used to think there was a beginning and a middle and an end'.[3] By emphasizing amendment of conventional fiction's chronological construction, Hardy incidentally indicates another area of modernist initiative in changing the form of the novel. This phase of innovation is further discussed in Chapter 3.

A third aspect of Scott-James's significance, however, is the element of reservation or qualification his views introduce into some of the distinctions just outlined. Woolf and other modernists acted on their belief in the need for change, and looked back disparagingly on authors such as Arnold Bennett who seemed to them too content with convention. Yet Scott-James suggests that such a complacent generation may never have existed. Though he hardly approved of the consequences, he indicates that long before Joyce and Woolf began publishing, 'the old fixed canons of taste' had 'lost their validity' and that it was not unusual to find a novelist who 'ignores the earlier conventions'. Perhaps the stylistic and structural innovation characteristic of modernism's greatest achievements needs to be seen as less unique or daring than it has sometimes been considered. Virginia Woolf, after all, remarks at the start of 'Modern Fiction' that 'it is difficult not to take it for granted that the modern practice of the art is somehow an improvement upon the old', but she soon goes on to admit that

> In the course of the centuries . . . We do not come to write better; all that we can be said to do is to keep moving, now a little in this direction, now in that. (p. 103)

As Woolf suggests, an urge to 'keep moving' is not unique to modernism: neither an urge for novelty nor a commitment to change are altogether new in literature. It may be that the differences between modernism and earlier writing are best considered relative rather than absolute, quantitative rather than altogether qualitative. This is a possibility to be kept in mind throughout analysis of modernism's stylistic, structural and linguistic transformations in Chapters 2, 3 and 4. Departures from the serial, chronological construction of storytelling, for example – its usual beginning, middle and end – are by no means uniquely the invention of modernist fiction. Likewise, according to one contemporary critic, Wyndham Lewis in *Time and Western Man* (1927), even the stream-of-consciousness technique – often held to be the principal innovation and distinguishing achievement of modernist fiction – had first been practised long before, by Charles Dickens in *Pickwick Papers* (1837). There is better evidence, as Chapter 2 explains, that it was first used extensively in French fiction in the late nineteenth century.

Nevertheless, even if the stream of consciousness was not the wholly original invention of Dorothy Richardson or James Joyce, it had not been employed previously in English writing on the scale, or with the flexibility, which those authors had established for it by the mid-1920s. The evidence of Scott-James helps to avoid crediting modernism with an absolute originality it did not possess, yet the range and scale of changes the movement introduced, and the regularity and radicalism with which these were put into practice, remain quite sufficient to set apart and make distinctive a period in the literary history of the twentieth century. If not always totally new in kind, modernist innovation *was* spectacularly, inescapably new in extent. Thomas Hardy was by no means the only critic who recognized a contemporary urge not just for change, but to 'change everything'. Herbert Read, for example, remarks in *Art Now* (1933) that

> there have of course been revolutions in the history of art before today. There is a revolution with every new generation, and periodically, every century or so, we get a wider or a deeper change of sensibility to which we give the name of a period ... But I do think we can already discern a difference of kind in the contemporary revolution: it is not so much a revolution, which implies a turning-over, even a turning-back, but rather a break-up, a devolution, some would say a dissolution. Its character is catastrophic ...
>
> The aim of five centuries of European effort is openly abandoned. (pp. 58–9, 67)

As Read suggests, innovations in contemporary fiction were only one aspect of a radical change in the period's sensibility as a whole, apparent in ways confined neither to the novel genre nor to writing in Britain. Fiction by Marcel Proust or André Gide in French, or by Thomas Mann or Franz Kafka in German, shares many characteristics of new forms appearing in the novel in English. T.S. Eliot's *The Waste Land* (1922) marks an analogous revolution – or in F.R. Leavis's term, 'New Bearing' – in English poetry. Ezra Pound's determination to 'make it new' and his memorably simple demand 'I want a new civilisation'[4] are likewise reflected in his own poetry – in the Imagist movement he helped to foster around 1910 and eventually, most substantially, in the *Cantos* he began to publish in 1917.

Read's 'revolution in the history of art', and modernist dispositions like Pound's for a 'new civilisation', are at least as apparent in fields beyond contemporary literature as they are within it, affecting almost every genre of artistic enterprise throughout Europe and eventually the United States. Equally radical changes were introduced to the structural constitution of contemporary music. The conventional structuring of tones in Western composition, the diatonic scale, was replaced in 1908 by Arnold Schoenberg with a free a-tonality – a kind of creative anarchy of semi-tones – which he organized around 1920 into a new serial arrangement of twelve tones, interrelated independently of traditional systems. As one later commentator expresses it, such innovations 'undertook a radical dismantling of the established syntax of Western music'[5] – what Herbert Read would have called a 'break up . . . a dissolution' of conventions of construction developed over centuries of European artistic endeavour.

This kind of 'dissolution' is equally clear in contemporary European painting. As in modernist fiction, artists made changes not necessarily in their subject or theme, or in the nature of what was represented: but in the form and structure of the representation: the style and strategy of the art itself. Pablo Picasso's early Cubist painting *Les Demoiselles d'Avignon* (1906–7) still – more or less – represents human forms, though the means by which it does so are changed so radically that even this is not wholly convincing or clear. The unitary perspective of painting, the tradition of seeing things from a single point in space, is abandoned in Picasso's work in favour of an apparent multiplication of points of view which allows the presentation of opposite sides of a face together in the same picture. Fundamental changes of this kind in the conventions of art greatly astonished the British public when they appeared in the exhibition of Post-Impressionist painting organized by Roger Fry in London late in 1910. This is usually thought to account for Virginia Woolf's choice, in her essay 'Mr. Bennett and Mrs. Brown', of December 1910 as an especially revolutionary time for the contemporary sensibility; a moment when, she suggests, 'human character changed' (I, p. 320).

Whether Woolf actually had Fry's exhibition principally in mind when she wrote 'Mr. Bennett and Mrs. Brown' is a matter further discussed in Chapter 2. At any rate, no matter how far she and other novelists were directly concerned with changes taking place in many other forms of contemporary European art, these do often ' provide illuminating analogues for innovations in their writing, as well as confirming the revolutionary nature of the period as a whole. Practically, however, there are difficulties in concentrating on modernist fiction while also keeping a spectrum of European arts in view. There are now, in any case, a number of critical studies which offer broad surveys of the diversity of change and the different forms modernist innovations took across the field of early twentieth-century art as a whole.[6] This study briefly refers to other art-forms where appropriate, while including the work of Marcel Proust as a major example of literary developments occurring elsewhere. Proust's fiction is in any case well worth examining, as in a number of ways it can be connected particularly closely and usefully with the British context. Especially in the areas of structure, chronology, and concomitant change in views of time, the innovations of modernism can be more fully and easily illustrated from Proust's *Remembrance of Things Past* (*A la recherche du temps perdu*, 1913–27) than with reference only to fiction in English. In these and other areas, his example appealed fairly directly to several English modernists themselves. Both Dorothy Richardson and Virginia Woolf record admiration for Proust. 'Oh if I could write like that', Woolf remarks, mentioning at certain stages an intention to try to do so – to adapt certain of Proust's styles for her own use.[7]

Such instances of admiration or possible influence among modernist writers, however, are significantly rare. Statements of antipathy or at best indifference are more regularly in evidence. Though Woolf admired Proust, she had much more equivocal feelings for Joyce. She praises him in 'Modern Fiction', but records in her diary finding *Ulysses* 'a mis-fire . . . diffuse . . . brackish . . . pretentious'. Joyce himself could see no particular merit in Proust's writing. D.H. Lawrence could see little merit in either Proust, Joyce, Dorothy Richardson or Woolf – who for her part remarks 'I can't help thinking that there's something wrong with Lawrence'.[8] In *Time and Western Man* and *Men Without Art* (1934) Wyndham Lewis suggests that there was a good deal wrong with almost all modernist authors – with Woolf, Lawrence, Joyce and Proust, as well as Gertrude Stein, Ernest Hemingway and William Faulkner from the United

States. His negative views of these figures, and of contemporary culture as a whole, are further discussed in Chapter 3.

Lawrence himself warned that novelists' comments on their work are never entirely to be trusted, and it is possible that the modernists may sometimes have borrowed more from each other than they were prepared to admit. Nevertheless, the statements quoted above do help to indicate that – unlike other contemporary movements such as Imagism, Futurism or Vorticism – modernism involved little direct association between the writers involved. It was never a movement fostered through personal contacts or collective agreement about aims, goals, ideas or styles. Modernism is a critical construct – a recognition, some years after writers completed the work involved, of substantial similarity or even a collective identity in the initiatives they took and the styles and concerns they made a priority. This, however, does not make less viable the idea of modernism or of its coherence as a movement. As the present study will show, developments individual authors made independently from each other are nevertheless clearly comparable, and often related to one another more or less logically and progressively, one change of style following incrementally from another throughout the early decades of the century. Yet modernist authors' relative independence from each other does raise one obvious question about their work. If mutual association or influence cannot much account for manifold similarities throughout this phase of contemporary writing, what can?

One answer, really as obvious as the question, has already been offered by Alan Friedman's remarks, quoted in the Preface. The originality of modernist fiction, for Friedman, is owed to the originality of 'the modern experience' itself, to 'causes' in its philosophy, psychology, science, society, economics and politics. Along with so much contemporary art, modernist fiction changed radically in structure and style because the world it envisaged changed radically at the time, as indeed did means of envisaging it. Analogous innovations in so many contemporary art forms may have arisen not from mutual influence – Joyce did not restructure his work only because contemporary painters had done so, nor vice versa – but from common apprehension of the shifting nature of life, and of methods of perceiving it, in the early twentieth century. In other words, if contemporary novelists 'changed everything' in their work, as Thomas Hardy suggests, it would be reasonable to suppose that this was simply because they perceived everything around them as changed – even, in Woolf's view, human character itself. Like many an obvious answer, this is one which needs to be considered further before it can be accepted as innocent of over-simplification. Nevertheless, there is much evidence which does support Friedman's conclusion, some of it also helping explain the present study's methods of analyzing the modernist period and its writing. Many contemporary commentators confirm the extent of new challenges to the period's life and thinking, indicating how inescapable the effects of the new industrialized, technologized modernity of life seemed at the time. Even by 1880, the German philosopher Friedrich Nietzsche was suggesting of 'Premises of the Machine Age' that 'The press, the machine, the railway, the telegraph are premises whose thousand-year conclusion no one has yet dared to draw'.[9] Over the next thirty years, many further forms of new technology impacted upon and transformed everyday life. By the early twentieth century, even before the First World War, the 'thousand-year conclusions' Nietzsche saw in the machine age had been many times further multiplied. Excited by this new technology and the accelerating pace of life and change it created, the Italian Futurist F.T. Marinetti was talking by 1913 of

the complete renewal of human sensibility brought about by the great discoveries of science. Those people who today make use of the telegraph, the telephone, the phonograph, the train, the bicycle, the motorcycle, the automobile, the ocean liner, the dirigible, the aeroplane, the cinema, the great newspaper (synthesis of a day in the world's life) do not realize that the various means of communication, transportation and information have a decisive influence on the psyche.[10]

Such 'decisive influences on the psyche' and on 'renewal of human sensibility' also figure in philosophy and other forms of systematic thinking at the time. Elsewhere in his Futurist Manifestos, Marinetti talks of 'The earth shrunk by speed' and suggests 'Time and Space died yesterday . . . because we have created eternal, omnipresent speed'.[11] As he indicates, technological change inevitably also became conceptual and philosophic: new speeds, a new pace of life, contributed to new conceptions of the fundamental co-ordinates of experience, space and time. Though contemporary philosophy by no means entirely shared Futurism's enthusiasms, it inevitably responded to the same set of conditions. Without accepting that time and space had died altogether, it did often suggest that they had ceased to exist in ways they had conventionally been understood, and that new forms and mutual relations had to be established for them. Several of the contemporary philosophers considered in Chapter 3 – particularly Henri Bergson, whose popularity spread from France to Britain in the early part of the century – engaged in new enquiries regarding the nature and relations of space and time. Spectacularly confirmed in 1919, the astonishing theories of Albert Einstein eventually made such enquiries a common concern for the age as a whole – a topic of daily interest and conversation, as well as frequent literary reference, throughout the 1920s. A contemporary critic writing about the novel in 1928, John Carruthers, records that 'space-time' had become a 'modern philosophical term that means so much' (p. 84). In her novel *Mary Olivier*, published in 1919, May Sinclair likewise suggests that time and space had somehow become general 'forms of thought – ways of thinking' (p. 227). Richard Aldington begins his First World War novel *Death of a Hero* (1929) by defining individual life itself as 'a point of light which . . . describes a luminous geometrical figure in space-time' (p. 11).

No novelist, thirty or even twenty years before, would have described life quite in those terms. As the examples of Aldington and the others quoted suggest, space and time occupied a peculiar position in the imagination of the 1920s, providing – often in the newly hyphenated form 'space-time' which Carruthers and Aldington use – a fashionable, trendy terminology particular to the decade. Its appeal also appears in the work of Joyce's acquaintance Carola Giedion-Welcker, who remarked of *Ulysses* in 1928 that

> the arguments between man and world, the spiritual core of all great novels, becomes in Joyce, a great poetic-philosophical revelation about the inner and outer world, about subject and object, about matter, space, and time. They are the problems of the present philosophical and physical theories.[12]

One of the most significant of narrative theorists, Mikhail Bakhtin, likewise responded to the dominance of such theories in the 1920s by referring to Einstein's ideas and coining the term '*chronotope* (literally, "time-space")' (p. 84) as a central category employed in his analysis of the novel. Destabilized by a complex of recent developments, and prominent in contemporary thinking, space and time offer appropriate categories of analysis for modernist fiction, and are used in this way – in a sense, to examine the period in terms it used to re-examine and reconfigure itself – in Chapters 2 and 3.

New concerns with space and time, however, were symptoms of still more fundamental changes of outlook apparent in the early twentieth century. As Giedion-Welcker suggests, interest in space and time in 'present philosophical and physical theories' belongs with something defined more generally as 'the arguments between man and world'. There is evidence that these arguments intensified, or at any rate changed in character, in the late nineteenth and early twentieth centuries. As Chapters 2 and 3 discuss, philosophers such as Bergson, Nietzsche and William James are all concerned with a change in something as fundamental as the relation of mind and world – a kind of epistemological shift, from relative confidence towards a sense of increased unreliability and uncertainty in the means by which reality is apprehended in thought. Examining this general shift, the work of such thinkers helps confirm the opening decades of the century as a time of changes as far-reaching or 'catastrophic' in philosophy, and in the outlook of the age as a whole, as those Herbert Read found in contemporary art, or Marinetti in 'human sensibility'. The modernist period is of the sort indicated by one of the most sophisticated of recent analysts of culture and history, Michel Foucault, when he remarks that

> within the space of a few years a culture sometimes ceases to think as it had been thinking up till then and begins to think in a new way. (p. 50)

While Foucault confirms a culture's capacity to change, radically and quickly, the way it conceptualizes reality and itself, he also cautions against certain ways of assessing such changes, and movements in culture generally. He raises in particular 'the problem of causality', adding that

> the traditional explanations – spirit of the time, technological or social changes, influences of various kinds – struck me for the most part as being more magical than effective. (pp. xii–xiii)

As Foucault suggests, there are some problems of logic and per-
suasiveness in 'traditional' attempts – such as the one suggested by
Alan Friedman, partly followed above – to explain art or culture in
terms of supposed 'causes'. The 'spirit of the time', for example,
the '*Zeitgeist*', is based upon observation of an age and then used
to explain what is observed, a process which can come close to
tautology. First, a particular shape and character are ascribed to
the *Zeitgeist* on the basis of certain cultural phenomena, then these
phenomena are themselves said to owe their particular shape and
character to the *Zeitgeist*. Tracing 'influences of various kinds' –
not from some general spirit of the age, but even from specific
thinkers within it – can also be problematic: if not, as Foucault
suggests, 'magical', at least less logical and straightforward than is
sometimes supposed. The critic Lionel Trilling warns against simple views of influence and suggests that it is necessary to

> question the assumption which gives the priority in ideas to the philosopher
> and sees the movement of thought as always from the systematic thinker, who
> thinks up ideas in, presumably, a cultural vacuum, to the poet who 'uses' the
> ideas 'in dilution'. (pp. 191, 190)

Trilling's warning might seem self-evident or unnecessary. Even if
novelists read philosophy at all, they are fairly unlikely to derive
their ideas solely from it, or to accept ones not at least partly
congenial to them already. Yet in the 1920s, as in other periods,
there was a widespread assumption that views current in literature
or elsewhere must have originated in philosophy or in some generally shared idea. D.H. Lawrence illustrates this when he remarks in
1923 that

> The metaphysic or philosophy may not be anywhere very accurately stated and
> may be quite unconscious, in the artist, yet it is a metaphysic that governs men at
> the time, and is by all men more or less comprehended and lived. Men live and
> see according to some gradually developing and gradually withering vision. The
> vision exists also as a dynamic idea or metaphysics – exists first as such. Then it
> is unfolded into life and art. (*Fantasia of the Unconscious*, pp. 9–10)

Like apostles of the *Zeitgeist*, Lawrence elevates the common
'vision' of an age into an idea or 'metaphysic' whose 'unfolding'
somehow controls, causes or accounts for the characteristics of the
age itself. His views are typical of the assumption that different

aspects of a culture must exist hierarchically, with philosophy or a 'metaphysic' as dominant forms at the top. As Foucault suggests, this assumption may arise because philosophy – with all the respectability of its classical past – seems the most exalted authority to choose as the origin of any dominant idea or vision whose appearance elsewhere has to be explained. The creation of a *Zeitgeist* may likewise result from some ghost of theology haunting literary analysis.

Some such exalted view of philosophy seems to have been held by Wyndham Lewis when he discusses the 'parallel manifestation' of certain ideas throughout the cultural field he analyses in *Time and Western Man*, and goes on to remark

> Point for point what I had observed on the literary, social and artistic plane was reproduced upon the philosophic and theoretic . . .
>
> There seemed no doubt, after a little examination of the facts, that the more august of these two regions had influenced the lower and more popular one. (pp. 218, 219)

Lewis's idea of 'parallel manifestation' is more promising than the one he concludes upon, allowing the relations between philosophy and literature or the wider outlook of the age to be perceived as reciprocal rather than primarily causal or hierarchical. As Trilling suggests, philosophers do not work in a 'cultural vacuum', but are themselves conditioned by history, expressing rather than creating the general circumstances and 'gradually developing and gradually withering vision' of their age. The views not only of philosophers, but of psychologists, scientists and other thinkers are likewise at least as likely to be a consequence as a cause of this vision. Considered in this way, however, as Chapters 2 and 3 further suggest, their work remains worth examining for its analogies or parallel manifestations of the concerns of contemporary literature. It can often be especially worthwhile in offering direct, 'undiluted' formulation of such concerns, or systematic versions of the general vision by which 'men live or see' at the time.

This vision, however, needs to be related not only to philosophy or other forms of thought, but – more importantly – to contemporary social, political and economic conditions. In this area, too, Foucault warns about the issue of causality, and the technologic or social changes he mentions need to be considered not necessarily much more likely than philosophic ideas to shape literature and culture altogether directly. An exception helps illustrate this general rule. The imagination of the Futurist Manifesto quoted earlier is almost overwhelmed by excitement about the invention of the racing car. Marinetti unreservedly approves of the new technologies, celebrates them throughout what he writes, and considers it right that they should shape and dictate vision in literature, art and the world in general. 'Time and Space died yesterday', he suggests, 'because we have created eternal, omnipresent speed': for the Italian Futurists, in other words, vision – or at any rate its co-ordinates, time and space – underwent a welcome change *because* of new technologies, industries and the conditions of modernity they created.

Modernist authors were confronted by much the same set of new conditions which excited the Futurists. They may even, at times, have shared in some of this excitement: it appears, for example, in Marcel's various enthralled visions of powered flight, or the speed of the motor car, in Proust's *A la recherche du temps perdu*. But the speeds and stresses of modern life, and the new technologies and forms of rational intelligence which supported them, were viewed a good deal more sceptically by many contemporary authors, the modernists in particular, especially after the First World War. Rather than celebrating the modern experience, modernist authors were often chiefly concerned about its threat to the integrity of life and the individual, and more likely to react against than to accept what Nietzsche calls the conclusions of 'the machine age'. Though much readier than R.A. Scott-James to welcome change in art – indeed to emphasize its necessity – they were not always any more disposed to approve of it in reality, and modernist innovation results at least as much from an urge to resist as to reflect changes in contemporary life. As the critic Peter Brooker suggests, modernism often seeks to 'prescribe . . . a "modern" art which would administer to and correct "the modern world", not collaborate with it' (p. 6). Fredric Jameson likewise indicates that much of modernism's enthusiasm for change in art can be seen to arise, partly unconsciously, from a need to compensate for – rather than just represent – changed conditions in modern experience. This need dictated the creation of new imaginative strategies able to deflect or neutralize the new pressures –

industrial, economic and ultimately political, as well as social and technologic – so marked in the machine age. Unlike Futurism, modernism neither welcomed nor accepted the death of space and time. Like much contemporary philosophy, it attempted instead a kind of surgery to keep these dimensions alive and open in human terms, reshaped in ways which could continue to allow individual life to be construed as integral and significant – at least in imagination, if often not in reality.

This reshaping largely defines the nature of modernist fiction's structural and stylistic developments, further explored in the chapters which follow. To questions about why modernism changed the novel, the obvious answer remains – though with some qualifications – the right one. As Friedman suggests, 'the roots of change in the novel lie tangled deep in the modern experience'. As Foucault warns, unravelling these roots is rarely a matter of tracing direct causes and effects, but of untangling the various shifts of emphasis, restructurings, myths and evasions through which modernism sought to accommodate and make tolerable contemporary reality and the modern experience in general. By looking for what aspects of this experience offer in the way of 'analogies' and 'manifestations' paralleling innovation in the novel – and by avoiding the temptation of turning correlation too easily into cause – justice can be done to the complex, fascinating processes through which modernist fiction encountered the history of its time.

—— 2 ——

# SPACE

Our mistake lies in supposing that things present themselves as they really are . . .

The kind of literature which contents itself with 'describing things' . . . is in fact, though it calls itself realist, the furthest removed from reality . . .

How could the literature of description possibly have any value, when it is only beneath the surface . . . that reality has its hidden existence . . .

It is only a clumsy and erroneous form of perception which places everything in the object, when really everything is in the mind.

(Marcel Proust, *Remembrance of Things Past*
(*A la recherche du temps perdu*), 1913–27)

illumine the mind within rather than the world without.
(Virginia Woolf, 'Phases of Fiction', 1929)[1]

Writing in 1932, the popular English novelist Hugh Walpole pointed to what he considered, for contemporary authors, '*the* question of all questions. What is reality in the novel?' (p. 25). By the time he wrote, many contemporary novelists had answered this question as suggested above – choosing, in Woolf's terms, to hold up the mirror of art not to reflect nature and the world without, but to illumine the mind within, to portray consciousness. Later commentators have usually considered these novelists' attempts to place 'everything in the mind' – rather than in 'the object' or in objective, realistic description – as a central, defining characteristic of modernist writing.

As Chapter 1 pointed out, this concentration within the mind was a feature of contemporary writing sufficiently striking to have become a subject of discussion even before Walpole raised his 'question of questions' in 1932. Assessing the state of the novel in

1926, Gerald Bullett talks of 'the subjective method' as 'so characteristic of our age' (pp. 12–13). In a study of the novel published in 1928, John Carruthers likewise remarks that priorities Virginia Woolf expressed in her critical writing at the time were 'another indication of the trend of modern fiction from objective to subjective, from outer semblance to alleged inner reality' (p. 71).

Carruthers's study emphasizes that although increased attention to inner reality was an obvious feature of writing by the mid-1920s, it had appeared not altogether suddenly, but as part of a longer trend. He suggests that for many years previously European fiction had shown 'a persistent tendency away from objectivity and towards the ever more minute and analytic exposition of mental life' (p. 64). Hugh Walpole likewise felt his 'question of questions' had preoccupied novelists for twenty years or more. New possibilities for the 'exposition of mental life' were most spectacularly exploited by Woolf and Joyce in the 1920s, but as these contemporary critics suggest, a movement towards their style of fiction, a gradual deployment of new forms and emphases, can be traced through a longer phase of development – evident in the work of earlier authors such as Henry James, Joseph Conrad, Ford Madox Ford, D.H. Lawrence, Dorothy Richardson and May Sinclair. Each of these authors introduced some of the transformations in the language and style of the novel necessary to encompass 'ever more minute' mental movements and inner realities. Following in detail the changes of technique appearing in these authors' work, this chapter traces the trend from objective to subjective, the spatial shift of attention from 'outer world' to 'inner world', before going on to consider contemporary factors which encouraged this move to be made.

## HENRY JAMES, JOSEPH CONRAD, FORD MADOX FORD

Another contemporary critic, C.H. Rickword, looked back in the 1920s to suggest that Henry James

> certainly was the first to realize that the interior drama might be rendered immediately by language . . . that the word was as capable of embodying mental as physical movements.[2]

Gerald Bullett also considers James an important source of the 'subjective method' he saw as characteristic of his age, and as 'the chief channel of its ubiquitous influence' (pp. 12–13). James's influence arose not only from his novels, but from the prefaces he began to publish for them early in the twentieth century, clarifying his ideas about fiction and his priorities as a writer. A motive in producing these prefaces was his conviction that novel-writing required firm principles and a controlling aesthetic to govern what seemed to him at times rather a haphazard practice. James saw the work of many of his contemporaries as only a 'lump of life', a raw, undifferentiated transcription of reality, too full of the shapelessness and lack of significance of actual experience to be fully accepted as art. Life itself he considered to be 'all inclusion and confusion', whereas art and writing should be 'all discrimination and selection', matters of 'propriety and perspective'. James sought to provide some of this selection and discrimination in his own novels by the use of 'a structural centre . . . [an] organic centre' – a character through whose perceptions and perspective the material of the fiction could be carefully shaped and focused. James talks of his 'instinctive disposition' for

> placing advantageously, placing right in the middle of the light, the most polished of possible mirrors of the subject . . . these persons are, so far as their other passions permit, intense *perceivers*, all, of their respective predicaments.

This disposition can be seen in James's work at least as early as *The Portrait of a Lady* (1881): in discussing his heroine in the preface, and his tactics in the novel generally, James talks of the need to 'place the centre of the subject in the young woman's own consciousness'. His disposition also appears in a particular form in *What Maisie Knew* (1897). In this case the organic centre, Maisie, is a child whose limited but suggestive perceptions are used to build up a highly ironic, provocative vision of the moral dilemmas surrounding her. As James himself suggests, however, the most 'unmistakeable examples' of his 'instinctive disposition' appear in later novels such as *The Golden Bowl* (1904) and, perhaps most clearly, in the use of his hero Lambert Strether in *The Ambassadors* (1903).[3]

Even in *The Ambassadors*, however, the role of 'intense perceiver' is not as uncomplicated as James's image of the polished mirror suggests. Strether's progress embodies James's general interest in how innocence encounters experience, an issue sometimes examined – as in this case – through the encounters of North

Americans with the complexities of an older civilization in Europe. Though Strether is hardly as innocent or uninitiated as the child Maisie, he is an emotionally rather inexperienced American adrift in a Paris whose complex allures and subtleties at first elude his grasp, leaving him unable to comprehend the true situation of Chad, the young American he tries to persuade to return to his family in Massachusetts. James reports of one of Strether's puzzling conversations that

> he was in fact so often at sea that his sense of the range of reference was merely general and that he on several different occasions guessed and interpreted only to doubt. He wondered what they meant. (p. 76)

Guessing, interpreting, doubting, and constantly unsure of the true nature of what is going on, Strether is always an intense perceiver, but – initially at least – no more than a rather hazy, particular mirror of his experience, and not a polished or neutral one. Talking to his sophisticated friend and confidant Maria Gostrey, Strether records of the complexities confronting him 'You see more in it . . . than I' and she replies 'Of course I see *you* in it' (p. 46). Something of the relation the remarks imply also exists between Strether and readers. Events, action and the other characters in the novel are presented almost exclusively through his view of them, yet readers' processes of deduction allow them to see more than Strether does at times, making them more intense or accurate perceivers of Chad's situation or Strether's own predicament than he is himself. *The Ambassadors* is in a way a detective story, in which Strether's understanding gradually catches up with truths sometimes known or guessed before he has discovered them. Resulting ironies and the sense of Strether's inadequacy help to withdraw attention from what he reflects as a 'mirror' of life in Paris, redirecting it onto the nature of the mirror itself – onto Strether's mind, its reactions, its developing capacity to grasp what is happening. Consciousness and its devices for assimilating complex experience, even its ability to do so at all, thus become 'the centre of the subject'. This satisfies the preference James expresses for 'the reflected field of life' rather than 'the spreading field, the human scene'.[4] It is also a twofold anticipation of later developments of modernism: not only, as contemporary commentators saw, in moving the attention of the narrative away from the external world and onto subjective consciousness, but also, consequently, in raising questions about how the areas of mind and world can be related; about how, and how accurately or completely, individual perception can reflect the world it encounters.

James, however, represents an early stage in the growth of these interests. *The Ambassadors* concentrates with a new exclusiveness on the vision of a single character: readers encounter little more of Parisian life and society than Strether does, and, except for deduction and implication, know no more than he does of the novel's 'human scene'. Yet the manner in which this vision is communicated remains relatively conventional. James employs few of the tactics later developed by modernist writers to communicate the inner mental experience of characters or their immediate thoughts as they occur. Strether's vision and perception is recorded throughout, but not in the form in which it immediately impinges on his mind, nor for the most part quite as he might express it in his own voice, but instead in the more objective, reporting terms of James as the author. *The Ambassadors* in this way provides an excellent illustration of the distinction the narrative theorist Gérard Genette draws, within the general category of 'point of view', between 'who sees' and 'who speaks'. The point of view, in *The Ambassadors*, is almost always Strether's, in the sense that he envisages and provides a focus for the action of the novel – functioning as what Genette calls a focaliser, a character whose 'point of view orients the narrative perspective' (p. 186). Yet although Strether 'sees' the action of the novel, it is James who speaks, reporting Strether's thoughts and vision. Perhaps the best metaphor for the novel's practice is provided not by James's reference to the 'polished mirror', but by the critic Hugh Kenner's view that James 'employ[s] a foreground character over whose shoulder auctorial infallibility permits us to look' (p. 79). Individual consciousness in James's fiction determines the field of the novel's vision, rather than the processes through which this vision is communicated.

Such tactics create for James a transitional role, poised between nineteenth-century and modernist fiction. *The Ambassadors* shares modernism's fascination with inner consciousness, intense perception and the nature of individual vision, and goes further than earlier fiction in making such matters an exclusive centre of attention for the novel. James also, however, retains a nineteenth-century disposition for an authorial voice which speaks from a position aloof from the events it reports; for an objective authorial infallibility even in reporting the subjective experience of a thoroughly fallible individual perceiver. Critics for some time after James wrote suggested that he had taken the novel and its capacities to present subjective experience as far as it was possible to go. Aware of techniques subsequently developed which undermine authorial infallibility and confine the novel further within the consciousness of characters, later critics have usually placed James as an early figure in the 'trend from objective to subjective' – as much a forerunner of modernist initiatives as a central figure in the movement itself.

Joseph Conrad is often considered a similarly transitional figure. Fredric Jameson, for example, suggests that

> Conrad marks . . . a strategic fault line in the emergence of contemporary narrative . . . in Conrad we can sense the emergence . . . of what will be contemporary modernism. (p. 206)

This new form of narrative Jameson sees emerging from what he calls, in discussing *Lord Jim* (1900), 'a structural breakdown of the older realisms' (p. 207). Older realism – the assumption, in Proust's terms, that 'things present themselves as they really are' – is undermined by several aspects of Conrad's writing in *Lord Jim*. Scepticism about how things present themselves is directly stated, for example, when Jim faces the Court of Enquiry set up to investigate his desertion of his ship, the *Patna*. The novel records Jim finding that the court

> wanted facts. Facts! They demanded facts from him, as if facts could explain anything! . . .
>
> The facts those men were so eager to know had been visible, tangible, open to the senses, occupying their place in space and time, requiring for their existence a fourteen-hundred-ton steamer and twenty-seven minutes by the watch . . . and something else besides, something invisible, a directing spirit of perdition that dwelt within. (pp. 27, 29)

For Conrad, as for Proust, the visible, tangible, object world is of less significance, almost of less reality, than what is invisible and dwells within. It is remarked of the range of spectators at

Jim's trial that 'the interest that drew them there was purely psychological' and that the enquiry's preoccupation with asking Jim purely factual questions is

> as instructive as the tapping with a hammer on an iron box, were the object to find out what's inside . . . the questions put to him necessarily led him away from what . . . would have been the only truth worth knowing. (p. 48)

Taciturn, evasive, and unable to string together more than a couple of broken sentences at a time to describe himself, Jim resembles an iron box in the hermetic surface he presents to outside scrutiny. Conrad's narrator Marlow, who communicates most of the story of *Lord Jim*, finds that much of what he tells has to be pieced together not from Jim himself but from the views of other characters who have encountered him. He supplements Jim's fragmentary testimony with the stories of the French naval Lieutenant who eventually rescues the *Patna*, and of Gentleman Brown, the pirate who eventually destroys Jim's sanctuary in Patusan, also offering briefer views of Jim from his employer Egström, from the German merchant Stein, even from the mad guano-picker Chester, as well as from the Court of Enquiry itself. These diverse accounts of Jim, however, provide only further tapping on the box: the psychological interest, what dwells within Jim, never seems fully exposed, at least for the characters within the novel.

The inclusion of so many narrators and points of view, however, fully exposes the impossibility of facts given the uncertainties of subjective, individual views of the world and the discrepancies which appear between them. Conclusions about Jim constantly vary depending upon the viewpoint recorded at the time. His nature, even his stature, remain persistently difficult to define, literally from the novel's first sentence to its last. *Lord Jim* opens with the observation that 'He was an inch, perhaps two, under six feet'. A sense of slight shortcoming in Jim himself is immediately introduced by his falling just short of the imperial measure of six feet. A shortcoming in the accuracy of perception, however, is suggested equally immediately by 'perhaps', indicating the viewpoint of a narrator unable to provide firm facts and forced to conjecture about appearances. Even Marlow, the principal observer of Jim, admits that it was 'impossible to see him clearly' (p. 255), adding

I don't pretend I understood him. The views he let me have of himself were like those glimpses through the shifting rents in a thick fog – bits of vivid and vanishing detail, giving no connected idea of the general aspect of a country. (pp. 62–3)

Marlow finds the task of narrator if anything even more difficult in Conrad's *Heart of Darkness* (1902). He confesses that during his time in an African colony any feeling that he 'belonged still to a world of straightforward facts' was one which 'would not last long' (p. 30) and admits to the immediate audience of his story that its central figure, Kurtz, may be 'impossible to see clearly':

'Kurtz . . . at the time I did not see – you understand . . . Do you see him? Do you see the story? Do you see anything? It seems to me I am trying to tell you a dream – making a vain attempt, because no relation of a dream can convey the dream-sensation, that commingling of absurdity, surprise and bewilderment in a tremor of struggling revolt, that notion of being captured by the incredible which is of the very essence of dreams' . . .

'... No, it is impossible; it is impossible to convey the life-sensation of any given epoch of one's existence, – that which makes its truth, its meaning – its subtle and penetrating essence. It is impossible. We live, as we dream – alone....'

He paused again, as if reflecting, then added –

'Of course in this you fellows see more than I could then. You see me, whom you know....'

It had become so pitch dark that we listeners could hardly see one another. For a long time already he, sitting apart, had been no more to us than a voice. (p. 50)

Marlow's doubts about truth, meaning and the visible, and his emphasis instead on the essence or sensation of dreams, anticipate Proust's conclusion that 'it is only beneath the surface . . . that reality has its hidden essence'. This emphasis, and much of the story, add significance to the coincidence that Conrad's novella first appeared in serial form in 1899, the same year as Sigmund Freud's *The Interpretation of Dreams*. Like Freud's work, *Heart of Darkness* looks beneath surface behaviour towards primal forces within the self and a core of being deeper and darker than had hitherto been generally supposed. The voyage up river into the interior of the colony is also Marlow's symbolic journey into himself, and his encounter with Kurtz – 'chief of the Inner Station' (p. 47), overwhelmed by madness and savagery – confronts him with a darkness from which he finds he cannot consider himself immune. The 'absurdity, surprise and bewilderment' of this discovery precipitate a near-fatal illness which further confirms his identification with Kurtz, who dies on the way down river. It is a discovery which can also be seen to anticipate modernist authors' deeper concern with character and the inner reaches of consciousness: how far such new interests can be traced directly to the influence of Freud is a question discussed later in this chapter.

The context of Marlow's storytelling also creates implications which go beyond individual psychology. Becalmed with him on a yacht on the Thames at nightfall, his immediate audience is made up of figures representative of affluent, stable British society – 'the Director of Companies . . . the Lawyer . . . the Accountant' (pp. 15–16). Yet Marlow opens his story with the judgement, while looking over the sombre Thames at London – now centre of the British empire, though once itself subjugated by the Romans – that 'this also . . . has been one of the dark places of the earth' (p. 18). The kind of diminished distinctions he implies between colonizer and colonized, civilization and barbarism, enlightenment and atavism, later came to concern modernist writers in various ways, especially after the outbreak of the First World War. In general, the imperial encounter with other, radically different societies, and the exploitative, commercial savagery with which these were suppressed and colonized – grimly exposed throughout *Heart of Darkness* – forced writers in the modernist period to reconsider the validity and value of any 'civilization' Europe could claim. In relation to society as much as the self, 'civilization' was a more uncertain term for the early twentieth century than it had been for the nineteenth. Conveniently published as the century turned, *Heart of Darkness* has often been interpreted by critics as clear evidence of this growing uncertainty.

Yet Marlow's questions about how much even his immediate audience can 'see' emphasize another kind of uncertainty: the difficulty of interpreting his story with confidence, in the ways suggested above or any others. Much of its 'darkness' derives not only from the story's subject but from the haziness or unreliability of its telling. As Marlow half-confesses in the passage quoted, it concerns an encounter with a dark, unseen side of himself, and with what lies beyond his powers of interpretation and communication: it is part of 'the essence of dreams', after all, to be opaque to the dreamer. Marlow's immediate listeners – and readers of the novel – must therefore work out for themselves what is often no more than implied in his narrative, such as the extent of his identification with

Kurtz. For example, when Marlow recounts seeing Kurtz seeming to stare at him out of the 'glassy panel' (p. 118) of his bereaved fiancée's door in Brussels, readers are left to deduce that Marlow is actually looking at a reflection of himself. At such moments, and many others throughout, the difficulty not of seeing Kurtz but of assessing Marlow himself becomes a central interpretative problem. Rather like Maria Gostrey in James's *The Ambassadors*, admitting that she can see more of Strether's story because she can see him in it, Marlow tells his listeners 'You fellows see more than I could . . . You see me'. It is essential to an understanding of the story that they should, even though Marlow has actually become as he speaks a vanishingly dark figure on the benighted Thames.

Like James in *The Ambassadors*, in other words, in *Heart of Darkness* as in *Lord Jim*, Conrad partly redirects the psychological interest of the novel upon the see-er and ways of seeing rather than only on the characters who are seen. Since neither Chad, Jim, Kurtz, nor the 'the human scene' in general are straightforwardly 'open to the senses', but almost opaque or impalpable, the motives and mental processes of the perceiver move naturally into the foreground. Both Conrad and James accepted a label borrowed from recent developments in visual art, 'Impressionist', as a description of their styles: it aptly suggests techniques which dissolve objectivity and leave the human scene of the novel suffused with the subjective vision of the figure observing or narrating it. Like the fiancée's door, the fiction of James and Conrad presents a 'life-sensation' in which, regardless of the ostensible subject, the nature, motives and consciousness of central observers or narrators are always reflected.

As the term 'Impressionist' helps to suggest, this modification in the manner of fiction at the turn of the century can be more widely considered in relation to the art and thought of the time. As Jameson indicates, it marks a significant 'fault line'; a break from earlier conventions or 'older realisms' which accepted relatively unproblematic contact between the mind and 'things as they really are'. The critic J. Hillis Miller concurs with Jameson in seeing Conrad's novels as sharply differentiated from earlier fiction in this way, suggesting that

> Victorian novels were often relatively stabilized by the presence of an omniscient narrator . . . a trustworthy point of view and also a safe vantage point . . . in *Lord Jim* no point of view is entirely trustworthy.[5]

Conrad actually departs further from convention than James in this respect. Whereas James stabilizes Strether's problematic perceptions with his own authorial voice, in *Heart of Darkness* and *Lord Jim* no narrator is omniscient. In the latter novel particularly, every voice and vision is idiosyncratic, and often highly particularized in style and language. As Jameson suggests, the breakdown of older realism which Conrad achieves is specifically structural, depending in the novels discussed, and in *Chance* (1913), on a construction which introduces a narrator to dramatize the uncertainties of perception itself. Conflicting or uncertain visions leave no world-view secure, and the fiction necessarily focused on the subjective processes through which reality may be known by each individual – processes which in the early twentieth century seemed increasingly complex, dream-dominated and dark.

Henry James saw Conrad's use of the narrator Marlow creating 'a prolonged hovering flight of the subjective over the outstretched ground of the case exposed'.[6] A comparable 'flight of the subjective' appears in the work of a novelist closely connected with James and Conrad, Ford Madox Ford. His critical study *Henry James* appeared in 1915, the same year as one of his best novels, *The Good Solider*. Like some of James's fiction, *The Good Soldier* traces the perplexities of a naïve, inexperienced North American encountering the complexities of European society – like James, or Conrad, Ford places his central figure in an alien, unfathomable environment in order to highlight the relativity and particularity of perception. The narrator of *The Good Soldier*, John Dowell, often admits to a puzzled, limited knowledge of English society, at one stage concluding that in certain areas 'Englishmen seem to me to be a little mad' (p. 137).

Ford collaborated with Conrad in writing novels such as *The Inheritors* (1901) and *Romance* (1903) and also, as he records in his dedicatory letter to *The Good Soldier*, in exhaustive studies of 'how words should be handled and novels constructed'. In some aspects, construction included, *The Good Soldier* particularly resembles *Lord Jim*. Dowell is perplexed yet fascinated by the silent, inscrutable, surprisingly unreliable Englishman Edward Ashburnham, much as Marlow is by Jim, and Dowell's notion that he is telling his story 'in a very rambling way', as if to 'a silent listener', makes *The Good Soldier* into the sort of 'free and wandering tale' which Marlow's after-dinner monologue, in Conrad's view, made *Lord Jim*.[7]

There are also, however, significant differences between *The Good Soldier* and *Lord Jim*. One of Marlow's difficulties, and a reason for including in his narrative so many testimonies other than his own, is his distance, emotionally and often geographically from Jim himself. Dowell, on the other hand, is consistently involved, personally and emotionally, in the events he recounts – principally his wife's protracted infidelity with Ashburnham – and always much concerned with his own responses to them. However much he reveals his own nature in the process, Marlow talks mostly about Jim rather than himself. Dowell is a more obvious, explicit centre of his own attention than is Marlow, at least in *Lord Jim*. In one way, this places *The Good Soldier* close in strategy to the sort of half-confessional, first-person narratives found in Victorian fiction – for example, in Charles Dickens's *David Copperfield* (1849–50) or *Great Expectations* (1860–1). By comparison such Victorian novels nevertheless remain, in Hillis Miller's terms, at least relatively stabilized by 'a trustworthy point of view and a safe vantage point'. Neither Pip's childhood perspective in *Great Expectations*, nor David's in *David Copperfield*, is entirely trustworthy either morally or perceptually; this unreliability, however, is carefully indicated by their later, narrating selves. One of the structuring principles of the sort of fiction in which they appear is that the narrator progresses, in the course of the story, from earlier existence as a child towards the sort of maturity possessed throughout by the older, narrating self who looks back on past limitations or mistakes. John Dowell does not achieve stability in this way, and his narrative never offers a safe vantage point. The eventual revelation of his wife's epic infidelity does show him the extent to which he has been an 'ignorant fool', but he remains thereafter only less ignorant, and not always a trustworthy observer of his world or himself, nor even a consistent one. Denial that 'analysis of [his] own psychology matters at all to this story', for example, is quickly followed by mention of a 'mysterious and unconscious self' and of 'unconscious desires' (pp. 88, 99, 100, 213).

Far from being irrelevant to the story, as he suggests, Dowell's psychology and the particularity of his outlook are central, unavoidable issues in *The Good Soldier*. Self-contradictory, frequently biased and jealous, and often ruled by unconscious desires he seeks to ignore, Dowell is an excellent example of an unreliable narrator. Such figures are often considered characteristic of modern fiction, and a decisive step in the breaking down of older realism, enforcing sceptical scrutiny of the means through which a story is told, as much as of what is told within it. Such scepticism installs in the fiction an epistemological doubt, an uncertainty about how completely or truthfully the world can be known or communicated through any individual's idiosyncratic vision of it. Though Ford's fiction may be less completely comparable to the work of Conrad and James than he suggests, he clearly shares in these authors' shifting of some of the novel's interest away from the perceived world in order to examine in more depth the nature of perception and the psychology of the perceiver. This shift further marks the 'fault-line' between Victorian and modernist fiction. As Gérard Genette suggests, the interest of narrative after the turn of the century was 'caught between what it tells (the story) and what tells it (the narrating)' and moved increasingly towards 'domination by the latter (modern narrative)' (p. 156).

Shifts of interest of this kind, from perceived to perceiver, from the world without to the mind within, had become such an obvious feature of contemporary fiction by the mid-1920s that Gerald Bullett could suggest in *Modern English Fiction* (1926) that

> the young intellectual who sits down to write his first novel instinctively inter-
> poses between us and the events of his story the consciousness of its chief
> character. (p. 12)

The fiction of Conrad, Ford, and James shows the origins and early forms of this instinct. The use of what James calls 'a definite responsible intervening first-person singular'[8] – figures such as Strether, Dowell or Marlow, who provide mirrors polished, cloudy, or warped through which the world of the novel is mediated – marks one stage in the development of the subjective method, the instinct for interposing consciousness whose dominance in the 1920s Bullett records. A comparison of Ford's *The Good Soldier* with some of his later fiction – particularly the *Parade's End* tetralogy (1924–8) – suggests ways in which novelists, by the end of the 1920s, had learned to enter more deeply and intimately into the consciousness of their chief characters or intervening first-persons singular.

In *Parade's End*, Ford records as follows, for example, the thoughts of his hero Christopher Tietjens, disturbed by his experience as a combatant in the First World War, and by the monstrous infidelities of his wife:

> Panic came over Tietjens. He knew it would be his last panic of that interview. No brain could stand more. Fragments of scenes of fighting, voices, names, went before his eyes and ears . . . Years before ... How many months? ... Nineteen, to be exact, he had sat on some tobacco plants on the Mont de Kats ... No, the Montagne Noire. In Belgium ... What had he been doing? ... Trying to get the lie of the land.... No.... Waiting. (pp. 492–3)

Frequent self-questioning and self-contradiction, and abbreviated, fragmentary sentences, repeatedly interrupted with ellipses, imitate the rhythm, hesitation and something of the nature of thoughts as they occur to Tietjens. Such passages appear frequently in *Parade's End*, and are often extensive: the reflections beginning above, for example, continue for more than two pages. They obviously represent a development from the tactics employed in *The Good Soldier*: this is no longer the manner of a narrator telling a story to a silent listener, but a style which follows the inner voice – if not always the actual words – of a character silently addressing himself. Ford's employment of this voice helps to indicate (and may itself have directly benefited from) some of the developments in fictional style made between around 1915 and 1928. To the subjective methods Ford might have learned from Conrad and James there were added, in this period, further techniques for entering the mind within, variously introduced by D.H. Lawrence, Dorothy Richardson, May Sinclair, Virginia Woolf and eventually, most comprehensively, by James Joyce.

## D.H. LAWRENCE

Critics are sometimes unsure how far D.H. Lawrence should be considered a modernist. He can be compared in this respect with E.M. Forster and Aldous Huxley, each of whom attracts similar or stronger doubts. In some ways, both Forster and Huxley are clearly enough concerned with the transformations of the modern age, Huxley perhaps more obviously in 1920s novels such as *Crome Yellow* (1921) or *Antic Hay* (1923) in which he satirizes the hectic new lifestyles and moralities which appeared after the First

World War. Forster belongs largely to the Edwardian age, and almost ceased writing fiction after *Howards End*, published in Virginia Woolf's epochal year of 1910. In his last novel, *A Passage to India* (1924), however, he goes on to provide a topical criticism of the divisive power structures of empire, while *Howards End* itself comprehensively examines the erosion of traditional life and values by a modern, materialist world of ruthless business and industrial development; of 'telegrams and anger'. Yet despite such contemporary concerns, neither Forster's fiction, nor Huxley's (at least until *Point Counter Point*, 1928) much show the characteristic which Virginia Woolf and most subsequent critics consider distinctively modern, or modernist: readiness to address a changing, challenging modern life by transforming not only the subjects and themes of art, but, more radically, its form and style. Critics such as Michael Levenson assign Forster to 'an ambiguous position in the history of modern fiction', on the grounds that 'he could never muster the conviction for a programmatic assault on traditional forms' and remained committed to 'an evolutionary rather than a revolutionary change' (1991, pp. 78–9). Though more 'revolutionary' in outlook, Huxley's relatively conventional satiric style merits a similarly ambiguous or peripheral position in relation to modernism.

There are similar ambiguities in Lawrence, whose work also shows some allegiance to traditional forms, but critics have usually seen him as a figure much more revolutionary than evolutionary in both outlook *and* style. David Daiches suggests that

> in his mature novels Lawrence was at least as revolutionary as Joyce . . . a great innovator, one who puts the novel form to genuinely new uses. (pp. 139–40)

In his survey *Modernism*, Peter Faulkner likewise sees Lawrence as 'a deliberate innovator in his method as a novelist', though adding that he had 'scant respect' for the modernists (p. 60), several of whom he criticized precisely because they were so firmly – Lawrence thought fussily – attentive to the minutest movements of inner consciousness. W.W. Robson's equable conclusion that Lawrence was 'profoundly traditional as well as profoundly modern' (p. 88) can perhaps be usefully accepted along with Daiches's view that innovative qualities may be chiefly apparent in Lawrence's mature novels, particularly *The Rainbow*

(1915) and *Women in Love* (1921), rather than necessarily throughout his writing. Earlier work such as *Sons and Lovers* (1913) is closer to traditional phases of writing. A partly auto-biographical novel about growing up towards maturity, it shares some characteristics with examples of the *Bildungsroman* (the novel of personal education and growth towards adulthood, such as *David Copperfield*, especially popular in Victorian times) which continued to appear in the early twentieth century.

*Sons and Lovers*, however, does show an early form of interests which extend throughout Lawrence's fiction, particularly his concern with close sexual relations and their consequences within the individual psyche. *Sons and Lovers* deals with the difficulties created for Paul Morel's affairs by his inability to separate himself and his affections sufficiently from his mother, a problem he remains long unaware of himself. Paul remains equally unconscious of his true feelings for Miriam, described as follows:

> He did not know himself what was the matter. He was naturally so young, and their intimacy was so abstract, he did not know he wanted to crush her onto his breast to ease the ache there. He was afraid of her. The fact that he might want her as a man wants a woman had in him been suppressed into a shame. (pp. 220–1)

In Paul's relations with Miriam and with his mother, *Sons and Lovers* introduces a problem which regularly recurs for characters in later novels. Like Paul, they often 'do not know themselves what was the matter', encountering strong forces and desires which nevertheless cannot be fully grasped or contained within their conscious minds. In *The Rainbow*, for example, Lawrence explains of Tom Brangwen that 'a daze had come over his mind, he had another centre of consciousness . . . unable to know anything' (p. 39). Lawrence likewise suggests of one of his heroines in *Women in Love*, Gudrun, that she 'knew in her subconsciousness, not in her mind' (p. 508), and remarks of the other, Ursula, that 'she could not imagine what it was. It merely took hold of her . . . beyond thought . . . she was translated beyond herself' (p. 221).

Such movements into 'another centre of consciousness . . . beyond thought' suggest that even in his mature fiction, Lawrence remained in part a traditional writer not so much despite as *because of* what seem profoundly modern – sometimes, in his own day, even profoundly shocking – interests in sex and the psyche.

Profoundly modern techniques, such as stream of consciousness, cannot be altogether adequately applied to characters whose most crucial experiences are often not conscious at all. Transcribing the inner voice of such characters does not help to gain access to aspects of their experience which cannot be reached or spoken within it. Instead, Lawrence has to remain aloof from his characters, reporting or dramatizing authorially what they cannot wholly know themselves; relying on the sort of authorial omniscience described in *Lady Chatterley's Lover* (1928) as the novelist's conventional licence 'to reveal the most secret places of life . . . the *passional* secret places' (p. 104). If Lawrence's tactics are 'profoundly modern', it is not always on account of the style through which he reports or describes consciousness and what lies beyond it, but often simply as a result of the extraordinary frequency with which such passages appear, at times almost overwhelming action and dialogue. Quantitatively, Lawrence entirely shares in modernism's shift of attention from outer world to inner space, at least in the mature novels *Women in Love* and *The Rainbow*, and in most of those that follow. In each, even single lines of conversation are often separated by whole paragraphs describing the unfolding complexities of the conversants' unspoken inner feelings.

Such passages, however, sometimes strain the patience of Lawrence's readers. Critics of Lawrence often suggest that his urgency in seeking out the deepest core of his characters' being leads him to employ a language overfraught with portentous vocabulary – repeatedly, ineffectually gesturing at 'dark', 'mystic', '*passional*' but ultimately vague or ungraspable emotions. Part of Ursula's experience of Birkin in *Women in Love*, for example, is floridly described in terms of 'rivers of strange dark fluid richness . . . full mystic knowledge of his suave loins of darkness . . . magical, mystical, a force in darkness, like electricity' (pp. 354, 358). Some explanation of this uneasy style is offered by another description of Ursula's relations with Birkin which suggests they are characterized by 'unspeakable communication . . . that can never be transmuted into mind content' (p. 361). Some of her communication with Birkin may be unspeakable not only for Ursula herself, but for the author, able to go only so far in communicating experience beyond thought, to do no more than gesture awkwardly at what lies in this region. Certain impulses, physical passions especially, lead not only beyond thought, but beyond what can be conventionally rendered in language, even by a reporting author – an inevitable problem for modernist writing, with its deepening fascination for the mind within, which is further considered in Chapter 4.

One of Lawrence's better solutions to this problem is not to attempt a report of characters' feelings but to dramatize them in symbolic episodes, such as the following account of cruel mistreatment of his mare – terrified of a passing train – by Gudrun's eventual lover Gerald:

> He held on her unrelaxed, with an almost mechanical relentlessness, keen as a sword pressing into her . . .
>
> Gudrun looked and saw the trickles of blood on the sides of the mare, and she turned white. And then on the very wound the bright spurs came down, pressing relentlessly. The world reeled and passed into nothingness for Gudrun, she could not know any more . . .
>
> The guard's van came up, and passed slowly, the guard staring out in his transition on the spectacle in the road. And, through the man in the closed wagon Gudrun could see the whole scene spectacularly, isolated and momentary, like a vision isolated in eternity. (p. 124)

Though Gudrun 'could not know' consciously what the scene means for her, its significance is made clear enough by her physical reaction to it. Blood drains from her face as it does from the sides of the mare: in 'another centre of consciousness', a level of physical cognition or even 'blood consciousness' as Lawrence sometimes calls it, she identifies herself with the horse, anticipating the destructive flaunting of cruelty and power which will characterize Gerald's relations with her. Especially in *The Rainbow* and *Women in Love*, Lawrence shows a particular talent for creating such symbolic scenes, at once relatively natural – simply a picture of a man controlling a horse at a level crossing, for example – yet highly endowed with wider significance about the emotions of characters and the unconscious forces which structure their relationships. Lawrence's tactic of frequently shifting his narrative's point of view – one employed throughout his writing, but illustrated especially clearly and complexly in the last lines of the extract above – contributes to the effectiveness of such symbolic scenes, adding a highly visual quality which helps their significance stand out 'spectacularly', as vivid visions isolated from the otherwise generally inward orientation of his fiction.

*The Rainbow* and *Women in Love* also benefit from Lawrence's development of a tactic much less often employed in *Sons and Lovers*, one able in certain instances to adapt language to represent inner thought and deeper movements of the psyche. Lawrence's use of this device is illustrated in the following account in *The Rainbow* of Ursula's passionate feelings for religion and for the early spring:

> The passion rose in her for Christ . . . But how did it apply to the weekday world? What could it mean, but that Christ should clasp her to his breast, as a mother clasps her child? And oh, for Christ, for him who could hold her to his breast and lose her there! Oh, for the breast of man, where she should have refuge and bliss for ever! . . .
>
> Again she felt Jesus in the countryside. Ah, he would lift up the lambs in his arms! Ah, and she was the lamb. Again, in the morning, going down the lane, she heard the ewe call, and the lambs came running . . . to the udder . . . sucking, vibrating with bliss . . . Oh and the bliss, the bliss! She could scarcely tear herself away. (pp. 286–7)

No matter how passionate an author Lawrence may be considered in general, the passion of this passage, as it begins by indicating, is Ursula's and not his. The voice in the passage which says 'oh' and 'ah' and 'oh, and the bliss, the bliss!' cannot therefore be plausibly ascribed to Lawrence as the narrator of the novel, nor can all the questions and exclamations which predominate throughout. Not, or at any rate not purely, representing the author's voice, the passage must in some way be transcribing Ursula's. But this is not conventionally marked for the reader, either in the form of direct speech – which would read '"Ah", she thought, "And I am the lamb"', with pronouns in the first person and verbs in the present tense – or indirect speech, which would give 'She thought that she was the lamb', with verbs in the past tense, pronouns in the third person, and the character's questions and exclamations deleted. Instead, much of the passage has characteristics of both direct and indirect recording of speech, or, in this case, of inner thought. Free Indirect Discourse is the name usually given to this technique of presenting a character's voice partly mediated by the voice of the author; instances where, as Gérard Genette puts it,

> the narrator takes on the speech of the character, or, if one prefers, the character speaks through the voice of the narrator, and the two instances are then *merged*. (p. 174)

The term Free Indirect Discourse is perhaps best reserved for instances where words have actually been spoken aloud, while instances such as the above, where a character's voice is probably the silent, inward one of thought, can be described as Free Indirect Style.

Free Indirect Style of this kind, transcribing unspoken or even incompletely verbalized thoughts, appears very frequently throughout *The Rainbow* and *Women in Love*. It is especially predominant in chapters (such as VI, 'Anna Victrix', or XI, 'First Love' in *The Rainbow*; or 30, 'Snowed Up' in *Women in Love*) where characters experience crises, or strong desires, or engage in extended inward reflection about their lives and relations. One such passage, again presenting Ursula's feelings, appears at the beginning of Chapter 15 of *Women in Love*, at an early stage of her 'deep and passionate' love for Birkin:

> She sat crushed and obliterated in a darkness that was the border of death . . . Darkly, without thinking at all, she knew that she was near to death. She had travelled all her life along the line of fulfilment, and it was nearly concluded. She knew all she had to know, she had experienced all she had to experience, she was fulfilled in a kind of bitter ripeness, there remained only to fall from the tree into death. And one must fulfil one's development to the end, must carry the adventure to its conclusion. And the next step was over the border into death. So it was then! There was a certain peace in the knowledge . . .
>
> Of the next step we are certain. It is the step into death . . .
>
> It was a decision. It was not a question of taking one's life – she would *never* kill herself, that was repulsive and violent. It was a question of *knowing* the next step. And the next step led into the space of death. Did it? – or was there – ?
>
> Her thoughts drifted into unconsciousness, she sat as if asleep beside the fire. (pp. 214–15)

In a letter of 1914, Lawrence suggested to his publisher that 'You mustn't look in my novel for the old stable *ego* . . . of the character', adding that it required 'a deeper sense than any we've been used to exercise' to create and sustain a recognizable individuality for characters.[9] The last lines, particularly, of the passage above show the deepening effected by Lawrence's Free Indirect Style, equipping his narrative with the potential to record what Ursula knows 'without thinking', following her thoughts in their drift towards the very edge of unconsciousness. The passage as a whole also illustrates one of the ways in which Lawrence's writing destabilizes the ego, dissolving any easy, secure sense of identity in the voice of author or character, increasingly fused together in various shades and tones of intermingling. The opening lines can be read as relatively stabilized, almost in the manner of a Victorian omniscient narrator, seeming to view Ursula from outside and simply reporting her condition as 'crushed and obliterated'. But the apparently objective 'she' in these lines quickly slides into the less definite 'one' and 'we': by 'she would *never* kill herself', even 'she' has become, in Free Indirect Style, almost a kind of equivalent for 'I', and the passage seems directed largely by Ursula's unspoken thoughts, as the last lines confirm. Exclamations, questions and italicized emphases – more plausibly features of character rather than author's discourse – help to trace this progression into Free Indirect recording of Ursula's own thoughts, but there remain intermediary stages in which author and character voice are almost impossible to identify or separate – for example, in the sentence 'And the next step was over the border into death'. Such '*merged*' or intermediary sentences allow the novel a certain freedom of suggestion, a possibility of statement precisely located neither with character nor author, but as if drawn from the whole atmosphere or situation the narrative develops. Much of Lawrence's moral and religious vision depends on this sort of freely located statement, one of the conditions of what is often called his 'prophetic' style. At the end of Chapter X of *The Rainbow*, for example, the voice which asks 'Can I not, then, walk this earth in gladness, being risen from sorrow . . . after my resurrection' is one which can be ascribed neither to Ursula, even in the 'visionary world' she inhabits at the time, nor to Lawrence himself, nor even to the risen Christ, belonging instead to a sort of 'visionary world' the whole novel creates for itself from the freewheeling interfusion of all its many voices.

Free Indirect Style is an extensive, distinctive feature of *The Rainbow* and *Women in Love*, extending into much of Lawrence's later fiction, such as *The Lost Girl* (1920) and *The Plumed Serpent* (1926), but it is by no means his invention. Following Mikhail Bakhtin's suggestion that the novel form fundamentally depends upon interminglings of languages (see also Chapter 4), recent narrative criticism and theory has increasingly concerned itself with forms of what Bakhtin calls the 'hybridization' of speech.[10] Narrative theory now sometimes envisages the merging of character and author discourse in some form of Free Indirect Style as a distinctive, even definitive, feature of fiction in general. Some such merging, at any rate, is evident long before Lawrence's appearance in the history of the novel: as Bakhtin himself points out, it is often clearly present in the fiction of Charles Dickens. It is also at times a feature of Jane Austen's style. As the last chapter suggested, many aspects of modernist style need to be seen not altogether as innovations, but as changes of emphasis – even as quantitative rather than wholly qualitative differences from earlier writing. In this way, though it is not at all new to the twentieth century, Free Indirect Style does help distinguish the work of the modernists from the 'relatively stabilized' fiction of their predecessors, if only on the grounds of the new frequency and extent of its employment – though perhaps also the particularity of its use as a register for unspoken thoughts, rather than only another way of recording dialogue. Free Indirect Style is used as a means of illumining the mind within not only in the mature fiction of D.H. Lawrence – and in the work of many contemporary modernists, such as Katherine Mansfield throughout her short stories – but in some of the other writing so far discussed. In *The Ambassadors*, for example, it is regularly used by James as a means of keeping the narrative close to the point of view of Strether, of allowing 'auctorial infallibility' to remain at the shoulder of the protagonist. Ford's use of the style in *Parade's End* is more extensive, forming a principal means of transcribing Tietjens's thoughts, as in the passage recording Tietjens's wartime 'panic', quoted earlier. Such passages seem to appear more frequently as Ford's novel-sequence progresses in the 1920s. By the last volume of the tetralogy, *The Last Post* (1928), his Free Indirect Style is not just a regular feature of his writing, but at times a very striking and even extravagant one. It extends into transcription of the inner thoughts of Tietjens's brother Mark, and of the highly idiosyncratic English of his French mistress: at one stage, the narrative enters into for a whole chapter (I, iii) the heavily dialectal voice of Tietjens's servants, one of whom reflects, for example, that

> if you 'as to 'ave Quality all about you in the 'ouse tis better not to 'ave real Quality . . . 'E coudn' say as 'ow 'e liked the job the Governor give 'im. He had to patch up and polish with beeswax – not varnish – rough stuff such 's 'is granf'er 'ad 'ad. An 'ad got rid of. Rough ol' truck. Moren n'undred yeers old. N'more! (pp. 704–5)

Even when, at the end of the First World War, Mark is so enraged at the peace made with Germany that he vows never to speak aloud again, his resolution passes almost unnoticed, so richly is his inner voice sustained by Ford's style.

Used with increasing diversity and extravagance throughout *Parade's End*, Free Indirect Style is a mark of Ford Madox Ford's increasing modernity in the 1920s – perhaps also of ways the stresses of the First World War force his characters to take refuge increasingly within the relatively safe sphere of their private consciousnesses. In its earlier uses by James and Lawrence, Free Indirect Style indicates an intermediary, half-way stage in the 'trend from objective to subjective'; from Victorian to modern. It shows Lawrence, in particular, poised as some of his critics suggest between nineteenth-century and modernist fiction. Free Indirect Style moves towards deep and full entry into a character's consciousness, yet cannot abandon altogether the authority of the author's own voice. Its use shows Lawrence still partly traditional in retaining an element of authorial infallibility, a stabilizing omniscience; yet also largely modern in using so extensively a language and style which offers a flexible means of transcribing inner thoughts and mental experience. A further, crucial step towards abandonment of the voice of authorial omniscience, towards complete containment of narrative within the minds of characters, remained to be taken by Dorothy Richardson in some of the early volumes of her thirteen-novel sequence, *Pilgrimage* (1915–67).

## DOROTHY RICHARDSON AND MAY SINCLAIR

This step is not immediately apparent in the first volume of *Pilgrimage*, *Pointed Roofs* (1915). Dorothy Richardson records her admiration for Marcel Proust's 'reconstruction of experience focused from within the mind of a single individual' and for Henry James's manner of 'keeping the reader incessantly watching . . . through the eye of a single observer'.[11] From the beginning, *Pilgrimage* is similarly focused through the mind and observation of Miriam Henderson, Richardson's chief, completely central, character. But J.D. Beresford makes a useful observation when he remarks in his Introduction to the first edition of *Pointed Roofs* that he finds it 'the most subjective thing I have ever read', while also describing it as 'realism . . . objective'.[12] As Beresford suggests, though Miriam Henderson's mind and subjective experience is consistently the centre of the novel's attention, it is nevertheless treated objectively enough at times. Initially, and at many stages throughout, Richardson relies like Henry James on authorial report to record the movements and contents of her protagonist's mind. She also, however, moves beyond such methods, as in the following passage, showing Miriam pondering her place in society:

> Never daring to tell anybody.... Did she want to tell anybody? To come out into the open and be helped and have things arranged for her and do things like other people? No.... No . . .
>
> Her thoughts hesitated ... Sivvle ... Something grand – all the grand girls were horrid ... somehow mean and sly ... Sivvle ... *Sivvle* ... *Civil*! Of course! Civil *what*?
>
> Miriam groaned. She was a governess now. Someone would ask her that question. She would ask pater before he went.... No, she would not.... (I, p. 31)

Exclamation, rhetorical questions, and italicized emphases resemble the devices of D.H. Lawrence's Free Indirect Style, while the frequent use of ellipses to indicate how 'her thoughts hesitated' are close to Ford's tactics in the passage quoted earlier from *Parade's End*. Elizabeth Drew might have had Ford or Dorothy Richardson specifically in mind when she commented in 1926 that

> the twentieth-century novel, indeed, might almost be identified with that device of punctuation so liberally employed by its creators, and called the Novel of the Three Dots. (p. 37)

Richardson's principal contribution to the twentieth-century novel, however, was neither a device of punctuation nor extended use of Free Indirect Style to communicate her heroine's thoughts, but the development of a new 'subjective method' different from any of those employed by James, Conrad, Ford or Lawrence. Her progress towards the use of this method can be traced through the various registrations of Miriam's impressions which take place in the following passage:

> She was surprised now at her familiarity with the detail of the room ... that idea of visiting places in dreams. It was something more than that ... all the real part of your life has a real dream in it; some of the real dream part of you coming true. You know in advance when you are really following your life. These things are familiar because reality is here. Coming events cast *light*. It is like dropping everything and walking backwards to something you know is there. However far

you go out, you come back.... I am back now where I was before I began trying
to do things like other people. I left home to get here. None of these things can
touch me here. (II, p. 13)

Miriam's impressions might be compared with Marlow's conclusions, quoted earlier from *Heart of Darkness* – or with the priorities
of modernism generally – concerning the intermingling of dream
into the heart of life and reality. Richardson's tactics at any rate
ensure that it is the dreamy or inner reaches of the self that passages
such as the above most bring to life. It opens objectively enough
with the pronoun 'she', though the three-dot device and the movement into the second-person 'you' form soon begins to indicate
transcription of Miriam's thoughts. 'You' is used much in the sense
of 'one' or even 'I', part of a subtle progression, a gradual slippage,
from third person towards first. This makes the eventual appearance
of 'I' in the last line seem quite natural, though it actually marks a
decisive change from an indirect register of Miriam's inner vision,
mostly mediated by the author, to a direct recording of her thoughts
themselves, supposedly in the form in which they occur to her.

Such sections of direct recording of thought – of Miriam's 'mind . . .
rushing on by itself' (I, p. 268) – appear more frequently as the
sequence goes on: perhaps as Richardson's confidence with 'the subjective method' grew, or as a general 'trend from objective to subjective' began to be more clearly shared by other contemporary authors.
At any rate, by *The Tunnel* (1919), the method of the passage above
turns up not just in occasional phrases, but sustained more or less
throughout whole chapters, or in long passages such as the following:

I *must* have been through there; it's the park. I don't remember. It isn't. It's waiting.
One day I will go through. Les yeux gris, vont au paradis. Going along, along, the
twilight hides your shabby clothes. They are not shabby. They are clothes you go
along in, funny; jolly. Everything's here, any bit of anything, clear in your brain; you
can look at it. What a terrific thing a person is, bigger than anything. How *funny* it is
to be a person. You can never not have been a person. Bouleversement. It's a fait
bouleversant. *Christ*-how-rummy. It's enough. Du, Heilige, rufe dein Kind zurück,
ich habe genossen das irdische Glück; ich habe geliebt und gelebet . . . Oh let the
solid ground not fail beneath my feet, until I am quite quite sure.... Hallo, old Euston
Road, beloved of my soul, my own country, my native heath. (II, p. 256)

Richardson alternates between use of the pronouns 'you' and 'I' to
represent the first person, while the more external, objective, 'she'

is entirely missing from this long passage, indicating suppression of the voice of aloof authorial report. Stabilizing authorial omniscience disappears, replaced by Miriam's 'registration of impressions' (I, p. 431) – the wandering, associative, '*Christ*-how-rummy' polyglot inner mutter through which her thoughts address themselves and swirl around the core of 'what it is to be a person'.

Marked by present-tense verbs and by use of the 'I' form to indicate an unmediated directness of thoughts as they occur, such writing in *Pilgrimage* is the earliest sustained example in English of the stream-of-consciousness form. (The terms 'stream of consciousness' and 'interior monologue' have since come to be used almost interchangeably by critics. Throughout this study, 'stream of consciousness' refers to the form of writing distinguished here in Richardson's work, while 'interior monologue' is used in a more general sense, to include other registers for inner consciousness as well.) The phrase stream of consciousness – not much appreciated by Richardson herself – was probably first used critically by May Sinclair in a review of early volumes of *Pilgrimage* in 1918 in which she explains that

> In this series there is no drama, no situation, no set scene. Nothing happens. It is just life going on and on. It is Miriam Henderson's stream of consciousness going on and on. And in neither is there any grossly discernible beginning or middle or end.[13]

Sinclair may have borrowed the concept of consciousness as a stream from the philosophy of Henry James's brother William. In *Principles of Psychology* (1890), William James remarks that

> consciousness, then, does not appear to itself chopped up in bits . . . it is nothing jointed; it flows. A 'river' or a 'stream' are the metaphors by which it is most naturally described. *In talking of it hereafter, let us call it the stream of thought, of consciousness, or of subjective life* . . .
>
> The wonderful stream of our consciousness. (I, pp. 239–43)

Later critics have come to consider the invention and use of a literary form of 'the wonderful stream of consciousness' as one of the central achievements of modernism: commentators even in the 1920s were quick to praise its improvement on earlier means of representing subjective life. For example, while claiming the

stream of consciousness as the invention of a Frenchman, Edouard
Dujardin, and discussing its later borrowing by James Joyce,
Valery Larbaud pointed out in 1925 the form's

> audacity; the possibilities it offers for forceful and rapid expression of the most
> intimate and spontaneous thoughts, ones which seem to arise outwith conscious-
> ness and apparently prior to being formed into organised discourse . . . a form
> which makes it possible to reach and seize upon thoughts springing up close to
> their source deep within the self.[14]

Larbaud also points out the form's 'novelty'. As he suggests, the
stream of consciousness is in one way a technical breakthrough; a
radical new step in the forceful expression of thought; a more direct,
intimate entry to consciousness than anything hitherto available to the
novel. Dorothy Richardson's disdain for the new phrase, however,
may indicate – and aspects of her writing confirm – that this 'new'
technique can also be seen to have evolved steadily, even inevitably,
rather than altogether suddenly and unexpectedly. The paragraphs
which appear throughout *Pilgrimage*, moving freely between 'she',
'you' and 'I', and sometimes remaining within the final 'I' form of
stream of consciousness, suggest the form develops as a kind of natural, logical continuation of earlier techniques for registering thoughts
deep within the self. Once Henry James had focused his fiction
around the mind and experience of a single individual; once Lawrence, Ford, and Richardson herself had expanded the use of Free
Indirect Style to allow narrative such extensive contact with the inner
voice of characters, the fuller entry to the mind offered by stream of
consciousness required only a couple of further transformations of the
language of the novel – changing of verbs into the present, and of the
'she' and 'you' pronouns into the 'I' which they had in any case always
strained towards representing. Sooner or later, such transformations
were bound to be made. The appearance of stream of consciousness
in English writing might thus be seen as evolutionary rather than
revolutionary – not so much a breakthrough, but an extension of the
developing literary history, and the evolution in fictional language, of
the first decades of the twentieth century; as a natural consummation
of general trends from objective to subjective.

There is a good deal of truth in this view, but important qualifications remain to be added to it. As always, the evolution of literary
history needs to be seen in the context of the wider historical and
political forces which condition the shapes imagination creates

for experience. As the work of a woman writer in representing a female character, *Pilgrimage*, in particular, needs to be placed in the context of the changing status, outlook and social role of women at the time, developments which affect modernist fiction – and literature throughout the early part of the twentieth century – vary widely and variously. In 1899, Henry James suggested that 'nothing is more salient in English life today . . . than the revolution taking place in the position and outlook of women' and that new possibilities for fiction would result.[15] Some of his expectations seemed to Elizabeth Drew to have been fulfilled by 1926, when she remarks in *The Modern Novel* that 'the full development of the intellect and imagination of women is possible now in a way it has never been before' (p. 105). As she suggests, by the 1920s characters even in novels by male authors had moved decisively beyond what she calls the 'definite design in conduct which all Victorian heroines follow' (p. 107) – though not necessarily always in favourable directions. The fiction of Aldous Huxley, Ford Madox Ford, Wyndham Lewis and others at the time is fraught with the menace of many *femmes fatales*, figurations of male anxiety about women's rejection of conventional 'designs of conduct' and gender roles, and their generally less passive attitudes during the suffragette period.

D.H. Lawrence appears more sympathetically interested in what he calls 'woman becoming individual, self-responsible, taking her own initiative', showing Ursula in *The Rainbow* determined and free enough to reject many Victorian designs in conduct, including the institution of marriage. Yet Lawrence remained suspicious of what he describes as 'the cold white light of feminine independence',[16] and has often been criticized for his portrayals of women – after her self-determination in *The Rainbow*, Ursula's final alliance with Birkin in *Women in Love*, for example, seems a compromise, a tame conclusion. 'The full development of the intellect and imagination of women' is a much more sustained, central achievement of *Pilgrimage*. Much of Richardson's narrative is concerned with Miriam's struggle to maintain an independent financial existence within the rigours of the English class system, and with her experience of new social possibilities for women at the time, even at the ordinary enough level of smoking in public or cycling alone. Miriam's convictions make her what she calls 'something new – a kind of different world' (I, p. 260); a 'new woman' (I, p. 436) whose struggle to develop intellect and imagination for herself disposes her firmly against the restraining attitudes of class and a society controlled by men, whom she sometimes finds 'simply paltry and silly – all of them' (II, p. 206). In her view, 'all the men in the world, and their God, ought to apologise to women' (I, p. 459).

Such struggles and resentments, central to the theme of *Pilgrimage*, also have significant consequences for its form – and for the forms of early twentieth-century fiction more generally. Rejection of restraining social conventions at this time extends into rejection of the conventions of fiction: as critics such as Jane Eldridge Miller have pointed out,

> the principal forms of nineteenth-century British fiction were, at the most basic level of narrative dynamics, inimical to the expression of feminist rebellion, for they inevitably moved toward or endorsed stasis, the status quo, and social integration through marriage, and thus ran contrary to the heroine's desire for independence, rebellion and social change . . .
>
> Novelists who wrote about rebellious women were forced to confront and respond to the implications of the formal conventions they had at their disposal. As a result, rebellion is not only thematised but often formalised, as the novelists themselves struggle with the constraints of tradition. (pp. 4–5)

For her part, Miriam feels there are 'whole heaps of books, millions of books I can't read' (I, p. 284), largely because they are written within male-dominated conventions and with

> some mannish cleverness that was only half right. To write books, knowing all about style, would be to become like a man. Women who wrote books and learned these things would be absurd . . . a clever trick, not worth doing. (II, p. 131)

Like her heroine, Dorothy Richardson was sceptical of contemporary, largely male, conventions in fiction, seeking instead, as she explains in her Foreword to *Pilgrimage*, 'a feminine equivalent of the current masculine realism . . . [a] feminine prose . . . moving from point to point without formal obstructions' (I, pp. 9, 12). Such priorities encouraged Richardson's development of the stream-of-consciousness form, its fluid nature – not 'chopped up in bits' or committed to 'stasis, the status quo' but shaped by an unconstrained, wandering, freely associative presentation of Miriam's thoughts – contributing to the unobstructed 'feminine prose' she demands.

Richardson's increased interest in consciousness, whether stream-like or not, can be seen to enact more generally her wish to escape conventions of 'current masculine realism'. Like Proust, Richardson sees a truer realism created by placing everything in the mind rather than in the object: her views of this matter, however, are appropriately considered not only in relation to Proust's, but to those of Virginia Woolf, another woman author of the period committed to writing specifically *as* a woman. Woolf remarks in *A Room of One's Own* (1929)

> If one is a woman one is often surprised by a sudden splitting off of consciousness, say in walking down Whitehall, when from being the natural inheritor of that civilisation, she becomes, on the contrary, outside of it, alien and critical. (p. 96)

Woolf's views suggest that male structuring of society – of Whitehall, of civilization generally – encourages women in particular to split off in consciousness from the external world. If women seek a room of their own, it is in the private domain of the mind that it may most easily be established, metaphorically at any rate. Women writers such as Richardson or Woolf may thus have been especially disposed to develop new narrative forms in which the workings of consciousness, split away from external reality and the object world, could be fruitfully sustained and explored. In Richardson's writing especially, the nature of such narrative forms may further reflect particular conditions imposed by a male-dominated world. One of the pressures this world exerts is in seeing women not just objectively, but quite often actually *as* objects, evaluated principally for external appearance, however inwardly or subjectively they may wish to see themselves. Much as Miriam resentfully retreats from this external evaluation towards subjective enclosure within her mind and self, some vestigial consciousness of it inevitably remains: her consciousness is therefore not only 'split off' from an external, male-dominated world, but partly split *by* it. Such a mixture of objective and subjective awareness of the self is probably present in any mind: regardless of gender, any sense of identity is partly split between external, public visions of the self and inward, private ones. *Pilgrimage* suggests, however, that the contemporary, rapidly changing situation of women made this split more acutely felt in female consciousness. Most attracted by the subjective privacy of an inner world, women were also most aware of the pressures on it from an outer one. Even when Miriam is most engrossed in her private thoughts, an awareness of herself from a more objective point of view can still intrude; an awareness of herself as 'she' as well as 'I'. This uneasy doubleness in identity keeps the 'she', 'you', and 'I' pronouns in tense yet fluid equilibrium in Richardson's writing, facilitating the transitions between them required for the final emergence of the stream-of-consciousness form. In such ways, although the form may have emerged logically and naturally from the evolving literary history of the early twentieth century, it is particularly natural and logical that it should have first appeared in *Pilgrimage*, a new woman's vision of a new woman's mind.

Many recent critics have traced connections of this kind between the emergence of modernism and issues of gender – often emphasizing, like Jane Eldridge Miller, the significance for modernist innovation of conflict between women's new outlooks in the early twentieth century and restrictions imposed by 'the principal forms of nineteenth-century British fiction'. Still the most comprehensive analysts of women's involvement in modernism, Sandra M. Gilbert and Susan Gubar point to a complex of literary and historical evidence for their argument – in *The Female Imagination and the Modernist Aesthetic* (1986) – that

> in their problematic relationship to the tradition of authority, as well as to the authority of tradition, women writers are the major precursors of all 20th-century modernists, the *avant-garde* of the *avant-garde*, so to speak. (p. 1)

Further evidence of this central involvement of the female imagination in the modernist aesthetic is provided by Bonnie Kime Scott's anthology, *The Gender of Modernism* (1990). Its wide range of statements by critics and by modernist authors themselves emphasizes how much further than has often been supposed 'the initial impetus for modernism came in fact from women writers' (p. 303), and how many of these writers should be seen as more than merely peripheral figures in the movement. Early, radical experiments with the language of fiction made by the Paris-based United States author Gertrude Stein, for example, can be seen as influential on later writing in a number of ways. Stein was a former student of William James, and the unpunctuated, associative, flowing quality of some of her writing contributes to a kind of early, idiosyncratic form of stream of consciousness. In the British context, Katherine Mansfield and Rebecca West each reshaped the conventional resources of fiction in examining women's experience, while May Sinclair remained close to Richardson in style and interest, as her early, intelligent review of *Pilgrimage*, quoted above, helps suggest.

Sinclair worked for the Women's Suffrage League, as well as in the first stages of the psychoanalytic movement. Her best novel, *Mary Olivier* (1919), is much concerned with constraining conventions imposed on contemporary women and the consequences for their consciousness and outlook. As in several of her other novels, she shows a heroine enduring a life of enforced renunciation and self-denial, her 'mind battering at the walls of her body, the walls of the room, the walls of the world' (p. 260). This 'battering' and the movements of Mary Olivier's mind generally are recorded in a variety of sensitive inner registers, often a Free Indirect Style and an expression in the second-person form of how 'your thoughts go on inside you' (p. 99). Like Richardson, Sinclair can move quickly from 'she' to 'you' to an 'I' form, as in the following passage recalling Mary's renunciation of a lover:

> She knew only one thing about perfect happiness: it didn't hide; it didn't wait for you behind unknown doors . . .
>
> If you looked back on any perfect happiness you saw that it had not come from the people or the things you thought it had come from, but from somewhere inside yourself . . .
>
> Not Richard. He had become part of the kingdom of God without ceasing to be himself . . .
>
> I used to think there was nothing I couldn't give up for Richard.
>
> Could I give up this? If I had to choose between losing Richard and losing this? (pp. 378–9)

Constraints on Mary's life and experience are generated not only by the general situation of women at the time, but by her particular position within a family dominated by strong religious faith, especially influential on Mary's childhood. Much of her later sense of release and genuine selfhood comes through discovering in writing and in art an escape from or a means of reshaping the constraints of reality and personal circumstance. Many of her problems, however, continue to arise from conflicts between the exigencies of religious faith, of art, and sometimes of sex. Along with the closeness with which Sinclair's writing follows the thought, language and point of view of a partly autobiographical central figure, these conflicts have often led to comparisons between *Mary Olivier* and a novel by an author she admired – James Joyce, who also follows, in *A Portrait of the Artist as a Young Man* (1916), evolution from a constraining childhood towards the free flight of art and creation. Comparisons with Joyce have not always been favourable to Sinclair, indicating a problem in the evaluation of the work of Dorothy Richardson as well as her own. Each author was considered important in her day, but their reputations had begun to be partially eclipsed by Joyce, even as early as 1925, as the following review of one of the volumes in Richardson's *Pilgrimage* series indicates:

> Probably no one has done more than Miss Richardson to transform modern fiction. She popularised, if she did not invent, the subjective novel, and genius, beside which her own meagre talents insignificantly fade, has been expended on it. Once, and not very long ago, Miss Richardson's novels, or rather the instalments of Miss Richardson's novel, were reckoned as quite important. She was parodied, discussed, esteemed. But now . . . Miss Richardson has failed to fulfil her earlier promise. The bleak truth is that Miss Richardson perfected a way of saying things without having anything to say . . . Is there anything there but an excellent manner execrably applied.[17]

Such bleak views of an excellent method no longer seem very close to the truth. Richardson's literary standing has recently been rightly restored by critics interested both in her transforming role in modern fiction, and in the issues of gender and class addressed in *Pilgrimage*. Joyce is nevertheless still judged the 'genius' of modernism, and the writer in whose work trends from objective to subjective received their most comprehensive and sophisticated embodiment. Even when insisting that a Frenchman was the original inventor of the stream-of-consciousness form, Valery Larbaud acknowledged that it received its fullest and finest employment in *Ulysses*.

## JAMES JOYCE

Joyce's writing did not immediately display the modernist techniques so fully and spectacularly deployed in *Ulysses*, but passed through several stages of the development, discussed above, which appeared in the work of his contemporaries. The short stories eventually collected as *Dubliners* (1914) are fairly conventional in their realistic, sometimes satiric, portrayal of drab lives in a city Joyce shows suffering from paralysis of will, energy and imagination. Joyce, however, also keeps most of his narratives quite closely focused around the minds and inward experiences of his protagonists – obviously in the opening three stories, written in the first person; in later stories more subtly, in frequent, extensive uses of Free Indirect Style, as well as authorial report of thought. An increasing reliance on this inward focus can be traced through the changes Joyce made in the draft novel, *Stephen Hero*, begun around 1904 and eventually transformed into *A Portrait of the Artist as a Young Man*, published in 1916. For the most part, *Stephen Hero* is a straightforwardly realistic narrative, presenting characters through report, dialogue and observation by a narrator who remains at an objective distance from the action. As Theodore Spencer explains in his introduction to *Stephen Hero*, which was eventually published in 1944, Joyce revised much of this draft material, 'aiming at economy, and . . . trying to place his centre of action as much as possible inside the consciousness of his hero' (p. 15). Some of the manuscript revisions to *Stephen Hero* indicate Joyce experimenting with Free Indirect Style: in *A Portrait of the Artist as a Young Man* itself, he omits some of the realistic detail of the earlier draft and practises a Jamesian exclusiveness of focus on – sometimes within – a single mind. Complete concentration on Stephen Dedalus makes him, in James's terms, the 'definite responsible intervening first person singular' around whom the material of the novel is entirely shaped.

A particular form of this concentration is immediately evident in Joyce's opening paragraph, as unusual as anything in the novel which follows:

> Once upon a time and a very good time it was there was a moocow coming down along the road and the moocow that was coming down along the road met a nicens little boy named baby tuckoo.... His father told him that story: his father looked at him through a glass: he had a hairy face.
>
> He was baby tuckoo . . .
>
> The Vances lived in number seven. They had a different father and mother. They were Eileen's father and mother. When they were grown up he was going to marry Eileen. He hid under the table. (pp. 7–8)

Without always recording his actual thoughts, this opening passage nevertheless dramatizes Stephen's consciousness through an infantile language whose simple vocabulary and observation and abrupt, arbitrary juxtapositions mimic the mental and linguistic habits of the child. This is a kind of mimicry Joyce scarcely returns to – or at least not so ostentatiously – in *A Portrait of the Artist as a Young Man*, but it is variously, extensively, employed in *Ulysses*. Gerty McDowell, for example, the girl Leopold Bloom meets on the beach in Chapter 13, 'Nausikaa', is introduced as follows:

> Gerty was dressed simply but with the instinctive taste of a votary of Dame Fashion . . . A neat blouse of electric blue selftinted by dolly dyes (because it was expected in the *Lady's Pictorial* that electric blue would be worn) . . .
>
> A sterling good daughter was Gerty just like a second mother in the house, a ministering angel too with a little heart worth its weight in gold. (pp. 455, 461)

Joyce himself remarked that '*Nausikaa* is written in a namby-pamby, jammy marmalady-drawersy style'[18] – a clichéd language designed to mimic the pretty, precious, cheaply romantic idiom of women's magazines such as *Lady's Pictorial*. A later section of *Ulysses*, Chapter 16, 'Eumaeus', set in the Cabman's Shelter, is equally occupied with endless, weary clichés. Exhausted himself at the time, Bloom suggests an explanation for this when

> To improve the shining hour he wondered whether he might . . . pen something out of the common groove (as he fully intended doing) at the rate of one guinea per column. *My Experiences*, let us say, *in a Cabman's Shelter*. (p. 750)

Bloom does not realize these ambitions in the course of the novel, but the chapter in which they are mentioned is written almost as if he had, and as if the chapter itself was the result. The passages introducing Gerty, or Stephen in *A Portrait of the Artist as a Young Man*, similarly seem as if written by the characters who appear in them; as if the characters were somehow helping to tell their own story, shaping its style around their distinctive linguistic habits and expressive idioms. Such mimicry is close to Free Indirect Style, which Gérard Genette sees as distinguished by the narrative 'taking on the speech of the character'. Yet it cannot be exactly labelled as Free Indirect Discourse or Style, since the narrative takes on Gerty's manner, or Bloom's, or Stephen's, without necessarily or consistently transcribing their actual speech or thought. Critical commentators on this aspect of Joyce's tactics have coined various other terms for it. Richard Ellmann describes it as a 'magnetization of style and vocabulary by the context of person, place, and time' (p. 146). Dorrit Cohn talks of 'stylistic contagion' (p. 33), suggesting that the speech habits of characters temporarily infect the narrative in which they appear. Hugh Kenner sees this sort of writing as a distinctive feature of Joyce's style, pointing to its 'characterising vocabulary'; the repeated inclusion of 'a little cluster of idioms which a character might use if he were managing the narrative'. Summing up such tactics, Kenner suggests that in Joyce's work 'words are in such delicate equilibrium that they detect the gravitational field of the nearest person' (pp. 16, 17).

Such 'gravitational fields' are neither altogether new, however, nor an invention of Joyce's. His stylistic imitation of characters' idioms extends what Mikhail Bakhtin sees as a perennial feature of the merging, intermingling systems of language fundamental to fiction. Bakhtin suggests that

> A character in a novel always has . . . a zone of his own, his own sphere of influence on the authorial context surrounding him, a sphere that extends – and often quite far – beyond the boundaries of the direct discourse allotted to him . . . this zone surrounding the important characters of the novel is stylistically profoundly idiosyncratic. (p. 320)

Many authors – Charles Dickens is again one of Bakhtin's examples – exploit this 'idiosyncratic zone' surrounding character. Once again, modernism may be best distinguished quantitatively rather than qualitatively from earlier writing: the 'gravitational fields' or spheres of influence exerted by characters within Joyce's writing may be neither unique nor new, but they are employed unusually frequently and extend unusually far. His idiosyncratic zones of language are not used exclusively to reflect the sphere of influence of characters, but even (as Ellmann suggests, and Chapter 4 discusses further), to indicate certain linguistic idiosyncrasies associated with particular places. Setting in a newspaper office in Chapter 7, ('Aeolus') for example, helps to account for the intrusion into the text of newspaper headlines and other fragments of journalese, sometimes even between single lines of dialogue. Nevertheless, it is most often the linguistic resources and habits of speech not of places but of individuals which shape the idiosyncrasies of Joyce's language. In this way, sometimes obliquely and subtly, the whole medium of Joyce's fiction is constructed to reflect the consciousness, inner discourse or cast of mind of its characters.

In much of *Ulysses*, of course, representation of consciousness is not oblique but clear and direct. Valery Larbaud and other critics in the 1920s praised Joyce not especially for his creation of a language of delicate equilibrium, but for the brilliant advances he made in the use of a stream-of-consciousness style able to 'seize upon' every thought or movement of characters' minds. Its potential is most apparent in the eighteenth and last chapter of *Ulysses*, 'Penelope'. Dorothy Richardson admired Joyce as one of the authors of the 'feminine prose' she advocated, and it may be appropriate that by far the longest sustained section of stream of consciousness in *Ulysses* communicates thoughts of neither of Joyce's male protagonists, Leopold Bloom or Stephen Dedalus, but of Bloom's wife Molly, somnolently, inwardly soliloquizing as her mind hovers on the edge of unconsciousness. As Richardson recommended, the prose of this section moves 'without formal obstructions': punctuation is almost entirely missing from the concluding sixty pages of *Ulysses*. Its absence suggests a mind flowing freely, associatively, sometimes arbitrarily between subjects, between thoughts, in flickering, almost seamless succession – as in the following passage, for example, in which Molly still seeks sleep:

> a quarter after what an unearthly hour I suppose theyre just getting up in China now combing out their pigtails for the day well soon have the nuns ringing the angelus theyve nobody coming in to spoil their sleep except an odd priest or two for his night office the alarmclock next door at cockshout clattering the brains out of itself let me see if I can doze off 1 2 3 4 5 what kind of flowers are those they invented like the stars the wallpaper in Lombard street was much nicer the apron he gave me was like that something only I only wore it twice better lower this lamp and try again so as I can get up early (p. 930)

As the above passage shows, 'Penelope' not only drops the formal obstruction of punctuation, it discards other formal constraints of grammar and coherence. Joyce's concluding stream of consciousness moves, as Larbaud suggests, beyond 'organised discourse' in its pursuit of 'thoughts springing up close to their source deep within the self', even leading towards what is formed 'outwith consciousness'. Joyce goes on to investigate the area beyond the conscious mind in *Finnegans Wake* (1939; further discussed in Chapter 4), though there are several points in *Ulysses* which anticipate this direction in his later writing: in Chapter 15, 'Nighttown', for example, and occasionally in some of the chapters which follow. *Ulysses* itself, however, ends at the point where unconsciousness, the sleep which has hovered around Molly throughout 'Penelope', finally overtakes her. Molly's soliloquy remains – just – within consciousness, a final consummation of the trends in early twentieth-century narrative to place 'everything in the mind' of characters and to suppress from view the stabilizing, controlling presence of an omniscient author.

Though *Ulysses* provides this consummate example of the stream-of-consciousness form, this should not obscure – as it sometimes seems to for critics the real variety of Joyce's writing throughout the novel. *Ulysses* is not only, nor purely except in its last chapter, a stream-of-consciousness novel. On the contrary, one of the strengths of Joyce's writing is its exploitation and integration within a single novel of the whole range of styles discussed so far. Their variety is in evidence, if not immediately from the novel's opening, certainly from its first introduction of its central figure:

> Mr Leopold Bloom ate with relish the inner organs of beasts and fowls. He liked thick giblet soup, nutty gizzards, a stuffed roast heart, liver slices fried with crustcrumbs, fried hencods' roes. Most of all he liked grilled mutton kidneys which gave to his palate a fine tang of faintly scented urine.
>
> 5   Kidneys were in his mind as he moved about the kitchen softly, righting her breakfast things on the humpy tray. Gelid light and air were in the kitchen but out of doors gentle summer morning everywhere. Made him feel a bit peckish.
>
> The coals were reddening.
>
> 10   Another slice of bread and butter: three, four: right. She didn't like her plate full. Right. He turned from the tray, lifted the kettle off the hob and set it sideways on the fire. It sat there, dull and squat, its spout stuck out. Cup of tea soon. Good. Mouth dry. The cat walked stiffly round a leg of the table with tail on high.
>
> 15   – Mkgnao!
>
> – O, there you are, Mr Bloom said, turning from the fire.
>
> The cat mewed in answer and stalked again stiffly round a leg of the table, mewing. Just how she stalks over my writingtable. Prr. Scratch my head. Prr.
>
> Mr Bloom watched curiously, kindly, the lithe black form. Clean to see:
> 20   the gloss of her sleek hide, the white button under the butt of her tail, the green flashing eyes. He bent down to her, his hands on his knees.
>
> – Milk for the pussens, he said.
>
> – Mrkgnao! the cat cried.
>
> They call them stupid. They understand what we say better than we
> 25   understand them. She understands all she wants to. Vindictive too. Wonder what I look like to her. Height of a tower? No, she can jump me. (pp. 65–6)

Bloom's first presentation to the reader is a parody of formal introduction, the excessively polite 'Mr Leopold Bloom' followed in lines 1–4 by the kind of authorial report of distinguishing characteristics, likes and dislikes, which often appears in Victorian fiction. Bloom's tastes, however, are comically insalubrious, undermining the formal tone of the passage's opening, though they curiously suggest a direction much of the rest of it will take: kidneys are followed into Bloom's mind by the narrative itself. By the end of the second paragraph, oddities and colloquialisms – 'Made him feel a bit peckish' – suggest it is moving towards a Free Indirect transcription of Bloom's thoughts. Though line 9 returns to what may be authorial objectivity, the movement into Bloom's mind continues in the next lines: 'she' is a pronoun without antecedent in the novel so far, one which, like the counting phrase 'three, four: right', makes complete sense only to Bloom. After returning to an objective, reporting voice in lines 11 and 12, the paragraph ends with the kind of abbreviated, telegrammatic sentences – 'Cup of tea soon. Good. Mouth Dry.' – which also appear at the conclusion of the whole passage. Some way from organized discourse, they are the principal device throughout the early part of the novel for representing Bloom's stream of consciousness and its barely verbalized movements.

The next section, from line 14, sees an intrusion upon Bloom's inner world by domestic reality, the cat determinedly forcing itself upon his thoughts. Joyce's fascination for sound, for phonetic music, creates in *Ulysses* a novel in which 'everything speaks in its own way' (p. 154), and it is typical that the cat moves beyond conventional miaowing to mkgnaoing, mrkgnaoing, and even, just after the passage quoted, mrkrgnaoing – no doubt in a feline attempt to demand 'milk now'. It is also typical that Joyce's communication of consciousness spreads beyond the strict confines of a single mind. Bloom's thoughts flow out not only to speculate about the cat's nature and perspective in lines 24–6 ('Wonder what I look like to her?') but even to encompass her possible thoughts and impulses – almost her language at 'Prr. Scratch my head. Prr'. Such extensions of consciousness over other creatures or objects in the characters' world frequently bring to life unlikely situations and points of view in *Ulysses*. Stephen, for example, imagines in Chapter 1 the words which might be spoken by a drowned corpse dredged back to the surface. Bloom's curious, kindly, mind repeatedly extends to encompass the likely thinking of other creatures or people – such as the 'blind stripling' whose thoughts and feelings he constructs at some length after a chance meeting (pp. 230–3).

Such interfusions of consciousness into context spread a bright cast of thought over the whole novel, a part not only of its communication of the mind within individual characters, but an enlivening of descriptions of the 'world without' in which they live. Even Bloom's kettle seems more than usually alive. And recording his reflections on the cat adds to more than just the warmth and intimacy of the passage's communication of Bloom's mind and inner world. Use of the cat's lowly point of view adds to the variety of perspectives used to delineate Bloom in his kitchen, and to the completeness with which he is seen from outside as well as in. Joyce explained that he sought to create in *Ulysses* a 'complete all-round character' and, of Bloom, that 'I see him from all sides, and therefore he is all-round'.[19] Typically of his writing, the above passage practises a kind of literary Cubism, an almost simultaneous use of alternative perspectives – points of view which repeatedly switch between cat, character and author; inner consciousness or objective distance. In its 'Cyclops' chapter (12), *Ulysses* warns against any narrow, single-minded or, literally, one-eyed view of reality. The novel's own practice works against any such narrowing of vision. No wonder Bloom, always fascinated by science, at one stage speculates about 'parallax' (p. 194) – changes in what is seen which are caused by alteration of the point of observation. *Ulysses* itself employs a kind of parallax to resist the paralysis of Dublin. However drab or static Dublin life may be in reality, its presentation is made lively and colourful by Joyce's parallactic tactics, constantly shifting the narrative through a spectrum of techniques and points of view.

Hugh Kenner provides an image which helps to define the operation of these techniques, perspectives and registers when he describes *Ulysses* as a sort of 'duet for two narrators' (p. 67). For the most part, each sentence in the passage quoted – or in the early part of *Ulysses* generally – can be assigned either to the author/ narrator who initially establishes an objective view of Bloom and his curious tastes, or to the subjective inner discourse of Bloom himself, a second voice constantly present in the novel. But there are also many areas – in lines 6 to 8, for example – which cannot be exclusively assigned to either voice, but are a mixture of both. Throughout *Ulysses*, the two voices of Joyce's duet often interfuse, harmonize and split apart again as they do in this passage, creating a range of modulations, a flickering movement into and out of characters' minds, sometimes even within a single line of text. The passage begins clearly enough with a parodic form of nineteenth-century narrative, and ends with a decisive movement into a thoroughly subjective, modernist, style: the forms employed between, however, demonstrate a full range of the possibilities – Free Indirect Style, authorial report of thought, stream of consciousness – developed or extended by modernist narrative in the early years of the century to deepen the novel's grasp of the minds of its characters. If, as Hugh Kenner suggests, *Ulysses* is 'the decisive English-language book of the century' (p. xii), this is not only for its outstanding achievement with the stream-of-consciousness form, but for its fluent movement among *all* the devices developed in the course of progress towards that most effective of inward styles. In this way, the passage not only introduces readers to Bloom. It also offers a kind of encyclopaedia of the new strengths and possibilities developed by fiction in English in the first decades of the twentieth century; an illustrated introduction to the new techniques created for narrative's steady movement from objective to subjective.

## VIRGINIA WOOLF

Virginia Woolf's fiction may have benefited from the example of *Ulysses*. Woolf admired Joyce for what she calls his attempts to come 'close to the quick of the mind'; 'to reveal the flickerings of that innermost flame which flashes its messages through the brain'; or to record 'the inner thought, and then the little scatter of life on top to keep you in touch with reality'.[20] But she also had reservations about *Ulysses*, as Chapter 1 pointed out, and the subjective method of her own novels differs significantly from Joyce's. Her particular style can be illustrated from the opening pages of *Mrs Dalloway* (1925):

> Mrs Dalloway said she would buy the flowers herself. For Lucy had her work cut out for her. The doors would be taken off their hinges; Rumplemayer's men were coming. And then, thought Clarissa Dalloway, what a morning – fresh as if issued to children on a beach.
>
> What a lark! What a plunge! For so it had always seemed to her . . .
>
> For having lived in Westminster – how many years now? Over twenty, – one feels even in the midst of the traffic, or waking at night, Clarissa was positive, a

particular hush, or solemnity . . . Such fools we are, she thought, crossing Victoria Street. For Heaven only knows why one loves it so, how one sees it so. (pp. 5–6)

The passage begins to move away from objective authorial report almost from its opening, with unexplained mentions of 'Lucy' and 'Rumplemayer's men' suggesting the frame of reference of Mrs Dalloway herself. The exclamations 'What a lark!' and 'What a plunge' and the rhetorical question 'How many years now?' belong still more clearly to the inner voice of the character. This voice, however, never replaces the author's completely, or for very long: on the contrary, the frequent cues such as 'thought Clarissa Dalloway', 'so it seemed to her', or 'Clarissa was positive' are a constant reminder of authorial organization and presentation of thoughts. Though in moving freely between 'she', 'we' and 'one' *Mrs Dalloway* seems close to the styles of Dorothy Richardson and May Sinclair, Woolf does not follow these authors in making further moves towards unmediated transcription of characters' minds in the first-person, present-tense form of stream of consciousness.

The six characters' monologues which Woolf presents in *The Waves* (1931) might seem closer to the subjective methods of Joyce or Dorothy Richardson, since thoughts and feelings are presented in the first person, in great detail, and largely uninterrupted by an authorial voice. Yet the inner life of each of Woolf's six characters is presented almost as if written in a letter. Their thoughts are carefully organized, clearly expressed, and show a sophisticated capacity to find metaphors for states of mind and the various pangs of contact between consciousness and the intractable world around it. As in *Mrs Dalloway*, Woolf's representation of thought in *The Waves* has none of the anarchic fluency of Molly Bloom's mind in *Ulysses*, nor the syntactic fragmentation which often marks entry to Leopold Bloom's. Far from a stream of consciousness which moves, as Larbaud suggests, beyond 'organised discourse', *The Waves* is so elegantly reflective and carefully structured that it comes as close as any novel to the condition of poetry. As in much of Woolf's work, subjective experience forms the whole substance of the novel, but a more general term such as interior monologue, rather than stream of consciousness, may be the appropriate term for the style in which it is recorded, both in *The Waves* and in Woolf's writing generally.

By comparison with stream of consciousness, Woolf's kind of interior monologue can appear a relatively conventional form. The repeated speech or thought cues in the above passage from *Mrs Dalloway* sometimes indicate an apparently direct transcription of the character's thoughts, as in the last sentences – almost a kind of direct speech, though without the conventional indication of quotation marks. The regular cues, however, also suggest that much of Woolf's representation of the 'innermost flame' of the mind is close to the familiar 'she thought to herself that' form of indirect discourse. Much the same tactics appear in *To the Lighthouse* (1927), at any rate in the novel's first and third sections. Woolf herself remarks of the latter novel that 'it is all in oratio obliqua' (indirect speech). J. Hillis Miller particularly admires Woolf's use of this form as a sensitive register for communicating inner experience, praising her

> indirect discourse, the consciousness of the narrator married to the consciousness of the character and speaking for it . . . *To the Lighthouse* is a masterwork of the exploration of the consciousness of others with the tool of indirect discourse.[21]

The capacity of these tools to reach 'the quick of the mind' in *To the Lighthouse* can be illustrated from the following passage from the first section of the novel, describing Mrs Ramsay at her triumphal dinner party:

> Everything seemed possible. Everything seemed right. Just now (but this cannot last, she thought, dissociating herself from the moment while they were all talking about boots) just now she had reached security; she hovered like a hawk suspended; like a flag floated in an element of joy which filled every nerve of her body fully and sweetly, not noisily, solemnly rather, for it arose, she thought, looking at them all eating there, from husband and children and friends; all of which rising in this profound stillness (she was helping William Bankes to one very small piece more and peered into the depths of the earthenware pot) seemed now for no special reason to stay there like a smoke, like a fume rising upward, holding them safe together. Nothing need be said; nothing could be said. (pp. 120–1)

'The world without' – second helpings and banal conversations about boots – is relegated in this passage to parentheses, emphasizing that Mrs Ramsay is mentally 'dissociated from the moment', free to float like a hawk, flag, or fume. Such similes describe the character's mind rather than recording thoughts plausibly arising within it, but there is also much in the passage which represents more directly the particular influence or 'gravitational field' of the character herself. In particular, the complicated syntax in the extended third sentence ('Just now . . .') and the rhythm which results strongly suggest associations and qualifications unfolding within Mrs Ramsay's pattern of thought. This is also present at least occasionally, as in *Mrs Dalloway*, in forms other than simple 'oratio obliqua': as Hillis Miller's metaphor of a 'marriage' between the voice of narrator and character actually suggests, Woolf's style moves at times beyond indirect discourse and towards Free Indirect Style.

Sometimes employing this form, sometimes the more ordinary oratio obliqua, writing such as the above is sustained throughout much of the first and third parts of *To the Lighthouse*. In its own way, it achieves as comprehensive an enclosure of narrative within individual consciousness as appears in *Ulysses* or *Pilgrimage*. The inner life exists so richly that 'nothing could be said' to equal it in direct speech, in the everyday external world. Woolf's style represents the mind of her central figure so thoroughly in the first part of the novel, also moving so fluently into and between the consciousness of several other characters, that the external, object world of boots and earthenware almost disappears – as at times it does in the third section, in which Lily Briscoe proves herself as adept as Mrs Ramsay at 'losing consciousness of outer things' (p. 181). The harsher physical realities Mrs Ramsay fears and her husband sometimes too insistently represents to her, fade from the novel. The insistent physical presence of the lighthouse across the bay, observed by all the characters, comes to provide an almost unique point of stable external reference – a 'stark and straight' (p. 211) object, a clear 'outer thing' to counterpoint the shifting tides of inner thought which flow around the novel in its first and third sections.

At the beginning of its second part, however, many of these functions and priorities are reversed. In the Ramsays' holiday home, 'one by one the lamps were all extinguished' (p. 143) as the family falls asleep, leaving the lighthouse beam the only illumination in the darkness of the night – and later many nights – shown passing through the house. With the characters asleep, or – later – departed or dead, Woolf's style changes radically from the subjective method of the first part. The second goes on to dramatize instead a world independent of individual consciousness – a world of outer things nevertheless made to seem not inert but sinisterly,

subtly alive and active. Woolf employs a style of sustained personification which endows mere objects with attributes – such as
will, reason or emotion – apparently appropriated from a now-
unconscious humanity. For example, it is observed that

> certain airs . . . entered the drawing room, questioning and wondering . . . the
> wind sent its spies about the house. (pp. 144, 151)

> Weeds . . . tapped methodically on the window pane. (p. 151)

> the Lighthouse . . . with its pale footfall upon stair and mat . . . the stroke of the
> lighthouse . . . laid itself with such authority on the carpet in the darkness . . . laid
> its caress and lingered stealthily and looked and came lovingly again . . . [and]
> leant upon the bed . . . sent its sudden stare over bed and wall. (pp. 144, 151, 157)

Airs, winds and the stroke of the lighthouse apparently walk at will
around the deserted house, while family life, human values, human
life itself, crumble under the constant questioning of wind and sky:
'Will you fade? Will you perish?' (p. 148). Casual recordings, in
brief parentheses, of the deaths of Mrs Ramsay and several members of her family emphasize the transient irrelevance of humanity
in an indifferent universe of stones, stars and things. Such brief
parenthetical asides – separating a diminished human domain from
a now-triumphant object world – entirely reverse the first section's
tactics in bracketing off an external world irrelevant to the flow of
characters' thoughts.

While the first and third sections of *To the Lighthouse* concentrate so comprehensively on the subjective life of the mind, in
other words, the second creates a style not so much objective as
adept at bringing objects themselves to life: at dramatizing, equally
comprehensively, a domain beyond consciousness hostile to its
order and light. So sharply divided in style between its three parts,
*To the Lighthouse* enacts formally the theme of Mr Ramsay's
philosophy: 'Subject and object and the nature of reality' (p. 28).
Even the novel's setting on an island, washed around by the endless chaos of the ocean, extends figuratively – in the manner of
some of Conrad's fiction – a sense of the mind and its orders
threatened by the randomness which surrounds it. Something of
this sense preoccupies Mrs Ramsay, even at her moment of greatest security, domestic order and social success, her triumphal
dinner party, when she feels that

inside the room seemed to be order and dry land; there, outside, a reflection in which things wavered and vanished, waterily . . . they were all conscious of making a party together in a hollow, on an island. (p. 112)

Juxtaposing order and chaos, subjectivity and objectivity, at the level of form as well as theme, *To the Lighthouse* provides a kind of paradigm for the new priorities of modernist fiction, for its growing inclination to turn from the world to the mind.

## BACKGROUND AND CONTEXT

So concerned in her fiction with disparities between the mind within and the world without, Woolf is also one of the clearest of critical commentators on wider conflicts between subjective and objective methods in the writing of her period. In her essay 'Modern Fiction' (1919), she defines as 'spiritual' the attempt by Joyce and others to come 'close to the quick of the mind', distinguishing their work from the 'material', realist style she sees characterizing the work of H.G. Wells, Arnold Bennett and John Galsworthy. In 'Mr. Bennett and Mrs. Brown' (1924) she goes on to discuss in more detail the inability of such realist methods to represent truly a hypothetical character, Mrs Brown. Methods which concentrate on factual, observable aspects of this character – her dress, appearance, background and material circumstances – allow the spirit or inner nature to escape. Too close attention to what is perceived precludes Woolf's favoured interest in the perceiver, the human subject with all his or her complex thought processes and emotions. Like Proust, Woolf considered it a mistake to place 'everything in the object' when 'really everything is in the mind': what she calls in 'Modern Fiction' the 'enormous labour of proving the solidity, the likeness to life, of the story' is therefore 'not merely labour thrown away, but labour misplaced'. 'Is life like this?' she asks. 'Must novels be like this?' In reply to her questions, Woolf provides a summary of her own priorities for modern fiction:

Look within and life, it seems, is very far from being 'like this'. Examine for a moment an ordinary mind on an ordinary day. The mind receives a myriad impressions – trivial, fantastic, evanescent, or engraved with the sharpness of steel. From all sides they come, an incessant shower of innumerable atoms; and as they fall, as they shape themselves into the life of Monday or Tuesday, the accent falls differently from of old . . . Life is not a series of gig-lamps symmetrically arranged; life is a luminous halo, a semi-transparent envelope surrounding us from the beginning of consciousness to the end. Is it not the task of the novelist to convey this varying, this unknown and uncircumscribed spirit, whatever aberration or complexity it may display, with as little mixture of the alien and external as possible? We are not pleading merely for courage and sincerity; we are suggesting that the proper stuff of fiction is a little other than custom would have us believe it.

It is, at any rate, in some such fashion as this that we seek to define the quality which distinguishes the work of several young writers, among whom Mr. James Joyce is the most notable, from that of their predecessors. (II, pp. 106–7)

Woolf's views in 'Modern Fiction' provide one of the most comprehensive, celebrated statements of the priorities of modernism. Several other modernist writers discussed or sought to redefine 'the proper stuff of fiction' – or dismissed some of Joyce's predecessors – in similar terms. Ford Madox Ford also considers John Galsworthy too little inclined to 'look within', describing him as 'a scientific observer' offering 'the Literature of organised materialism . . . simply the results of his observations in life'. D.H. Lawrence attacks a lifelessness in Galsworthy's characters which he attributes to 'the collapse from the psychology of the free human individual into the psychology of the social being'. Such beings, in Lawrence's view, suffer from being 'too much aware of objective reality' and too involved in the 'materialist' disposition of their age. Henry James's negative assessment of some of his contemporaries likewise arises largely from a view that their work reflects 'simply the results of . . . observation of life'. In his essay 'The Younger Generation' (1914), James extends to Arnold Bennett and other contemporary novelists the kind of criticisms he had made earlier of Wells – that their realist styles provided only a shapeless 'lump of life', encumbered with 'innumerable small facts and aspects'. This sort of meticulous attention to the external, perceived world omitted James's preferred interest in the 'intense perceiver' around whom experience could be 'wrought and shaped' into art.[22]

Comments by some of the novelists the modernists attacked often confirm such differences in their outlook. Hugh Walpole, a prominent novelist himself in 1910, briskly dismisses the modernist answer to the 'question of questions. What is reality in the novel' which he asks in his open *Letter to a Modern Novelist*. He tells the determinedly modern author he addresses

All that *your* school of novelists has to say about the novel seems to us nonsense . . .

I find your novel unreal just as you find mine to be so. (pp. 6, 25)

John Galsworthy and H.G. Wells defend some of the preferences modernism rejected. Galsworthy admits that it is not the individual psychology of characters which interests him, so much as their existence as types, through whom he could satirize a whole society. H.G. Wells similarly sees his subject as 'contemporary social development and its problems', suggesting that he would 'rather be called a journalist than an artist'. Though ready to admire Conrad for his 'depth' and 'subjective reality', Wells claims in *Kipps* (1905) that 'the business of the novelist is . . . facts' – obviously not a business of much interest in Conrad's fiction, either to his hero in *Lord Jim*, questioning whether 'facts could explain anything', or to Marlow in *Heart of Darkness*, finding little viable contact with 'a world of straightforward facts'.[23]

Such radical differences between the modernists and some of their contemporaries established terms for a debate about 'the proper stuff of fiction', the true locus of reality in the novel, which has continued throughout the twentieth century. Philip Henderson and Wyndham Lewis in the 1930s, and Angus Wilson and J.B. Priestley in the 1950s, along with many more recent commentators, all return to re-examine the views Woolf expresses in 'Modern Fiction' and 'Mr. Bennett and Mrs. Brown'.[24] Many of these reassessments have found injustices in Woolf's approach. In particular, Woolf seems to miss the point of much of Bennett's fiction, which follows the French writers he admired in treating 'the fabric of things', the material environment, not as separate or a distraction from human nature, but as a principal shaping force upon it. And Woolf's conclusion – supported by Lawrence and Ford – that Bennett, Galsworthy and Wells were 'materialists' can seem an odd accusation to make of Edwardian writers who along with E.M. Forster often explicitly attacked the rampant materialism of their age. Galsworthy does so throughout the satire of *The Forsyte Saga* (1906–29), and Wells equally directly in novels such as *Tono-Bungay* (1909), critically surveying 'the whole of this modern mercantile investing civilisation' (p. 186). Yet Bennett's emphasis on environment, and the other authors' concerns with contemporary society, did oblige them, as Woolf says, to 'describe . . . describe . . . describe' (II, p. 322) the material facts and circumstances of their characters, allowing a kind of materialism to dominate their work at the level of style and vision. In a way, this does make their fiction inadvertently complicit with the very aspects of modern life they sought to criticize, emphasizing the material world and marginalizing the inner life or spirit of the individual much as contemporary social forces did in reality.

Nevertheless, as later commentators have pointed out, however justifiable Woolf's views may be, they have often been used too sweepingly to glorify modernist writing at the expense of Edwardian or later fiction whose more traditional aims could be adequately realized within conventions established in the Victorian period. The modernist writers considered in this chapter did much more, in the ways suggested, to develop new priorities, styles and languages for the novel, but this did not grant them unique or exclusive access to 'the proper stuff of fiction'. Woolf's views are best used not necessarily to evaluate, but, as she suggests, to 'distinguish the quality' or characteristics which set Joyce and the modernists apart from their predecessors and many of their contemporaries. 'Modern Fiction' and 'Mr. Bennett and Mrs. Brown' provide clear statements not only of Woolf's own position, but of the priorities which distinguished, in general, a modernist writing no longer satisfied with 'observation of life' but determined to 'look within' instead.

Novelists, of course, have always looked within and examined the mind, and the early twentieth century saw only the new kind of concentration and exclusiveness in doing so which Woolf indicates. Her essays also point to factors at work in the early twentieth century which may have encouraged this new concentration. In 'Mr. Bennett and Mrs. Brown', her demand for new fictional styles and structures is made on the grounds that the life the novel sought to reflect had itself been 'a little other than custom would have us believe it' ever since December 1910, the date she claims 'human character changed' (I, p. 320). Such exact dating of such a radical change has provoked much attempted explanation by critics. As Chapter 1 observed, most assume that Woolf must have had in mind the exhibition of Post-Impressionist paintings, on show in London at the time and organized by her friend Roger Fry, as the source of new visions strange and revolutionary enough to change humanity's apprehension of itself. A fuller explanation should probably recognize 1910 as a turbulent time of agitation by trades unions, by the Home Rule movement in Ireland, and – probably most significantly for Woolf – by the Suffragettes, in many violent demonstrations on the streets of London. And by December – following the General Election in that month – it had become clear that the Liberal Government could abolish the powers of the House of Lords if forced to do so in order to carry through its programme of radical social reform. Some of the hierarchies, stratifications and gender divisions of British life, deeply inscribed in novelists' views of character and relationship, probably seemed as a result more shifting and precarious during or after December 1910 than they ever had before. For some authors this may have been an incentive to turn their attention towards the depths of inner nature rather than continue to look out upon an uneasy society in which the individual's place had become increasingly uncertain.

Woolf's own view of a changed contemporary life, however, may have been principally focused neither upon aesthetics nor politics but on psychology. In a draft, unpublished form of 'Mr. Bennett and Mrs. Brown', she explains that the rapidly changing views of 'human character' which she felt novelists had to take account of resulted from what she calls 'scientific reasons' such as the influence of Sigmund Freud. Her essay 'Modern Fiction' likewise concludes that a distinguishing feature of the new writing she admires and recommends is that 'for the moderns . . . the point of interest lies very likely in the dark places of psychology' (II, p. 108). Other contemporary commentators shared this view, as Chapter 1 pointed out – Elizabeth Drew, for example, explaining that modern novelists found 'the older technique too clumsy for their purposes' because of an 'engrossing interest' in 'conscious and deliberate psychology' (p. 248).

As Woolf and Drew suggest, modernism's urge to examine the mind more completely and constantly than earlier fiction seems likely to have been influenced by the extent to which psychology had become an area of 'conscious and deliberate' study, and of widespread public interest, especially by the 1920s. *The Interpretation of Dreams* and other investigations of the unconscious which

Freud had begun to publish in 1896 were quickly influential out-with the English-speaking world, and fairly quickly within it. English translations of Freud's work – some of it already familiar from Havelock Ellis's studies of sexuality – began to appear in English in 1909.[25] By 1913 May Sinclair was helping establish the first psychoanalytic clinic in London. Dorothy Richardson reviewed books on psychoanalysis for *Dental Review*, later commenting on a whole atmosphere of 'Freudianity' (I, p. 12) which had grown up by the end of the First World War. Looking back in 1928, John Carruthers similarly – though more sceptically – suggests that when the work of Freud and his followers 'reached England and America in translation . . . psycho-analysis became for a time an appalling craze' (p. 56). Much the same view of Freud's ubiquitous influence in the years around the First World War can be found in Richard Aldington's war novel *Death of a Hero* (1929), which shows in its early pages Freud's theories achieving in certain areas of society the status of a fashionable if rather shallow cult. Ford Madox Ford indicates something similar in *Parade's End* when he shows Christopher Tietjens's fashionable wife Sylvia deciding to 'pin [her] faith to . . . Freud' (p. 37). Freud's particular hold on the popular mind in the 1920s is confirmed by D.H. Lawrence, who suggests of certain of his ideas that

> the Oedipus complex was a household word, the incest motive a commonplace of tea-table chat . . .
>
> Does it need a prophet to discern that Freud is on the brink of a *Weltanschauung* . . .
>
> The old world is yielding under us. (*Fantasia of the Unconscious*, pp. 197–8)

The appearance of this *Weltanschauung* (world-view) in contemporary fiction can be traced in several ways, both general and specific. In general terms, several authors show a new readiness to discuss and examine what Ford Madox Ford calls in *The Good Soldier* 'that mysterious and unconscious self that underlies most people' (p. 100). Interest in this aspect of the self leads modernist authors to emphasize areas of experience previously of much more limited concern to the novel. Still assessing fiction largely in terms of its older conventions, E.M. Forster remarks in *Aspects of the Novel* (1927) that sleep is an area generally ignored by novelists, who make 'no attempt to indicate oblivion or the actual dream world' (p. 61). Yet what Proust calls 'the world in which we live when we are asleep' (II, p. 84) is quite often an interest of *A la recherche du temps perdu*, which sometimes analyzes the nature of sleep and dreams for several pages at a time (e.g. II, pp. 1012–18). The subject is immediately introduced in the novel's opening paragraph, showing how Proust's narrator and hero Marcel falls asleep when a child. Throughout, sleep and dream continue to provide Marcel with a favoured, fascinating means of 'escape from the perception of the real' (II, p. 84), one which at times colours the novel's own perceptions of consciousness and reality. Of one dream Marcel records, for example, it 'had the clarity of consciousness. By the same token, might consciousness have the unreality of a dream?' (II, p. 1018).

Conrad's equation of life, dream and reality in *Heart of Darkness*, and Richardson's in *Pilgrimage*, have already been discussed. Unreality and dream, if not quite oblivion, are also occasional interests of *Ulysses*, especially in the phantasmagoric, dream-like 'Nighttown' chapter (15). Warped by the hallucinations and suppressed obsessions of its characters, 'Nighttown' anticipates the extended entry into 'night language' made by Joyce after the publication of *Ulysses*, in his 'Work in Progress' which continued in the 1920s, eventually published as *Finnegans Wake*. Except for 'Nighttown', however, *Ulysses* does not entirely confirm Elizabeth Drew's 1920s judgement that 'Joyce apparently accepts the Freudian dogma that the activities of the subconscious mind are the true personality' (p. 88). The stream of thoughts he records are subvocal, but not by any means always subconscious. As discussed earlier, much of *Ulysses* is in the form of stream of consciousness – not, as in *Finnegans Wake*, of unconsciousness – and abandons its protagonists at the moment oblivion or unconsciousness overtakes them.

More thoroughgoing acceptance of 'Freudian dogma' and more specific connections with the ideas of the new psychoanalysis do appear in modernist fiction. In Woolf's *Mrs Dalloway*, Septimus Warren Smith's treatment for shell-shock and general mental debility by Sir William Bradshaw – 'the ghostly helper, the priest of science' (p. 104) – reflects the expanded influence of psychoanalysis brought about by the need to treat traumatized victims of the First World War. The doctor in Rebecca West's *The Return of the Soldier* (1918) likewise pronounces on a case of 'shell-shock' in thoroughly Freudian terms. Freud himself remarked how greatly the war had helped to further his work, and interest in the psycho-analytic movement generally. May Sinclair's direct, personal interest in the new movement is emphasized by Jean Radford in her introduction to Sinclair's *Life and Death of Harriett Frean* (1922), when she points out that

the new science of psychoanalysis offered her a theory of mental functioning, and she drew in particular on the Freudian notions of repression and sublimation.

Each of these 'notions' can be seen to be particularly examined in a single novel. *Mary Olivier* is an extended study in sublimation. Its heroine diverts into learning, literary activity, and the life of the mind energies which family life, religious belief and constraints on women's behaviour otherwise allow little outlet in personal development or sexual fulfilment. *Life and Death of Harriett Frean* offers a grimmer view of a heroine for whom – as the title begins to suggest – life scarcely exists independently of a deathly, repressive proclivity which gradually extinguishes vital instincts altogether.

Contemporary commentators, such as Drew and Carruthers, often saw D.H. Lawrence's work shaped at least as much as Sinclair's by the new theories of mental functioning. In particular, Paul Morel's lingering possession by his mother makes *Sons and Lovers* seem almost a casebook illustration of Freud's idea of the Oedipus complex, while the general emphasis on sexuality throughout Lawrence's fiction seems to ally it more widely with some of Freud's views of the roots of personality and behaviour. Lawrence's interest in 'another centre of consciousness . . . beyond thought' also shows his fiction moving towards darker areas of mental life towards which Freud's work had drawn new attention. Some of this sense of a previously ignored depth in human experience is figured in Gerald's disquieting discoveries in the 'Water Party' chapter of *Women in Love* – one which further illustrates Lawrence's talent for creating complex implications around plausibly natural action; for creating highly symbolic scenes. Out on the lake, Gudrun waits in a boat uncertainly balanced upon 'the surface of the insidious reality', while Gerald seeks his drowning sister in the depths beneath, returning appalled by

a whole universe under there . . . so endless, so different really from what is on top . . . you're as helpless as if your head was cut off. (pp. 203, 206)

The scene has particular implications, first of all, for Gerald himself. Like the episode discussed earlier in which he viciously struggles with his horse – a creature often used in Lawrence's writing to represent 'something else besides mind and cleverness'[26] – 'Water Party' indicates a kind of self-division in Gerald. His frightened response to the unfamiliar, subaqueous universe, 'so different from what is on top', indicates the extent to which his own severe rationality, his life in the head, has cut him off from deeper, elemental parts of his own nature. Like Marlow's journey upriver into the interior in *Heart of Darkness*, his plunge beneath the surface of the lake challenges him with a depth and darkness in experience he had not hitherto acknowledged.

In another way, this new universe Gerald encounters – dark, fluid, vast, yet hidden beneath an apparently safe, smooth surface – can be seen as more widely emblematic of the deeper, less rational mind and self which interested Lawrence throughout his fiction, and whose existence Freud's work helped establish as part of the general outlook of the twentieth century – part of its readiness to believe, with Proust, that 'it is only beneath the surface . . . that reality has its hidden existence'. The episode can also be seen as typical of a widespread employment of symbol, not only in Lawrence's work, but in modernist writing generally. More than earlier fiction, modernist novels rely on ordinary enough episodes or things – the lighthouse or rainbow immediately highlighted by Woolf and Lawrence in their titles, for example – which are endowed with a symbolic significance leading far beyond the 'surface of the reality' which contains them. Such tactics may also have been encouraged by Freud's work in the interpretation of dreams, in which symbols and their significance often have an important role.

Other phases of Lawrence's writing, however, challenge any view of Freud as a decisive or unique influence on modernism's tactics, or on its general trend from objective to subjective, certainly where Lawrence himself is concerned. Through his German wife Frieda, Lawrence was aware of Freud's ideas earlier than most British writers, but rather than wholly welcoming them he complained about the 'vicious half-statements of the Freudians' and acknowledges only that 'what Freud says is always partly true'. Rightly, in Lawrence's view, Freud's work highlighted areas of mind and self beyond complete rational, intellectual control, but it was exactly these areas which Freud sought to *submit* to rational, intellectual analysis. For Lawrence, this was a threat to the deepest sources of spontaneity, life and vitality, since it returned to consciousness and intellect the very areas of experience crucially liberated from them. Lawrence considered 'the first bubbling life in us, which is innocent of any mental alteration, this is unconscious', whereas the systematic, rational aspect of Freud's thought made it for him the kind of process which threatened to subject 'everything spontaneous to certain machine principles called ideals or ideas'.[27] As far as Lawrence relied on ideas of mind in his own highly idiosyncratic studies, *Fantasia of the Unconscious and Psychoanalysis and the Unconscious* (1923), these are taken very much less from Freud, criticized throughout, than from the German biologist, Ernst Haeckel. His suggestion that unconscious forces originate not only within the mind but in the ganglionic cells easily adjusts with Lawrence's own belief in 'blood consciousness' and his opinion that

> real knowledge comes out of the whole corpus of the consciousness; out of your belly and your penis as much as out of your brain and mind. The mind can only analyse and rationalize.[28]

Virginia Woolf's views of psychoanalysis in *Mrs Dalloway* are hardly more favourable than Lawrence's, partly on account of a similar mistrust of its rationalization of areas where more natural feelings – even simple sympathy – might be more appropriate. The analytic approach of Sir William Bradshaw, priest of science, makes him an unsympathetic figure, and an unsuccessful one: none of the various counsellings of the medical profession can reach Septimus Warren Smith's disturbed mind, or save him from suicide. In 'Mr. Bennett and Mrs. Brown', Woolf also shows in the end more doubt than conviction about the likely value of Freud for her contemporaries. References to him were deleted from the final version of the essay: even in its draft form, Woolf questions in relation to Freud 'how much we can learn from science . . . and make use of . . . and make our own'.[29]

The question is a crucial one, relating not only to the likely influence of Freud but to the discussion, in the last chapter, of how literature can be validly assessed in terms of the wider context of an age and its possible influences. That discussion decided –

contrary to the views of Wyndham Lewis, and many critics before and since – that figures such as Freud may confirm the ideas of novelists, but are rarely a sole source or cause of them. Though some of Freud's thinking seems so relevant to *Heart of Darkness* – and its narrative has so often been discussed in terms of Freud and psychoanalysis – Conrad's novella first appeared *simultaneously* with *The Interpretation of Dreams*, and not in any direct way as a result of Freud's ideas. Among writers working after Conrad, no doubt these ideas did contribute to or confirm an inclination to move from objective to subjective, in ways suggested above, in the early decades of the twentieth century. But as Lionel Trilling remarks, neither Freud nor any other thinker creates ideas in a vacuum, nor single-handedly builds the consciousness of an age. On the contrary, all thinkers are themselves conditioned in outlook and imagination by the nature and dominant concerns of the historical period in which they write. This shapes their work, as well as being shaped by it. Freud was at most a partial rather than an ultimate *cause* of the new literary apprehension of human character Woolf saw originating in December 1910: he remains a good witness to the nature, direction and effects of particular forces and habits of mind which existed at the time. Seeing Freud in this way – as Lawrence suggests, as a significant part of the *Weltanschauung* of the time – allows the new delvings into consciousness in modernist fiction to be understood not as isolated phenomena, but part of the wider movement of contemporary thought; part of the more general conditions to which 'the old world yielded'. One or two other thinkers are worth considering in this way – as witnesses to, as well as architects of, the *Weltanschauung* of the early twentieth century – before going on to examine the historical, political and social conditions which informed their individual views and the modernist movement generally.

The ideas of Friedrich Nietzsche were widely disseminated in Britain after the translation from German of *Beyond Good and Evil* (1886) in 1907 and the popularization of his work in the journal *The New Age* around the same time. By 1915, as Wyndham Lewis claims in the second volume of *Blast*, Nietzsche had 'had an English sale such as he could hardly have anticipated' (p. 5), and there is much evidence of the interest of his philosophy to a number of contemporary authors as well as Lewis himself. The critic John Carey, for example, claims that 'all Lawrence's central

concepts are derived from Nietzsche' (p. 75): Lawrence did at any
rate admire Nietzsche, and he examines the Nietzschean idea of
'Wille zur macht' (will to power) at several points in his fiction,
notably in *Women in Love* (e.g. p. 167).

More generally, Nietzsche's ideas are often given as much credit
as Freud's for establishing intellectual conditions under which 'the
old world yielded'. Two of his contributions to such conditions can
be usefully related to modernist fiction. The first is his pronounce-
ment that 'God is dead'. Nietzsche, of course, was by no means
unique in observing the faithlessness of the modern age, but the
radical scepticism of his philosophy sums up concisely and memorably, in the idea of the death of God, the effects of a decline in
religious faith originating well before the twentieth century began.
It had gathered pace in the 1860s, after Charles Darwin demon-
strated that species evolve through secular processes of natural
selection, rather than divine ordering and control: by the end of
the nineteenth century, there must have been a familiar ring to
Miriam Henderson's musings in *Pilgrimage*:

> distinguished minds . . . thought Darwin was true . . . No God. No Creation . . . It
> was probably true ... only old-fashioned people thought it was not. It was true.
> (I, pp. 169–70)

Yet from the point of view of the early twentieth century, the
Victorian period seemed in retrospect to possess a stability and
certainty which later events had made harder and harder to sustain. The 'enormous criticism going on of faiths upon which men's
lives and associations are based',[30] which H.G. Wells saw around
him in the early years of the twentieth century, expanded still
further as a result of the shock to religious and moral assumptions
created by the First World War. Looking back from the perspective of the 1920s, Elizabeth Drew remarks on how 'solidly sure of
itself' the Victorian age seemed, and on how 'the Victorian novel
shared in the general self-confidence' (p. 32). Writing in 1928, John
Carruthers found that in comparison with the Victorians his time
was 'riddled with disbelief', adding that 'the novels of to-day directly mirror the conditions of religious, moral and political in-
stability in which we all perforce live' (pp. 24, 27).

As he suggests, some of the changes in the contemporary novel
can be seen 'mirroring' an age of declining religious faith and

moral certainty. The regular absence from early twentieth-century fiction of what Hillis Miller calls the 'stabilising presence' of an omniscient author perhaps mirrors loss of faith in an omniscient deity. Without this figure of ultimate authority, and related assumptions about the coherence and meaning of life, the particular viewpoint of the 'first-person singular', in Henry James's terms, becomes as 'definite and responsible', as any other – increasingly, the only valid arbiter of experience. The new emphases on such viewpoints, discussed above in the work of James, Ford and Conrad, shows early twentieth-century fiction's increasing reliance on ways individual vision can create coherence and meaning; ways a stabilizing centre can still be established, within the individual, in a universe which lacks absolute, overall principles of order and control.

A second aspect of Nietzsche's significance lies in his questioning not only the existence of God, but of coherence and meaning in any form, or at least in any sphere beyond the individual mind. His philosophy challenges all forms of ultimate authority or truth: Nietzsche denies not only that 'facts could explain anything', but that any facts or certainties exist meaningfully at all. He asserts that

there are *no eternal facts*, just as there are no absolute truths . . .

What are man's truths ultimately? Merely his *irrefutable* errors.[31]

Nietzsche sees the universe as structureless, irrational, and quite independent of the shapes and categories which human consciousness tries to ascribe to it – an activity undertaken merely in order to satisfy the mind's private craving for comprehension and order. 'The understanding does not draw its laws from nature', Nietzsche explains, 'it prescribes them to nature' – a nature with which the mind can enjoy no authentic contact. Nietzsche suggests that

sense impressions naïvely supposed to be conditioned by the outer world are, on the contrary, conditioned by the inner world . . . we are always unconscious of the real activity of the outer world.[32]

Such views were supported elsewhere in the philosophy of the time. William James remarked in 1904 that 'the notion that even the truest formula may be a human device and not a literal transcript has dawned on us',[33] and Henri Bergson (further considered in Chapter 3) held comparable views about distorted connections between mind and outer world created by 'human device'. The work of such philosophers expresses the epistemological crisis or shift mentioned in the last chapter – a turning away, as the twentieth century began, from the stabler assumptions through which the external universe had most often been perceived in the vision of the nineteenth.

Similar scepticism about the process or even possibility of true perception, and similarly radical challenging of the validity of 'true formulae' and 'the laws of nature', show this epistemological shift extending into the field of contemporary science. Science had often offered the late Victorians what seemed an order, an authority, and a hope for progress which could at least partly substitute for religious faith. Yet even by 1886 Nietzsche was remarking that

> it is perhaps just dawning on five or six minds that physics too is only an interpretation and arrangement of the world . . . and *not* an explanation of the world.[34]

By the early years of the twentieth century, the minds most ready to accept Nietzsche's sort of scepticism often belonged to the most advanced scientists. Science, at the time, seemed enthusiastically ready to investigate and emphasize its own limitations and ultimate uncertainties. By 1923, Heisenberg's Uncertainty Principle had established, with all the rigour and logic of mathematics, the incapacity of science to establish anything about the physical universe with absolute rigour, logic, or certainty. Heisenberg's work developed in part from challenges to absolute or universal laws expressed in Albert Einstein's Theories of Relativity – Einstein suggesting that no law or observation could be universally reliable, but depended, among other factors, on the position of the individual observer. His conclusions quickly interested not only scientists, but found a much wider appeal: as described in Chapter 1, ideas of relativity had reached and excited a huge audience by the early 1920s.

The appeal of Relativity was immediate enough to suggest to D.H. Lawrence that it expressed some general temper in the contemporary outlook. He remarked in 1923 that

Everybody catches fire at the word Relativity. There must be something in the mere suggestion which we have been waiting for . . . Relativity means . . . there is no one single absolute central principle governing the world . . .

Really, an anarchical conclusion . . .

So, there is nothing absolute left in the universe. Nothing . . .

I feel inclined to Relativity myself . . . But I also feel, most strongly, that in itself each individual living creature is absolute: in its own being. And that all things in the universe are just relative to the individual living creature . . .

There is only one clue to the universe. And that is the individual soul within the individual being. That outer universe of suns and moons and atoms is a secondary affair. (*Fantasia of the Unconscious*, pp. 177–9, 147)

As Lawrence helps to suggest, science as well as contemporary philosophy, Einstein's work as well as Nietzsche's, left 'nothing absolute in the universe'. Whether or not this was a conclusion the age was 'waiting for', there is much evidence of its general recognition at the time, in the work of other modernist novelists as well as Lawrence himself. Joyce remarks in *Stephen Hero*, for example, that 'it is a mark of the modern spirit to be shy in the presence of all absolute statements' (p. 183). 'Science and religion', according to Virginia Woolf, 'have between them destroyed belief . . . all bonds of union seem broken, yet some control must exist'.[35]

In the passage quoted, Lawrence indicates where this sort of vestigial control or stability might still be found – in 'the individual soul in the individual being'. Proust's work likewise stresses the importance of concentration on this 'clue'. Marcel remarks in *A la recherche du temps perdu* that in

the current philosophy of the day . . . it was agreed that intelligence was in direct ratio to the degree of scepticism and nothing was considered real and incontestable except the individual tastes of each person. (I, p. 304)

Since 'nothing was considered real' beyond individual taste or vision, and little possibility seemed to exist for authentic contact with 'the real activity of the outer world', what Marcel calls the 'realist . . . form of perception which places everything in the object' is not so much 'clumsy and erroneous' but simply impossible or invalid. Marcel emphasizes this conclusion himself when he records the capacity of his thoughts to form a sort of recess, in the depths of which I felt that I could bury myself and remain invisible even while I looked at what went on outside. When I saw an external object, my consciousness that I was seeing it would remain between me and it, surrounding it with a thin spiritual border that prevented me from ever touching its substance directly; for it would somehow evaporate before I could make contact with it. (I, p. 90)

May Sinclair's heroine in *Mary Olivier* likewise ponders the philosophical conclusion that

all that is perceived in space or time, and with it all objects . . . have no existence grounded in themselves outside our thoughts. (p. 247)

The urge among modernist authors to 'look within' and place 'everything in the mind' thus mirrors and extends contemporary thinking which considered there may have been nowhere else rewardingly or even possibly to look; little wholly sure or convincingly real beyond the individual mind. The 'outer universe' seemed drained of order and meaning in an increasingly secular age; no more than 'a secondary affair' for the shifting epistemologies of the early twentieth century; perhaps even, as Marcel suggests, beyond genuine contact of any kind. In the face of such diminished belief and dismantled certainty, modernism could use only the individual soul as a remaining 'clue to the universe'. Inevitably, the envelope or recess of consciousness seemed the most natural, promising space for the modernist novel to represent.

This promise was confirmed by other factors, inscribed not only in contemporary science and philosophy but in the everyday experience of modern life. Some of its particular pressures on women were considered earlier: there were also certain stresses which affected the population more generally. Some of these are clearest in Lawrence's fiction, which shows even the individual soul as a precarious refuge from modern industrialism. With black coal pits standing out sharply against an open green background, even the landscape of some of Lawrence's fiction emphasizes the dark threat to nature imposed by the spreading industrialization of 'the machine age'. Such threats to physical nature obviously extend to disturb human nature as well. In *Sons and Lovers*, Paul Morel gloomily considers that 'he was a prisoner of industrialism . . . taken into bondage' (pp. 113–14) just as much as his father, a miner, had been. In *The Rainbow*, Ursula likewise resents and fears

> human bodies and lives subjected in slavery to that symmetric monster of the colliery . . .
> No more would she subscribe to the great colliery, to the great machine which has taken us all captives. In her soul, she was against it . . . she knew it was meaningless. (p. 350)

Lawrence's most sustained attack on the great machine of industrialism is developed through the figure of Gerald Crich, the colliery owner in *Women in Love*. Determined to create more wealth from his workers, Gerald exploits enthusiastically technologies newly available in the modern machine age which help him to reject the more liberal, paternalistic capitalism his father used in managing the family's colliery. Gerald's new expertise makes him 'the God of the machine' (p. 250), remorselessly rationalizing the pit on purely economic and technological principles, unquestioningly subordinating the welfare of his workforce to improvements in efficiency:

> He had conceived the pure instrumentality of mankind. There had been so much humanitarianism, so much talk of sufferings and feelings. It was ridiculous. The sufferings and feelings of individuals did not matter in the least . . . What mattered was the pure instrumentality of the individual. As a man as of a knife: does it cut well? Nothing else mattered . . .
>
> It was this inhuman principle in the mechanism he wanted to construct that inspired Gerald with an almost religious exaltation . . . he found his eternal and his infinite in the pure machine-principle . . . the substitution of the mechanical principle for the organic, the destruction of the organic purpose, the organic unity, and the subordination of every organic unit to the great mechanical purpose. It was pure organic disintegration and pure mechanical organisation . . .
>
> There was a greater output of coal than ever. (pp. 250–1, 256, 260)

Gerald's obsession with 'mechanical control' arises from – and adds to – an alienation from his own deeper feelings which has disastrous results: as his lover Gudrun realizes, Gerald's 'machine principles' are eventually thoroughly realized in himself. 'The Geralds of this world', she reflects, 'turn into mechanisms . . . become instruments, pure machines, pure wills' (p. 524). Cold and mechanical in his emotions, Gerald dies an appropriately icy death, frozen in the snowy wastes of the Alps. Long before Gerald's actual death, however, most worthwhile life has been drained out of his workers, forced themselves to become 'instruments, pure machines':

> the miners were reduced to mere mechanical instruments. They had to work hard, much harder than before, the work was terrible and heart-breaking in its mechanicalness.
>
> But they submitted to it all. The joy went out of their lives, the hope seemed to perish as they became more and more mechanized. (p. 259)

Similar anxieties about the denaturing processes of industrialized society appear in *The Plumed Serpent* – '*deliver me from man's automatism*' is one of its heroine's pleas – and extensively in *Lady Chatterley's Lover*, which laments that

> all vulnerable things must perish under the rolling and running of iron . . . [in] a world of iron and coal, the cruelty of iron and the smoke of coal, and the endless, endless greed that drove it all. (pp. 123, 149)

Lady Constance Chatterley flees with her lover Mellors this world of 'the mechanical greedy, greedy mechanism and mechanized greed' (p. 123) presided over by her husband Clifford. He considers the miners in the same terms as Gerald in *Women in Love*:

> he saw them as objects rather than men, parts of the pit rather than parts of life, crude raw phenomena rather than human beings. (p. 16)

Crippled literally by the First World War, Clifford is presented figuratively as further maimed by a commitment to profit and the industrialized machine which leaves him less than fully human. Constance reflects that

> Clifford was drifting off to this other weirdness of industrial activity, becoming almost a *creature*, with a hard, efficient shell of an exterior and a pulpy interior, one of the amazing crabs and lobsters of the modern, industrial and financial world, invertebrates of the crustacean order, with shells of steel, like machines, and inner bodies of soft pulp. (p. 114)

Deeply inscribed in Lawrence's writing, such concern about humanity becoming like machines – or disfigured by hard, efficient shells concealing pulpy or empty interiors – also appears elsewhere

in modernist fiction. In Conrad's *Chance* (1913) the corrupt finan-
cier is said to be 'a mere sign, a portent. There was nothing in him'
(p. 70), and is aptly named 'de Barral'. *Heart of Darkness* shows
Kurtz – another character who exploits humanity in the quest for
'something that is really profitable' (p. 110) – eventually appearing
to Marlow to be 'hollow at the core' (p. 95). T.S. Eliot takes from
*Heart of Darkness* his epigraph for 'The Hollow Men', a poem
which goes on to examine inner emptiness as the general condition
of a spiritless modern humanity. Eliot also presents this condition
in 'Rhapsody on a Windy Night', in which the speaker records how

> . . . the hand of the child, automatic,
> Slipped out and pocketed a toy that was running along the quay.
> I could see nothing behind that child's eye.
> I have seen eyes in the street
> Trying to peer through lighted shutters,
> And a crab one afternoon in a pool,
> An old crab with barnacles on his back
> Gripped the end of the stick which I held him.[36]

Once again, the individual is shown as empty within – like Gerald,
'a hollow shell' with a 'dark void' at its centre (p. 363). There is
apparently nothing behind the child's eye, and the speaker comes
closer to genuine contact – almost a kind of handshake – with the
crab than with any of the people in the poem, variously occluded
behind doors and shutters. As human beings grow empty within a
shell-like exterior, shelled creatures like the crab come to seem
more nearly human. A similarly reciprocal exchange of qualities
occurs between machines and human beings. Machines and things
are personified, taking on what would normally be human attributes: it is the toy, rather than the child, that runs along the
quay, while elsewhere in the poem streetlamps speak and doors
seem to grin. Human beings are fragmented – presented only as
eyes or hands rather than whole, integrated beings – and mechanical; empty behind their eyes and 'automatic' in their actions.
While things are personified, people are reified, made thing-like.

Reification – the portrayal of people as things or objects – is in
the sense discussed above a literary device. In a comparable sense,
however, in the view of Karl Marx, it is also a real condition of
modern labour, forced to make itself into a usable commodity
which can be sold for wages. Marx explains that

within the capitalist system all methods . . . distort the worker into a fragment of a man, they degrade him to the level of an appendage of a machine . . .

*The means of production*, the *material conditions of labour*, are not subject to the worker, but he to them. This in itself . . . entails the personification of things and the reification of persons. (I, pp. 799, 1054)

Reification in economic terms is reflected in literary ones, most clearly in Lawrence's writing. The industrialized world Gerald Crich creates – making people interchangeable with things, or treating 'a man . . . as a knife' – clearly exposes the denaturing, reifying conditions of modern industrial labour. Eliot's poetry, however, indicates wider contemporary awareness of the consequences of such conditions, as does Conrad, not only in *Heart of Darkness* but in novels such as *Nostromo* (1904), which gives another account of the corruption of mining wealth, and *The Secret Agent* (1907), one of whose central figures is described as

like an automaton . . . this resemblance to a mechanical figure went so far that he had an automaton's absurd air of being aware of the machinery inside of him. (p. 162)

Alternating employment of subjective and objective perspectives in *To the Lighthouse* – and the appropriation of the human world by objects and things in the novel's middle section – show some consciousness of reification in Virginia Woolf's writing. Lawrence, Conrad and Woolf also share with modernism more generally a disposition not just to represent reifying forces but to find means, at least in imagination, to compensate for them. Modernism's use of symbol might be seen in this way – as an attempt to re-endow with human significance a physical world of increasingly alien, threatening, objects and things.

More generally, a need to compensate for the reifying forces of modernity can be seen as a further, fundamental source of the determination to 'look within'. This compensatory function of modernist innovation is further clarified by *The Political Unconscious: Narrative as a Socially Symbolic Act* (1981), in which the Marxist critic Fredric Jameson traces ways the reifying nature of 'social relations in late capitalism' (p. 42) informs modernism and its styles. 'Modernism and reification', he suggests, 'are parts of the same immense process which expresses the contradictory inner logic and dynamics of late capitalism' (p. 42). Jameson, however, demonstrates that modernism is not simply a reflection of the reifying logic of late capitalism, but an attempt to balance, even neutralize it. He sees modernism as

> a revolt against . . . reification and a symbolic act which involves a whole Utopian compensation for increasing dehumanization on the level of daily life . . .

> modernism can . . . be read as a Utopian compensation for everything reification brings with it. (pp. 42, 236)

Jameson finds one example of such compensation in the work of Henry James, whose insistence on 'polished perceivers' and the subtleties of fine inner conscience he sees as one of the 'more desperate myths of the self' (p. 221) that modernism is forced to generate – as an attempt to create in art a free, integral selfhood lost in a reified reality. Jameson's views are shared by another Marxist critic, Terry Eagleton, who states that 'James's work . . . represents a desperate, devoted attempt to salvage organic significance wholly in the sealed realm of consciousness' (p. 141). Such compensatory or mythologizing reliance on 'the sealed realm of consciousness' appears not only in James's fiction, of course, but throughout modernism: Miriam Henderson provides a kind of theoretical justification for it when she muses in *Pilgrimage*

> Everything's here, any bit of anything, clear in your brain; you can look at it. What a terrific thing a person is, bigger than anything. (II, p. 256)

Placing 'everything in the mind', the 'sealed realm of consciousness', helps modernist narrative restore a sense of significance to the individual, making it seem possible to believe admiringly in 'what a terrific thing a person is' – regardless of how diminished (or in Miriam's case, severely financially constrained) actual life in an industrialised modern world may be. Appropriately, it is Gerald – thoroughly in accord with the negative forces of industrialism – who is so shocked to discover the dark reaches of a 'whole universe' beneath the visible surface of experience. Like Miriam Henderson, other modernist characters – and modernist novels generally – find more congenial this enlarged sense of the space of the self, promising a domain in which the individual can be freed from the object world and a reality ruled by 'the logic and dynamics of late capitalism'. An age which threatened to leave nothing behind the eyes of its inhabitants inevitably encouraged literary strategies which could reach some inviolable innermost flame of consciousness. Something had to be found to continue illumining a 'first-person singular' still 'definite and responsible' despite forces threatening to reduce individuals to the sum of their usable functions, or to negate feeling in favour of instrumentality. D.H. Lawrence's letter to his publishers in 1914 not only warns that 'the old stable *ego*' may be harder to find than ever, but also promises a 'deeper sense than any we've been used to exercise', one still able to reveal characters as 'the same single radically unchanged element'.[37] His views are representative of a whole phase of modernism's attempt to recreate a fuller, non-crustacean humanity for a modern life brittle on the exterior and hollow or pulpy within; to use deeper senses, formal shifts, and subtler strategies to compensate for the disintegral pressures of late capitalism on the self. Such pressures are often examined satirically or directly in the work of Edwardian novelists such as Bennett, Wells, Galsworthy or Forster: for the modernists, it seemed preferable to reconfigure a securer sense of the individual through reshaping some of the strategies of fiction itself; to move the attention of the novel towards the safer realms of inner consciousness. Ironically, of course, as Gerald's experience in 'Water Party' perhaps warns, the further modernist fiction chose to 'look within' the closer it risked coming to depths of consciousness towards which the 'first person singular' could be neither definite nor responsible; towards forces within the self possibly as disturbing to the 'old stable ego' as any arising from the external circumstances of the modern industrial world. As Eagleton remarks, however, and as this study suggests throughout, modernist fiction's attention and the thought it transcribes usually remain – just – within or on the borders of the 'realm of consciousness', rather than extending very far into the darker spaces of the unconscious mind, at least until Joyce's 'Work in Progress' and *Finnegans Wake* (see Chapter 4).

Fredric Jameson's relation of modernism to contemporary economic and political history also helps locate the movement within the wider evolution of literary history. In particular, it allows modernism to be seen as a late extension of Romanticism, or perhaps a modified replacement for it. Modernism offers 'Utopian compensation' for the dehumanizing nature of life in a late phase of industrialism: Romantic poetry undertook a comparable task in response to a much earlier phase, developing most strongly just after the Industrial Revolution at the end of the eighteenth century. When large sections of the population were being forced away from the land and into dismal factory employment in cramped, grimy cities, poetry which located humanity in a natural, green environment offered an ideal compensation for the kind of denaturing which was actually taking place. In this and other ways, Romantic poetry provided a congenial vision of the status and significance of the individual at a time when in reality huge numbers of individuals were being reduced to insignificant units within the system of wage slavery. The Romantic vision not only placed individuals back in a natural environment, it showed them in empathetic, mutually signifying contact with this environment. As critics have often observed, the natural world functions for the Romantics as a kind of mirror, reflecting and enlarging the shape and the drama of the individual soul, and *vice versa*. Through such pastoral connection, the individual seemed neither dehumanized nor diminished, but a central, significant pulse of ego, drawing a whole vision of the world around the self.

The post-Industrial Revolution, Romantic phase of the late eighteenth and early nineteenth centuries was followed by further technologic revolutions which left the green world of nature more distant than ever and the population still more firmly centred in cities. In Conrad's *The Secret Agent*, Dorothy Richardson's *Pilgrimage*, Woolf's *Mrs Dalloway*, Joyce's *Ulysses* or many other novels, it is the complex, challenging life of the city which most often provides the background of modernist fiction, and in the view of many commentators a principal influence upon it. Raymond Williams considers that 'the key cultural factor of the modernist shift is the character of the metropolis' – a 'dynamic common environment' which nevertheless eroded any real sense of community and left 'elements of strangeness and distance, indeed of alienation' central to urban experience (p. 91). Walter Benjamin likewise records a sense of isolation, paradoxically heightened by proximity to masses of people, as an inevitable aspect of life in the modern city. If inner vision and 'the individual soul within the individual being' seemed to modernist writers the only 'clue to the universe', it was partly because contact with other souls or a wider sense of community seemed least viable where they might have been thought most easily available – within the mass of people in the expanding cities of the early twentieth century.

Benjamin quotes another German socialist, Friedrich Engels, talking of

> A city like London, where one can roam about for hours without reaching the beginning of an end, without seeing the slightest indication that open country is nearby. (p. 166)

Even when modernist writing seeks to escape the metropolis or to re-establish contact with a green world beyond city boundaries, nature no longer offers the potential it did for the Romantics. The black collieries which scar Lawrence's green landscapes; the rust-coloured suburban sprawl which threatens the rural refuge of Forster's *Howards End*; 'the red suburban stain which fouls the fields' (p. 22) in West's *The Return of the Soldier* – all illustrate the dwindling possibility of finding any landscape empty enough, benign enough, safe enough from the modern industrial and financial world, to fulfil the needs of a consoling Romantic vision. The English landscape ceases to seem open, or a liberation of the soul, but crowded and restricting instead. On his nocturnal hunt in Lawrence's short story 'The Fox' (1923), for example, Henry finds a 'network of English hedges netting the view': as a result, 'suddenly it seemed to him England was little and tight, he felt the landscape was constricted . . . tight with innumerable little houses' (p. 121). Significantly, no English landscape can satisfy Virginia Woolf's requirement in *To the Lighthouse* for a setting unsullied by human activity – a setting of absolute loneliness for Mr Ramsay to walk and brood in – and she has to go as far as the Hebrides to find one.

Even a more inviolate and lonely landscape, however, is no longer consoling as it was for the Romantics. Particularly in the second part of the novel, Woolf's vision is largely anti-pastoral and anti-Romantic. As discussed earlier, Woolf's style in this section brings to life a natural world which – far from demonstrating sympathy or connection with the individual soul – systematically diminishes and marginalizes consciousness and human agency. The second section eventually makes completely explicit the impossibility of any longer discovering in external nature a viable space for consoling reflections of the self:

the sea tosses itself and breaks itself, and should any sleeper fancying that he might find on the beach an answer to his doubts, a sharer of his solitude, throw off his bedclothes and go down by himself to walk on the sand, no image with semblance of serving and divine promptitude comes readily to hand bringing the night to order and making the world reflect the compass of the soul . . .

those who had gone down to pace the beach and ask of the sea and sky what message they reported or what vision they affirmed had to consider . . . the silent apparition of an ashen coloured ship . . . a purplish stain upon the bland surface of the sea as if something had boiled and bled, invisibly, beneath. This intrusion into a scene calculated to stir the most sublime reflections and lead to the most comfortable conclusions stayed their pacing. It was difficult blandly to overlook them, to abolish their significance in the landscape; to continue, as one walked by the sea, to marvel how beauty outside mirrored beauty within.

Did Nature supplement what man advanced? Did she complete what he began? With equal complacence she saw his misery, condoned his meanness, and acquiesced in his torture. That dream, then, of sharing, completing, finding in solitude on the beach an answer, was but a reflection in a mirror . . . contemplation was unendurable; the mirror was broken. (pp. 146, 152–3)

Finding the mirror of nature broken, and no longer assured of its external space, modernist vision had little choice but to turn even further than the Romantics to inner space as a dimension in which to console and make significant the self – in which to answer doubts and 'bring the night to order'. This is very much the conclusion Woolf herself indicates in *To the Lighthouse* when instead of beauty and order outside she talks of

the vision within. In those mirrors, the minds of men . . . dreams persisted . . . good triumphs, happiness prevails, order rules . . . [there was] some absolute good, some crystal of intensity, remote from the known pleasures and familiar virtues, something alien to the processes of domestic life, single, hard, bright, like a diamond in the sand, which would render the possessor secure. (pp. 150–1)

It was suggested earlier that the preoccupation in *To the Lighthouse* with 'subject and object and the nature of reality' provided a kind of paradigm of modernist interests. Sections such as the above show the novel offering not only a paradigm but an explanation for the modernist imperative to 'look within'. Looking elsewhere, either at the natural world or the objects constituting it, ceased to offer either happiness or order: only 'the vision within' offered anything to 'render the possessor secure'. Following this vision in its first and third sections, *To the Lighthouse* demonstrates the direction followed by modernist narrative in general as a compensation for the new hostility and emptiness in the object world which Woolf dramatizes in the novel's second part.

The first of the passages quoted above also indicates an immediate historical reason for finding 'the minds of men' a necessary refuge from an intractable, fractured external reality. The 'ashen ship' and the 'purplish stain' on the surface of the sea bear to the shores of the Hebrides traces of a final, previously unimaginable disaster of the modern industrial and financial world – the First World War. As John Carruthers described in the 1920s, wartime saw 'a few million lives tossed away for no reason that . . . anyone . . . has yet been able to discover' (p. 25). It was a time when men took refuge within the hard shell of tanks from machine guns, shells and other forms of death delivered with the newly technologized efficiency of the machine age; a time when, as Woolf remarks in *To the Lighthouse*, 'flesh turned to atoms which drove before the wind' (p. 150). The experience of such a time offered the sharpest demonstration of 'the logic and dynamics of late capitalism' in turning individuals into a meaningless, almost worthless commodity, mere atoms of flesh. Given the stresses of such a period, the simplest explanation of the movement of modernist narrative considered in this chapter can be provided by Andrew Marvell's suggestion in 'The Garden' (1681) – a poem also written in a period of historical upheaval – that

> . . . the mind, from pleasure less
> Withdraws into its happiness;
> The mind, that Ocean . . .[38]

Confronted by a sea of troubles darkly stained by the war, the mind in the early twentieth century had obvious reason to withdraw to the oceanic spaces within itself and to pursue the streams of consciousness running through them. War and 'the modern industrial and financial world', however, had consequences not only for modernism's commitment to 'the vision within', but for the overall structure of its narratives. This aspect of modernism, and its sense of time and history, are considered in the next chapter.

# TIME

As there is a geometry in space, so there is a psychology in time.
(Marcel Proust, *Remembrance of Things Past*
(*A la recherche du temps perdu*), 1913–27, III, p. 568)

Time, unfortunately, though it makes animals and vegetables bloom
and fade with amazing punctuality, has no such simple effect upon the
mind of man. The mind of man, moreover, works with equal strangeness upon the body of time. An hour, once it lodges in the queer
element of the human spirit, may be stretched to fifty or a hundred
times its clock length; on the other hand, an hour may be accurately
represented on the timepiece of the mind by one second. This extraordinary discrepancy between time on the clock and time in the mind
is less known than it should be and deserves fuller investigation.
Virginia Woolf, *Orlando* (1928), p. 69

## STRIKING CLOCKS AND NEW CHRONOLOGIES

This chapter gives the 'discrepancy' outlined above in *Orlando* the
fuller investigation Virginia Woolf claims it deserves. Since modernism was disposed, as Chapter 2 explained, to place 'everything
in the mind', it would be logical to expect it to favour – in the terms
*Orlando* outlines – 'time in the mind' rather than 'time on the
clock'. And indeed there is much evidence throughout modernist
fiction of just this sort of preference – Gudrun's views of Gerald in
*Women in Love* (1921), for example, are worth considering at
greater length in this context. As Chapter 2 suggested, they are
typical of modernism's general concern about the reification and
mechanization of 'the modern industrial and financial world': they
also introduce a particular – related – dislike of time on the clock.
Gudrun reflects:

> Oh God, the wheels within wheels of people, it makes one's head tick like a clock, with a very madness of dead mechanical monotony and meaninglessness. How I *hate* life, how I hate it. How I hate the Geralds, that they can offer one nothing else . . .
>
> The thought of the mechanical succession of day following day, day following day, *ad infinitum*, was one of the things that made her heart palpitate with a real approach of madness. The terrible bondage of this tick-tack of time, this twitching of the hands of the clock, this eternal repetition of hours and days – oh God, it was too awful to contemplate . . .
>
> How she suffered, lying there alone, confronted by the terrible clock, with its eternal tick-tack. All life, all life, resolved itself into this: tick-tack, tick-tack, tick-tack; then the striking of the hour; then the tick-tack, tick-tack, and the twitching of the clock fingers.
>
> Gerald could not save her from it. He, his body, his motion, his life – it was the same ticking, the same twitching across the dial, a horrible mechanical twitching forward over the face of the hours . . . across the eternal, mechanical, monotonous clock-face of time. (pp. 522–3)

Summing up her horror of the machine-like nature of her lover, Gudrun's reflections also introduce – in imagining Gerald as a 'pure will' that works 'like clockwork, in perpetual repetition' (p. 524) – a wider uneasiness about bondage to time, and a particular questioning of time counted out by the tick-tack and twitching fingers of the clock. Comparable anxieties about clocks and clockwork appear with striking frequency throughout modernist writing. In James Joyce's *A Portrait of the Artist as a Young Man* (1916), the image chosen to represent hell is of the unceasing 'ticking of a great clock' (p. 133). Clocks occupy an equally threatening role in Virginia Woolf's fiction. In *The Waves* (1931), one of the things which most upsets Bernard is 'the stare of clocks' (p. 25), while in *Orlando* clocks are capable of striking 'like thunder . . . like a meteor' (pp. 226, 227). Woolf's central figure finds

> the clock ticking on the mantlepiece beat like a hammer . . . the clock ticked louder and louder until there was a terrific explosion right in her ear. Orlando leapt as if she had been violently struck on the head. Ten times she was struck. In fact it was ten o'clock in the morning . . .
>
> 'Confound it all!' she cried, for it is a great shock to the nervous system, hearing a clock strike. (pp. 210–11, 216)

Clocks are also a shock to the 'nervous system' in Joseph Conrad's writing: a surprising number of crises in his fiction involve them in one way or another. In *Under Western Eyes* (1911), Razumov finds himself so unnerved by the crucial encounter with Haldin in his lodgings that he drops his watch before he can find out the time. Looking 'wildly about as if for some means of seizing upon time which seemed to have escaped him altogether', he fixes on something which he has never previously noticed – 'the faint sounds of some town clock tolling the hours' – and finds that 'the faint deep boom of the distant clock seemed to explode inside his head' (pp. 59, 61). In *Nostromo* (1904), Captain Mitchell's interrogation by Sotillo's troops is strangely interrupted by Sotillo himself using his prisoner's 'sixty-guinea gold half-chronometer' (p. 278) as a means of threatening him, then becoming so mesmerized by the quality of its mechanism that he forgets Mitchell altogether. The hero of *Lord Jim* (1900), also briefly imprisoned, inexplicably finds that it is only while tinkering with 'a nickel clock of New England make' that the 'true perception of his extreme peril dawned upon him': after he has 'dropped the thing like a hot potato' (p. 192), he seeks his escape. Another odd episode earlier in the novel shows Captain Brierly neatly charting his ship's position 'with a tiny cross and . . . the date and time' (p. 50), carefully tying his chronometer, a reward for outstanding service, to the rail of his ship and then jumping overboard to lose himself forever in the shapeless vastness of the sea.

Clocks turn up most frequently and sinisterly in Conrad's *The Secret Agent* (1907). They share with other machines in the novel the kind of readiness to take on human attributes which, as Chapter 2 pointed out, often accompanies reifying transformations of people into things or machines in modernist writing. Many scenes in *The Secret Agent* resound to music produced automatically by a mechanical bar-room piano – a 'lonely piano' which chooses, apparently of its own accord, the right time for striking 'a few chords courageously', or for playing 'suddenly all by itself a valse tune with aggressive virtuosity', or for falling silent, 'as if gone grumpy' (pp. 72, 58, 248). A clock in the Verloc's house similarly appropriates human attributes, suggesting by its 'lonely ticking' that it wants to steal into the bedroom 'as if for the sake of company' (p. 149). Later in the novel, just after Mrs Verloc's murder of her husband, a more sinister ticking suggests – figuratively at least – that another clock's urge to take over a human place in the household has been violently, murderously realized:

Nothing moved in the parlour till Mrs Verloc raised her head slowly and looked at the clock with inquiring mistrust. She had become aware of a ticking sound in the room. It grew upon her ear, while she remembered clearly that the clock on the wall was silent, had no audible tick. What did it mean by beginning to tick so loudly all of a sudden? Its face indicated ten minutes to nine. Mrs Verloc cared nothing for time, and the ticking went on . . . tic, tic, tic . . .

Her fine, sleepy eyes, travelled downward on the track of the sound, became contemplative on meeting a flat object of bone which protruded a little beyond the edge of the sofa. It was the handle of the domestic carving knife with nothing strange about it but its position at right angles to Mr Verloc's waistcoat and the fact that something dripped from it. Dark drops fell on the floorcloth one after another, with a sound of ticking growing fast and furious like the pulse of an insane clock. (pp. 213–14)

Characters in modernist fiction outwith the British context are often as disposed as Conrad's to look at the clock with 'inquiring mistrust', or sometimes just to drop it altogether. In F. Scott Fitzgerald's *The Great Gatsby* (1926), at the crucial moment when at last he meets Daisy again, Gatsby dislodges his host's 'defunct mantelpiece clock' (p. 93), which threatens to smash in pieces on the floor. In William Faulkner's *The Sound and the Fury* (1929), Quentin Compson actually does begin his final, fatal day at Harvard by smashing the glass of his watch and tearing off the hands, though continuing to worry about 'the blank dial with little wheels clicking and clicking behind it' (p. 76).

It is not only characters in modernist fiction who are inclined to find the clock a shock to the nervous system, or to retaliate by trying to destroy it. In *Aspects of the Novel* (1927), the figure E.M. Forster holds responsible for having 'smashed up and pulverised [the] clock and scattered its fragments over the world' (p. 48) is not a character, but a novelist – Gertrude Stein. Characters' hostility to clockwork can be seen as a figuration or symbol of a changed attitude to time more generally evident in the novels in which they appear, and in their structure particularly: hostility to the clock, within modernist texts, is matched by their authors' reluctance to rely on chronological sequence as the basis of their construction. As Chapter 2 explained, Forster was on the whole a traditional rather than a modernist writer: he therefore found the new, clock-pulverizing attitudes disturbing, as he considered the structure of the novel to depend on what he calls 'sequence in chronology' (p. 49) – on an element of story which he thought can be defined. It is a narrative of events arranged in their time sequence – dinner coming after breakfast, Tuesday after Monday, decay after death, and so on. (p. 35)

Modernist fiction rarely abandons story altogether, or smashes up the clock entirely, but it often abandons the arrangement of 'events in their time sequence' – the kind of 'mechanical succession of day following day' Gudrun sees as part of the 'terrible bondage' of the clock. Lawrence himself believed that the 'idea of time as a continuity in an eternal straight line has crippled our consciousness cruelly' and thought it worth escaping the 'manner of on-and-on-and-on, from a start to a finish'. Virginia Woolf similarly complains in her diary about the 'appalling narrative business of the realist: getting on from lunch to dinner: it is false, unreal, merely conventional'.[1] Her own programme for the novel, set out in her essay 'Modern Fiction' (1919), includes the view that 'life is not a series . . . symmetrically arranged' (II, p. 106). Much of her fiction, and modernist writing generally, gives up or amends the kind of vision of life as a series of events and consequences which had conventionally structured the novel in the nineteenth century. The progressive, sequential development of the *Bildungsroman*, for example – tracing a character's life, step by step, over many years from birth to maturity – is in sharp contrast to Joyce's *Ulysses* (1922), or Woolf's *Mrs Dalloway* (1925), each of which follows protagonists through only a single day of their lives.

These and other novels in the 1920s show the final results of innovations in chronology and structure developing more or less progressively – like the movements into interior monologue and stream of consciousness discussed in Chapter 2 – throughout the earlier years of the century. In several ways, Marcel Proust's *A la recherche du temps perdu* provides an ideal starting-point for an analysis of these developments. Proust, first of all, is as clear as any modernist author in rejecting conventional temporality and sequence in chronology. In *A la recherche du temps perdu* he seeks explicitly to create a fiction which 'suppresses the mighty dimension of Time' – one able to 'make visible, to intellectualise in a work of art, realities that were outside Time' (III, pp. 1087, 971). In undertaking this task, Proust's writing illustrates many of the techniques available to writers trying to suppress or reshape the dimension of time – so many, in fact, that

Gérard Genette, in *Narrative Discourse* ('Discours du recit', 1972) bases a whole theory of the novel on examples drawn from Proust, using *A la recherche du temps perdu* as a kind of inventory of narrative techniques and strategies.

Another advantage of Proust's work, emphasized by Genette, is that it shows that modernist techniques for suppressing time are not necessarily new inventions, but often extensions or adaptations of characteristics inherent in the novel form itself. Discussing the historical origins of the form, Mikhail Bakhtin suggests that 'The novel, from the very beginning, developed as a genre that had at its core a new way of conceptualising time' (p. 38). Genette likewise sees as a 'core' of the novel its potential to manipulate time. What he calls 'anachrony' – departure, in narrative, from the order in which events supposedly occurred – he defines as 'one of the traditional resources of literary narration . . . one of the constitutive features of narrative temporality' (pp. 36, 85). As these two theorists confirm, one of the most obvious appeals of narrative in general is its capacity for reshaping into a desired or significant order a flow of life which – in actuality's casual juxtapositions and bland successions – may offer little particular shape or significance in itself. Proust did not discover this capacity. His status as a precursor of modernism's escapes from 'life as a series' is owed to the scale and dexterity, rather than any absolute novelty, with which this capacity is exploited.

His anachronic tactics rely heavily, after all, on the perfectly traditional device of first-person narrative. More or less by definition, narrators of novels in the third person are not involved personally in the story they relate. From a position of aloof, objective distance, they can be expected to present events in an orderly way, most often in the sequence in which they supposedly occurred, Tuesday following after Monday, decay after death, and so on. Fiction in the first person, on the other hand, may plausibly be arranged more idiosyncratically, especially as most first-person narrators retain an awareness of two strands of time rather than one – of the time of narrating, as well as the time during which the events of the story occurred. What happens on Monday can be recorded on Tuesday, but first-person narrators may well begin with Tuesday, with the time of writing, rather than with Monday.

They may further disrupt the chronology of events by following the order in which they are recalled, rather than the order in which

they occurred. Proust's narrator Marcel remarks that reality 'takes
shape in the memory alone' (I, p. 201) but adds that

> our memory does not as a rule present things to us in their chronological
> sequence . . .
>
> we relive our past years not in their continuous sequence, day by day. (I, p. 622;
> II, p. 412)

Marcel's narrative is shaped and ruled by the randomness of memory's ordering as much as by chronological sequence. Proust further disrupts conventional chronology by investigating a form of
memory which dislocates experience, and narrative, unusually
powerfully, immersing the novel in a 'time in the mind' quite separate from what is happening in external reality. Marcel indicates
the nature of this memory when he remarks

> the better part of our memories exists outside us, in a blatter of rain, in the smell
> of an unaired room or of the first crackling brushwood fire in a cold grate . . .
> Outside us? Within us, rather, but hidden from our eyes in an oblivion more or
> less prolonged. It is thanks to this oblivion alone that we can from time to time
> recover the person that we were, place ourselves in relation to things as he was
> placed . . . In the broad daylight of our habitual memory the images of the past
> turn gradually pale and fade out of sight. (I, p. 692)

'Habitual memory', or 'voluntary memory' (I, p. 47) – the memory
of the intellect which deliberately chooses to think of certain past
episodes – produces only the palest, the most desiccated vision of
the past. Involuntary memory, on the other hand – the kind of
association triggered almost automatically by a sound, a smell, a
blatter of rain, or an otherwise random sensual experience in the
present – does not simply or deliberately *call* to mind some remembered scene or detail. Instead, it so suffuses the mind with floods of
old sensation that characters are left virtually transformed into earlier versions of themselves. This happens at several stages of *A la
recherche du temps perdu*: when Swann's remembered passion for
Odette is triggered by hearing the Vinteuil sonata, for example; or in
Marcel's rediscovery of a continuity of present experience and past
sensation when he catches his foot on a paving stone at Guermantes.
Most famously, he is borne back into an 'identical moment' in his
childhood in Combray when he tastes once again a 'petite
Madeleine' cake dipped in tea. He discovers that

all the flowers in our garden and in M. Swann's park, and the water-lilies on the Vivonne and the good folk of the village and their little dwellings and the parish church and the whole of Combray and its surroundings, taking shape and solidity, sprang into being, town and gardens alike, from my cup of tea. (I, pp. 50, 51)

Here past time is shown continuing to exist not only in the recesses of the mind, but virtually in the body – digested, deeply engrained, within the physical structure of the self.

Neither the existence of this involuntary memory nor even its literary use are wholly Proust's discovery. Charles Dickens points to much the same phenomenon when in *David Copperfield* (1849–50) his hero remembers a stage of his courtship of Dora and remarks that

the scent of a geranium leaf, at this day, strikes me with a half comical half serious wonder as to what change has come over me in a moment; and then I see a straw hat and blue ribbons, and a quantity of curls, and a little black dog being held up, in two slender arms, against a bank of blossoms and bright leaves. (p. 456)

As in *A la recherche du temps perdu*, a sensual stimulus, scent in this case, is sufficient to transport the narrator almost into reinhabiting the past. Such transport in Dickens, however, briefly disturbs the narrator without much dislocating the narrative. This proceeds for the most part chronologically throughout *David Copperfield* – from David's birth, through his youth, towards the stability and maturity of the moment at which he writes. In the instance above, there is only the briefest of deviations into the moment of writing – a reference to 'this day' – before returning to the account of relations with Dora, resplendent in her straw hat and curls. And this memory of Dora occurs exactly in its proper place in the chronological sequence of episodes in David's life.

In *A la recherche du temps perdu*, on the other hand, memory has a central role not only in the emotional life of the narrator, but in structuring the text. This is immediately apparent in the 'Overture' to *A la recherche du temps perdu*. It begins with a general reflection on dream, memory and sleep, then their functioning is examined in a variety of remembered episodes and scenes, ranging freely between childhood and adulthood. The narrator moves on into more general recollections of childhood in Combray, returning at the end of the 'Overture' to the 'one day', many years later, when he encounters the Madeleine and brings his childhood back to life. The next section of the novel, 'Combray' goes on to give a longer account of these same early years. The first fifty pages of the novel thus confront the reader with what are called 'shifting and confused gusts of memory' (p. 7), recorded in a narrative which moves very freely between them. Even by the end of the 'Overture', consummated by the Madeleine's coalescence of past and present, *A la recherche du temps perdu* has engaged thoroughly and successfully in the search promised in its title. Ruled by memory's powerful connection of past and present, it continues throughout to search out past or lost times – eventually, as the novel's last section demonstrates, largely recovering them in a 'Time Regained' through the process of the fiction itself.

As Genette suggests, *A la recherche du temps perdu* is

> undoubtedly, as it proclaims, a novel of Time lost and found again, but it is also, more secretly perhaps, a novel of Time ruled, captured, bewitched, surreptitiously subverted, or better: *perverted.* (p. 160)

Opening up multiple, interweaving pathways into the past, Marcel's memory not only recovers lost times, but generally frees his narrative from bondage to the tick-tack of the clock or the mechanical succession of the calendar. As Genette shows at length in *Narrative Discourse*, Proust's multiplying anachronies go far beyond the simple alternations of a narrating present and a remembered past. Instead, Proust sets one memory on top of another, or allows a flashback to intermingle indistinguishably with a flash forward, or surreptitiously lets a narrative of remembered experience catch up and overtake the point in time from which the memory began. Such tactics leave the temporality of any event fluid and difficult to specify, fulfilling the novel's ambition to 'suppress the mighty dimension of Time'. As Genette remarks, Proust 'made clear, more than anyone had done before him and better than they had, narrative's capacity for *temporal autonomy*' (p. 85) – an achievement which 'anticipates the most disconcerting proceedings of the modern novel' (p. 67).

Proust occupies in this way a pivotal position between fiction of the nineteenth century and modernism. Several aspects of *A la recherche du temps perdu* resemble the nineteenth-century *Bildungsroman*. Like *David Copperfield*, it is a highly personal story, almost an autobiography, following the progress of a hero from childhood to adulthood, from naïvety to maturity. Yet if *A la recherche du temps perdu* is not entirely original in subject, its treatment of it nevertheless moves towards modernism's characteristic commitment to change and innovation in form. As Genette suggests, by extending so widely and variously narrative's potential for 'temporal autonomy', Proust provides models for the 'disconcerting proceedings' of many later modernist writers. In particular, *A la recherche du temps perdu* demonstrates the full potential of memory in departing from the chronological sequence of narrative – in making the past of any character wholly recoverable, through deliberate or involuntary association, at any moment in the present time of the story. Marcel talks of memory's potential to lift a character out of the present moment almost like a rope: D.H. Lawrence uses much the same image to indicate the strength and completeness of memory's connection of past and present. In *Women in Love*, he describes Gudrun, seeking sleep, as

> conscious of everything – her childhood, her girlhood, all the forgotten incidents ... it was as if she drew a glittering rope of knowledge out of the sea of darkness, drew and drew and drew it out of the fathomless depths of the past, and still it did not come to an end, there was no end to it, she must haul and haul at the rope of glittering consciousness, pull it out phosphorescent from the endless depths of the unconsciousness. (p. 391)

For modernist narrative, seeking to place 'everything in the mind', memory offers the ideal means of including the past alongside present experience. As fiction in the early years of the twentieth century moves further within the consciousness of characters, and even towards their unconsciousness, the 'rope' of memory is increasingly employed to hold past and present together. For modernist novelists, memory becomes an essential structuring device in the creation of a 'time in the mind' able to move – through the randomness of recollection – away from 'mechanical succession' and the oppressive control of the clock.

Several of Joseph Conrad's novels provide early examples of this in the British context, partly through their reliance, in Henry James's phrase, on an 'intervening first-person singular' – a figure in the fiction who shapes and structures the narrative supposedly independently of the more aloof vision of the author. In *Lord Jim*,

for example, use of the narrator Marlow makes the novel into a
first-person narrative, though of an unusual kind – one in some
ways still freer than Proust's to move randomly among various
episodes in the story. From the start of the fifth chapter to the end
of the thirty-fifth, *Lord Jim* is supposedly Marlow's spoken narrative, a yarn spun out 'in detail and audibly' (p. 31) after dinner in
some distant part of the world, with 'refreshments' to help him
through what Conrad suggests in his 'Author's Note' is three hours
or so of speech. Taking the form of a huge letter Marlow subsequently writes to a privileged member of his circle of after-dinner
listeners, the last ten chapters of the novel highlight the particular
characteristics of the earlier oral narrative. With Marlow writing
rather than speaking, this latter section of his story more or less
follows the chronological order of events during Jim's adventurous
life in Patusan. This relative straightforwardness – and the dominance of Jim's romantic imagination in shaping life in his colourful
new domain – leaves *Lord Jim* itself resembling in its closing stages
the kind of 'light holiday literature' (p. 11) which initially turned
Jim's mind towards the idea of an adventurous life at sea.

Earlier, Marlow's after-dinner monologue presents readers and
listeners with something more complex and challenging. First-
person narrators with the leisure to write events down have the
opportunity to order them carefully and chronologically if they
choose – as Marlow does in his concluding letter. Narrators delivering a story orally, on the other hand, may be more plausibly
expected to recount events simply in the order in which they occur
to them: an order ruled by memory, and by associations between
events possibly more powerful than any created by their simple
successiveness in time. At any rate, it is the process of Marlow's
recollection of events, and of the ways in which he found out about
them, that dictates the order of their presentation in his monologue – at times apparently almost regardless of the actual chronology of their occurrence. Details about the survival of Jim's ship,
the *Patna* – which might have been expected to follow the account
of its striking a submerged object at the end of Chapter 3 – are
delayed until Chapters 12 and 13, for example. This happens to be
the point in his monologue when Marlow recalls meeting, 'a long
time after' (p. 107), the French Lieutenant who almost single-
handedly rescued the ship as it drifted on the open seas. Drifting
apparently randomly between episodes in this way, and perhaps

increasingly influenced by those 'refreshments' – ironically specified as 'a glass of mineral water of some sort to help the narrator on' – Marlow's narrative quickly becomes what Conrad himself described as 'a free and wandering tale' (p. 7).

The randomness of its movement between episodes, however, is of course only apparent. Departures from chronological order allow Conrad much opportunity to stress moral points in the story – in the above instance, to enforce comparison or contrast of the French Lieutenant's supposed heroism with Jim's disgrace in his trial, recounted in Chapter 14, immediately after the French Lieutenant's story. Mutual significance, rather than simple succession in time, dictates Conrad's juxtaposition of episodes: like Proust, he is less interested in 'the mighty dimension of time' than in connections and patterns of association which transcend or suppress it. Just as Jim hastily gets rid of a clock while escaping imprisonment in Patusan, Conrad shows himself ready, in *Lord Jim* and elsewhere, to dispose of conventional, serial construction in favour of something less constrained by the 'mechanical succession' of chronology.

Some of the principles underlying this readiness were later summed up by Conrad's occasional collaborator, Ford Madox Ford. In *Joseph Conrad: A Personal Remembrance* (1924), Ford remarks of their work together

> it became very early evident to us that what was the matter with the Novel, and the British novel in particular, was that it went straight forward, whereas in your gradual making acquaintanceship with your fellows you never do go straight forward . . . To get . . . a man in fiction you could not begin at his beginning and work his life chronologically to the end. You must first get him in with a strong impression, and then work backwards and forwards over his past. (pp. 129–30)

Working 'backwards and forwards over the past' in this way is a tactic Ford employs himself in *The Good Soldier* (1915), a novel whose resemblance to *Lord Jim*, as Chapter 2 explained, extends beyond theme to include structure as well. Like Conrad, Ford shows a narrator perplexedly grasping at various explanations while attempting to assemble a coherent picture of a character who fascinates him but eludes complete understanding. Sometimes this involves collating and juxtaposing episodes separated by years in their actual occurrence. This 'free and wandering' strategy is made to seem natural by means of much the same device as Conrad uses in *Lord Jim*. Though Ford's narrator, John Dowell, does not actually deliver his story to a circle of after-dinner listeners, he carefully stresses that he proceeds – and abandons chronological order – as if he did so:

> I have, I am aware, told this story in a very rambling way so that it may be difficult for anyone to find their path through what may be a sort of maze. I cannot help it. I have stuck to my idea of being in a country cottage with a silent listener, hearing between the gusts of the wind and amidst the noises of the distant sea, the story as it comes. And, when one discusses an affair – a long, sad affair – one goes back, one goes forward. One remembers points that one has forgotten . . . one recognises that one has forgotten to mention them in their proper places . . . I console myself with thinking that this is a real story and that, after all, real stories are probably told best in the way a person telling a story would tell them. They will then seem most real. (p. 167)

In a way, Dowell's remarks raise once again '*the* question of all questions. What is reality in the novel?' which Chapter 2 quoted Hugh Walpole asking writers in the early twentieth century. Dowell acknowledges that there *are* 'proper places' for episodes in a story – presumably in the chronological order in which they occurred. But he also suggests that 'real stories' do not ideally follow this order. Realism – 'what will seem most real' – may not be created by following it. Typically of the tensions underlying the development of modernism, Dowell indicates a gap between 'proper' or established conventions of fiction and what is real; between the novel's traditional strategies for representing the world and a world which seems to have outgrown them, or to be out of step with them. Like Virginia Woolf, Ford and Conrad find the stuff of fiction ideally 'a little other than custom would have us believe it' and the custom of 'going straight forward', representing 'life as a series', particularly to be avoided. The way they do so in *Lord Jim* and in *The Good Soldier* shows them occupying, as in another way does Proust, a transitional role in the growing 'temporal autonomy' of modernist narrative. In one way, their departures from serial, chronological order create highly unconventional novels. Yet these departures are also – as in the passage above – carefully and plausibly explained: even fractured, wayward forms of construction can seem legitimate, natural, even conventional, if they are seen as aspects of oral narrative. In this way, Conrad and Ford simultaneously serve both propriety and novelty, convention and innovation.

Both authors went on to experiment further, and in some ways more radically, with fictional structure and chronology. In Conrad's *Nostromo*, a spoken narrative does appear briefly, in Captain Mitchell's garrulous account of revolution in an imaginary South American republic, Costaguana. His story, however, actually provides what is called a 'more or less stereotyped relation of the "historical events"' (p. 389), though one shown to represent these events distortingly and inadequately. It is elsewhere in the novel, without the sanction of a narrator, that Conrad decisively departs from chronological order. This departure could nevertheless still be seen as plausible enough in another way, serving a mimetic function in Conrad's representation of a South American history which he shows as too lacking in coherence to be easily reduced to conventional order, logical or chronological. Something of this view of their history is after all shared by recent South American novelists themselves, notably Gabriel García Márquez and Mario Vargas Llosa.

*The Secret Agent* is set firmly in London, yet, as in *Nostromo*, its third-person narrative extensively interrupts or warps chronological sequence. Conrad describes one of his principal characters, Chief Inspector Heat, seeming to rise above 'the vulgar conception of time' (p. 78), and the novel itself often follows him in this direction. When Heat encounters the anarchist Professor, for example, the narrative interrupts their conversation to loop back and follow at length Heat's thoughts about the earlier part of his day, and about how he was informed of the attempted bombing of Greenwich Observatory. As Genette points out in discussing Proust, such flashbacks – and anachronies in general – are not new in fiction, but part of the traditional resources and appeal of narrative. Yet there is a certain novelty in the extravagance with which they are employed in *The Secret Agent*. Between a single question and answer, Heat's conversation with the Professor is interrupted by no less than seven pages of his retrospection, as if deliberately demonstrating his conclusion that 'ages . . . could be contained between two successive winks of an eye' (p. 79). At several other points, the novel provides further evidence for Heat's view that there may be 'unexpected solutions of continuity, sudden holes in space and time' (p. 76). Like the interruptions to Heat's conversation with the Professor, other characters' thoughts and recollections repeatedly create startling anachronies, dissolving conventional narrative continuity or leaving it riddled with holes, gaps or loops. *The Secret Agent* thus amends conventional chronology not, as in *Lord Jim*, by means of the fickle memory of a narrator, but by following the mental processes of characters within the story whose thoughts often depart, in voluntary or involuntary memory, from the moment it has reached. *The Secret Agent* is in this way closer than *Lord Jim* to later modernist devices, disrupting chronology through the idiosyncrasies of characters' inner consciousnesses rather than their speech or storytelling. In Conrad's *Heart of Darkness* (1902), Marlow concludes that 'the mind of man is capable of anything – because everything is in it, all the past as well as all the future' (p. 52). *The Secret Agent* shows Conrad relying, actually more than in *Heart of Darkness* or *Lord Jim*, on the infinite capability of inner consciousness to coalesce past and present, to incorporate earlier experience into present thought.

Heat's thoughts, however, are still reported in the third person. As later novels entered more fully into the minds of individual characters, through devices such as stream of consciousness, they became more and more free to abandon serial chronology and pursue random associations within mind and memory. This development can be illustrated by comparing *The Good Soldier* with Ford's later *Parade's End* (1924–8). As Chapter 2 pointed out, *Parade's End* shared the increasing inwardness of fiction in the 1920s in moving through Free Indirect Style and interior monologue into the inner space of characters' minds. Mental processes feature more fully in *Parade's End* than in *The Good Soldier* or in Conrad's fiction, resulting at times in more thoroughgoing disruption of serial chronology; more frequent and minute insertion of past experience into the story's present. The sort of recursive, looping tactic Conrad uses to insert past events into the present of Heat's conversation with the Professor is employed frequently and at still greater length throughout *Parade's End*. Ford's protagonist Christopher Tietjens provides what is almost a theoretical description of his author's strategy when he suggests to his lover Valentine

> You cut out from this afternoon, just before 4.58 . . . I heard the Horse Guards clock.... To now.... Cut it out; and join time up.... It *can* be done.... You know they do it surgically; for some illness, cut out a great length of the bowel and join the tube up. (p. 285)

The kind of temporal surgery Tietjens describes is actually performed by the chapter in which his suggestion is made. It begins
and ends with his return home at 3.30 a.m. and his subsequent
departure for the trenches. Between, the narrative goes back
through Tietjens's recollections to events earlier in the evening,
and earlier in the day, including those around 4.58 p.m., tracing
them in fragments of Free Indirect Style, reported thought and
memory. Some of these events are in any case already familiar
from their recollection by Valentine in the previous chapter.
Throughout *Parade's End*, by entering characters' thoughts in this
way, whole sections are cut from the slack bowel of time and
reshaped through memory into loops which delve back into the
past and then proceed forward again until they have caught up
with the moment of consciousness at which the retrospection
began.

Several characters in *Parade's End* comment with surprise on
the fascinatingly anachronous nature of thought and its capacity to
warp or telescope time – perhaps incidentally indicating something
of Ford's own relish for his new techniques. Tietjens's wife, for
example, remarks to herself after an elaborate set of reflections,
'Good God! ... Only one minute.... I've thought all that in only
a minute' (p. 417). After a wide-ranging reflection of her own,
Valentine is likewise surprised to realize that 'she had thought all
that in ten seconds . . . that was what thought was' (pp. 518–19).
Such comments reflect the same kind of conclusion reached by
Virginia Woolf when she remarks in *Orlando* that 'an hour may be
accurately represented in the timepiece of the mind by one
second'. Demonstrating and reflecting on 'what thought was' in
this way, *Parade's End* largely shares the full, modernist 'temporal
autonomy' developed in the work of Woolf and Joyce – the capacity, if not to suppress altogether the mighty dimension of time, at
least to represent principally 'time in the mind' rather than only
'time on the clock'.

Throughout the 1920s, Virginia Woolf established her own ways of
cutting and stitching up time – of escaping 'the appalling narrative
business of the realist' in proceeding straightforwardly from lunch
to dinner. In the same entry in her diary in 1928 she resolves 'I will
read Proust I think. I will go backwards and forwards'. Much of her
fiction reflects Proust's emphasis on memory and his conclusion

that 'we relive our past years not in their continuous sequence'. In the novel finished shortly before this diary entry was made, *Orlando*, she suggests

> Memory is the seamstress, and a capricious one at that. Memory runs her needle in and out, up and down, hither and thither. We know not what comes next, or what follows after. Thus, the most ordinary movement in the world, such as sitting down at a table and pulling the inkstand towards one, may agitate a thousand odd, disconnected fragments . . . our commonest deeds are set about with a fluttering and flickering of wings, a rising and falling of lights. (p. 55)

Like Proust, Woolf finds associations with the past triggered powerfully yet almost arbitrarily by events in the present – powerfully enough to ensure that, in *Mrs Dalloway*, 'people . . . came back in the middle of St James's Park on a fine morning – indeed they did' (p. 9). Memory functions equally strongly in *To the Lighthouse* (1927). While painting her picture Lily Briscoe turns over in her mind a sudden memory of Mrs Ramsay sitting on the beach and asks

> D'you remember? . . . Why, after all these years had that survived, ringed round, lit up, visible to the last detail, with all before it blank and all after it blank, for miles and miles? (p. 194)

However inexplicable this sort of involuntary connection seems, it is also inescapable. While continuing with her painting in the present, Lily is simultaneously carried back almost physically into the past:

> at the same time, she seemed to be sitting beside Mrs Ramsay on the beach . . . as if a door had opened, and one went in and stood gazing silently about. (pp. 194–5)

Such moments, Lily reflects, are 'extraordinarily fertile . . . like a drop of silver in which one dipped and illumined the darkness of the past' (p. 195). They are certainly extraordinarily useful in Woolf's fiction, as in modernism generally. Like Proust, she uses the memory as a seamstress to cut and reshape sections taken out of the ordinary, sequential passage of time. 'Fertile moments' in the present offer a door through which the past experience of characters can be illumined, allowing a full sense of their earlier lives to be presented within the single days of consciousness she concentrates on in *Mrs Dalloway*, and in a way in *The Waves* (1931); or the two days in *To the Lighthouse*. Concentrating on the 'myriad impressions', memories included, daily passing through the mind, Woolf achieves her ambition of going back as well as forwards, firmly rejecting 'life as a series' yet managing to retain a full sense of the life of her characters.

Something similar is achieved by Joyce in *Ulysses*. Joyce's narrative progresses steadily enough through Bloom's day in Dublin, 16 June 1904, but it also ranges widely over his remembered earlier life, freely exploiting his mind's capacity to stray in imagination or memory far from the actual external events unfolding around him. His stream of consciousness continually recovers past events, associated and juxtaposed with present ones. Chapter 6, 'Hades', for example, finds Bloom a mourner at Paddy Dignam's funeral, yet also moving back in memory to the suicide of his father long before; to the burial of his infant son Rudy, ten years previously; to earlier times with Molly, living in Lombard Street West. Such past details are sufficient to provide a picture of a life as complete as in any Victorian *Bildungsroman*, yet very differently presented; constantly, immediately illumined through the fertile movements and moments of Bloom's mind in his single day in Dublin.

The potential of such illumination of the past is perhaps most fully realized at the end of *Ulysses*, in the freewheeling movements of Molly Bloom's mind, turning over and mixing thought and memory on the edge of sleep in 'Penelope', the last chapter. In its concluding pages, she associates with the present not a single set of recollections but at least two different eras of earlier experience. Her mind moves back, first of all, to Bloom's proposal to her, '16 years ago my God' – i.e. in 1888 – and to the way she 'wouldnt answer first only looked out over the sea and the sky . . . thinking of so many things he didnt know' (pp. 931–2). These things include memories of another still earlier phase of her life – her youth in Gibraltar, a location which helps to create a sense of universality at the end of *Ulysses*. Certain versions of the story of Odysseus (which Joyce of course follows carefully throughout *Ulysses*), tell of a final voyage taking him beyond the rock of Gibraltar – in myth, the Pillars of Hercules, which marked the point at which the known world opened out into chartless, unknowable, oceanic infinity. Moving in his last chapter towards a point marking the end of knowable space, Joyce also goes as far as possible towards the limits of specific or specifiable time. Molly's memories of accepting Bloom's proposal in 1888 are interfused with an earlier saying 'yes' to a lover in Gibraltar; perhaps also with a reaffirmation of her relationship with Bloom in the present of 1904. But in moving between Ireland, Gibraltar and the open sea beyond, and between 1904, 1888 and earlier, Molly's mind so interweaves memories and recollections – even remembered recollections – that it creates for the novel an affirmative, comedic conclusion largely beyond particular time as well as space. Molly's concluding 'yes' is spoken to no single man, nor at any specific moment, but to all human relationships. In various plans for *Ulysses* which he later allowed to be made public, Joyce indicates a particular time of day for each of the novel's chapters except the last, for which he either – in one plan – stipulates no particular time, or – in another – inserts in place of an hour of the day the symbol $\infty$ to represent infinity.[2]

Rather than bringing the action of *Ulysses* firmly to a close at the end, Joyce thus opens it out beyond constraints of geography or chronology. If *A la recherche du temps perdu* is in Gérard Genette's view a novel of 'temporal autonomy' – of 'time ruled, captured, bewitched, surreptitiously subverted' – then so surely is *Ulysses*. Molly Bloom's soliloquy consummates the modernist desire, discussed in Chapter 2, to 'look within' at inner consciousness: it also realizes as fully as possible the disposition discussed in this chapter to be freed of the mechanical rule of the hours; to rely on the time of the mind rather than the mechanism of the clock. Obviously, the two movements – towards inner consciousness, and away from clocks and mechanical succession – are closely related. Streams of consciousness and interior monologues offer not only a fluent entry to the mind's present movement, but to the depths of past experience, revitalized by association with immediate impressions. Some of the contemporary pressures encouraging fiction to 'look within', discussed in the last chapter, are therefore also relevant to the restructurings of fiction examined above. There were also, however, factors in the life of the early twentieth century which may be related more specifically to contemporary hostility towards the clock, and to modernism's consequent quest for 'temporal autonomy' and 'time in the mind'. These factors are discussed in the next two sections.

## THE TIME PHILOSOPHY

The most prolific contemporary commentator on the issue, Wyndham Lewis, had no doubt about the factors responsible for a new concern with time in the life and art of the 1920s. In his huge, 450-page assessment of contemporary culture, *Time and Western Man* (1927), Lewis explains that the new conception of time which he sees as such a distinctive feature in the writing of his period directly resulted from 'what was originally a philosophic theory used currently in the practice of the arts of expression, and become a second nature for the practitioners' (p. 149). The philosophic theory that Lewis believes so universally (and, in his view, damagingly) influential was the 'philosophy of *psychological time*' (p. 102), as he calls it, expounded in the work of Henri Bergson. Lewis considers Bergson

> more than any other single figure ... responsible for the main intellectual characteristics of the world we live in, and the implicit debt of almost all contemporary philosophy to him is immense. (p. 166)

In Lewis's view, 'practitioners' of Bergson's thinking in the literary sphere include, among others, Proust, Gertrude Stein and, above all, James Joyce. In his extended 'Analysis of the Mind of James Joyce' in *Time and Western Man*, Lewis remarks

> I regard *Ulysses* as a *time-book*; and by that I mean that it lays its emphasis upon, for choice manipulates, and in a doctrinaire manner, the self-conscious time-sense, that has now been erected into a universal philosophy. This it does beneath the spell of a similar creative impulse to that by which Proust worked . . .

> Without all the uniform pervasive growth of the time-philosophy starting from the little seed planted by Bergson, discredited, and now spreading more vigorously than ever, there would be no *Ulysses*, or there would be no *A La Recherche du Temps Perdu*. There would be no 'time-composition' of Miss Stein; no fugues in words. In short, Mr. Joyce is very strictly of the school of Bergson-Einstein, Stein-Proust. He is of the great time-school they represent. His book is a *time-book*, as I have said, in that sense. He has embraced the time-doctrine very completely. (pp. 100, 106)

The question of whether Joyce or others need be seen as 'practitioners' in a school established by Bergson can be left aside for the moment. Lewis is right at least in pointing out the extent to which

Bergson's philosophy bears comparison with various aspects of modernist fiction – in particular with the attitudes to time outlined in the last section. One of the cores of Bergson's thinking is its resistance – like modernist writers' – to conceptions of time or life as a series; as a succession of separate, clearly divisible events. Any such thinking he considers to be covertly, misleadingly based on habits of mind appropriate only for conceptualizing space. In *Time and Free Will* (*Essai sur les données immédiates de la conscience*, 1889) he suggests that

> time, conceived under the form of a homogeneous medium, is some spurious concept, due to the trespassing of the idea of space upon the field of pure consciousness. (p. 98)

This 'spurious concept' leads to the error of supposing time a quantity or commodity, something that can be divided up and parcelled out like a piece of material. The principal agent – or really villain – in making such divisions is of course the clock, magisterially dissecting time into lumps, units and numbers. In this role the clock is a particular focus for Bergson's criticism, his philosophy regularly indicating the obstacles it creates for the true, mental experience of time which he calls 'duration' (*durée*). He remarks, for example,

> When I follow with my eyes on the dial of a clock the movement of the hands . . . I do not measure duration . . . Outside of me, in space, there is never more than a single position of the hand . . . Within myself a process of organization or interpenetration of conscious states is going on, which constitutes true duration . . .
>
> states of consciousness, even when successive, permeate one another, and in the simplest of them the whole soul can be reflected. (pp. 107–8, 98)

Bergson sees the trespass of space upon thinking about time resulting from the intellect's disposition to define, divide and categorize. Time should be truly understood, he considers, not through this divisive intellect, but by means of intuition, able to apprehend the permeation of conscious states; the seamless flow of creative evolution and becoming.

Such views of continuity and duration establish a central role for memory in Bergson's work, which considers that – in an evolving flow of conscious states – past ones do not disappear, but coexist with and interpenetrate those in the present:

Behind the memories which crowd in upon our present occupation and are
revealed by means of it, there are others, thousands on thousands of others,
below and beneath the scene illuminated by consciousness. Yes, I believe our
past life is there, preserved even to the minutest details; nothing is forgotten; all
we have perceived, thought, willed, from the first awakening of our consciousness, persists indefinitely.[3]

Bergson's conviction that 'nothing is forgotten' coincides with
Gudrun's realization in *Women in Love* that 'everything . . . all the
forgotten incidents' are actually still available to present consciousness, able to be drawn back by the 'glittering rope' memory reaches
into the fathomless depths of the past. His explanation of the connection of present occupation and past life likewise offers a
philosophic version of Lily Briscoe's discovery, in *To the Lighthouse*, that 'fertile moments' in the present open doors upon the
past – or of Marcel's experience with the Madeleine in *A la recherche du temps perdu*. Like Proust, Bergson considers present
sensual stimuli automatically opening up powerful recoveries of the
past, offering in *Time and Free Will* his own example of this process:

I smell a rose and immediately confused recollections of childhood come back
to my memory . . . I breathe them in with the very scent; it means all that to me.
(p. 161)

Bergson's belief that time exists truly as duration, within the self,
and that the conscious states constituting this duration are seamlessly continuous, coincides not only with modernism's suspicion
of the clock but also with some of the movement's other priorities.
It matches both the assumption that the truest experience is found
by looking within, and that this mental experience is stream-like
and continuous in nature. Though the phrase 'stream of consciousness' belongs to William James, the idea that consciousness is not a
chain of separate items, but a constant flow of memories and
impressions, is equally Bergsonian. Molly Bloom's final soliloquy
gives an example of the sort of conscious activity, eliding distinctions between separate thoughts and between past and present,
which Bergson saw as the true life of the mind (at least as far as it is
possible to transcribe this in language). In this way, *Ulysses* or
other modernist novels could indeed be seen as 'time-books',
much as Wyndham Lewis claims. In *Time and Free Will*, Bergson
specifically asks for 'some bold novelist', able to show the 'infinite

permeation of a thousand different impressions' by 'tearing aside the cleverly woven curtain of our conventional ego' (p. 133). His request seems directly answered by modernism's movements beyond what D.H. Lawrence calls 'the old stable ego'[4] and by its development of techniques able to record the 'myriad impressions' Woolf sees daily passing through the mind.

Bergson's potential appeal for the modernists also goes some way beyond his views of time. His preference for intuition, rather than intellect or rational analysis, is developed further throughout his philosophy and widely shared and echoed in modernism. The modernist period shows throughout a tendency to move away from the rational, logical and deductive, in favour of the intuitive, the unconscious and the emotional. This appears fairly generally in Lawrence's writing, summed up in the complaint in *Lady Chatterley's Lover* (1928) that 'the mind can only analyse and rationalize', leaving humanity 'over-conscious' and 'on the spontaneous, intuitive side dead' (p. 39, 159). Proust similarly prefers spontaneous, automatic memory rather than 'the memory of the intellect'. A character in Richard Aldington's *Death of a Hero* (1929) remarks that it is 'so much better to trust to the deeper instincts than to talk about things with "the inferior intelligence"' (p. 25), and in *The Return of the Soldier* (1918) Rebecca West is equally suspicious of 'the whole hostile reasonable world' (p. 178). Reasoning and intellect are likewise not much approved in *To the Lighthouse*. Part of Mrs Ramsay's virtue is that 'her simplicity fathomed what clever people falsified' (p. 34): part of her husband's limitation is his determination to rationalize, categorize and define.

Bergson's interest for modernism thus extends well beyond his ideas of time (other relevant phases of his thinking are considered in Chapter 4). The way his ideas were communicated added further to his appeal. Philosophy might seem too abstract and esoteric to have much direct contact with popular or literary thinking. Yet Bergson's views are expressed unusually accessibly, often even poetically, and at the turn of the century they reached an audience much wider than the usual one for formal philosophy. Bergson occupied at the time a position comparable to Roland Barthes or Jacques Derrida in the later twentieth century – complex, challenging thinkers whose ideas are nevertheless influential within popular culture as well as academic circles, making them almost figures of fashion. Bergson's lectures at the Collège de France in the 1890s were hugely well-attended, almost society occasions, and his published work rapidly ran through several editions, both in the original and in English translation. There is plenty of evidence that his ideas were widely disseminated at different levels of society in the years which followed – Bergson turns up, for example, as a promising subject for tea-time chat among Princeton undergraduates in F. Scott Fitzgerald's *The Beautiful and Damned* (1922). There is also evidence that contemporary authors were more or less directly in touch with his thinking – T.S. Eliot was familiar with Bergson, and William Faulkner remarks that he agreed with 'Bergson's theory of the fluidity of time'.[5] Even Wyndham Lewis attended Bergson's lectures, despite his hostility. So did Marcel Proust, a distant cousin of Bergson's by marriage. A significant minor character in the early part of *A la recherche du temps perdu*, Bergotte, is sometimes said to be modelled on Bergson: at any rate, Marcel ponders at length the validity of Bergson's theories of memory in the 'Cities of the Plain' section of the novel (II, pp. 1016–17). A familiar interest in Bergsonian ideas can also be deciphered from Joyce's writing. The sixth section of *Finnegans Wake* (1939) mentions 'the sophology of Bitchson' in the course of discussing psychological time and the relation of time to space – a debate figured as the 'dime-cash' problem, of much concern to 'windy Nous' (pp. 56, 149).

As well as the 'sophology of Bitchson', *Finnegans Wake* also discusses the 'theorics of Winestain' (p. 149). In the view of Windy Nous, or Wyndham Lewis, the 'theorics' of Einstein were probably partly derived from Bergson's philosophy,[6] and certainly reversed any falling away in popular interest in his work. Even though Bergson's own fame and fashionableness might otherwise have slightly faded, Einstein's popularity in the 1920s reinvigorated a 'time-school' which Lewis saw including several other contemporary philosophers, such as Samuel Alexander and A.N. Whitehead, as well. Lewis explains the expanding influence of 'the school of Bergson-Einstein' by remarking that

> The philosophy of the space-timeist is identical with the old . . . bergsonian philosophy of *psychological time* (or *durée*, as he called it). It is essential to grasp this continuity between the earlier flux of Bergson, with its Time-god, and the einsteinian flux, with its god, Space-time. (p. 102)

Lewis's assumption of identity, or 'great orthodoxy' (p. 218) among all these contemporary thinkers is in one way simply wrong. Bergson's insistence that ideas of space must be kept separate from concepts of time differs quite clearly from the views of later thinkers. Einstein, in particular, encouraged the habitual hyphenation 'space-time' in the 1920s, establishing the idea of a unified medium in which time figures as a fourth dimension alongside the three of space.

Such differences between Bergson and the 1920s space-timeists were carefully pointed out by Bertrand Russell, and ought to have been clear enough in philosophic circles in any case. Nevertheless, Lewis was not the only one to ignore them, and they may have been still more easily overlooked in the popular mind. Bergson himself, after all, attempted to find a resemblance between Einstein's ideas and his own in his study *Durée et Simultanéité* (1922), though he did later acknowledge that the attempt had not been altogether successful. And Einstein's public pronouncements might easily have encouraged a feeling that his work followed from and confirmed other recent theories of time, Bergson's in particular. Einstein once remarked, for example, that

> The really important factor is ultimately intuition . . . The subjective sensation is a reality.

> There is only a psychological time, different from the time of physicists.[7]

With all the supposed weight of scientific truth, pronouncements of this sort offered – actually rather as Lewis suggests – powerful substantiation of psychological or durational time, rather than time on the clock or the time of physicists, as the true measure of experience.

Einstein's fame carried into the 1920s a huge wave of popular excitement and interest in such issues. When his theories were apparently confirmed by observations made during the solar eclipse of May 1919, as one contemporary commentator, Alexander Moszkowski, expresses it

> a wave of amazement swept over the continents . . . During that time no name was quoted so often as that of this man. Everything sank away in face of this universal theme which had taken possession of humanity . . . Relativity had become the sovereign password. (pp. 13–14)

Though Einstein's ideas were difficult to grasp, there soon appeared a huge literature of explanations and introductions – such as Moszkowski's *Einstein the Searcher* (1921) or Bertrand Russell's *The ABC of Relativity* (1926) – to ensure that, as Lewis puts it,

> within a few years of the arrival of Einstein upon the european scene, the layman, I suppose, knows more about Relativity physics than any layman has ever known about the newtonian cosmology. (p. 11)

Lewis, therefore, had good reason to suggest in *Time and Western Man* that Einstein's influence may have revived Bergson's – certainly that Relativity kept new ideas of 'psychological time' in the forefront of popular interest in the 1920s. *Time and Western Man* could even have gone further in considering how other recent thinkers might have contributed to this interest. Lewis might have examined more thoroughly some of the figures concerned in the epistemological shift – the radical challenge to the validity, even the possibility, of human understanding of the universe – whose appearance in the late nineteenth and early twentieth centuries was discussed in Chapter 2. A suspicion of conventional views of time was bound to figure in a shift of opinion which questioned – as mere 'human device', without universal validity – any means by which consciousness envisages and establishes its place within nature. Nietzsche's radical scepticism inevitably includes questioning of the conventional meaning of time, which he saw lacking natural or absolute existence and simply prescribed upon the world for human convenience. Nietzsche particularly attacks the erroneous assumption of the existence of 'divisible time spans' and 'divisible spaces', which he considers aspects of a more generally misleading 'presumption of eternal truths, and space, time, and causality as absolute and universally valid laws'. Rather than some divisible medium, Nietzsche considers 'in truth we are confronted by a *continuum* . . . a flux'; a 'course of *becoming*'. This continuum Nietzsche sees submitted to 'arbitrary division and dismemberment' by the habits of the intellect.[8] Such ideas place his thinking quite close to Bergson's concept of time as a continuous durational evolution of consciousness and experience. The assertion that time is an invented, arbitrary category, rather than an absolute or universal one, also coincides with Einstein's views – at least as they were summed up by Bertrand Russell in *The ABC of Relativity*:

The time-order of events is in part dependent upon the observer . . .

The universal cosmic time which used to be taken for granted is thus no longer admissible. (pp. 44, 50)

Conventional temporality was challenged in another way, around the turn of the century, by the work of Sigmund Freud. In Freud's view, past and present are crucially connected, though not necessarily in chronological sequence. The past not only continues to exist – though mostly buried in unconscious memories – it is largely the expanding effects of past psychic events which continue to shape and structure present personality. Distant events, Freud shows, especially those in childhood, are often more influential in this way than more recent ones: pain or pleasure thirty years ago may be more important, and in some ways closer to the present, than the events of yesterday. The origins of such distant yet inescapable influences can also be recovered in the present. At least occasionally, in 'fertile moments', or pulled up on the right 'glittering rope', the past can be exhumed – allowed to 'reappear in the light',[9] principally through the agency of dreams. For Freud, dreams offer as powerful a means of recovering the past as memory does for Bergson. He suggests in *The Interpretation of Dreams* (1899)

What we have long ceased to think about, what has long since lost for us all importance, is constantly recalled by the dream . . .

Nothing which we have once psychically possessed is ever entirely lost. (pp. 11, 15)

In *Women in Love*, when Gudrun finds that 'everything . . . her childhood, her girlhood, all the forgotten incidents' still exist in 'the sea of darkness . . . the fathomless depths of the past . . . the endless depths of the unconsciousness', her discovery belongs as much with the idea of a rope of dreams outlined by Freud as to the faculty of memory stressed by Bergson. It may be significant that several of the moments in modernist writing when chronological order is most comprehensively abandoned or transcended occur, as in Gudrun's case, when characters hover on the edge of sleep or dreams. Marcel is in this condition throughout the time-wandering 'Overture' to *A la recherche du temps perdu*; Molly Bloom shares it in the time-denying conclusion to *Ulysses*; and when rising furthest above 'the vulgar conception of time' in *The Secret Agent* it is of

'long and terrifying dreams dreamed in the instant of waking' (p. 78)
that Chief Inspector Heat finds himself thinking. In *Aspects of the
Novel* (1927), E.M. Forster particularly indicates dreamers, as well
as artists and lovers, as 'partially delivered from . . . tyranny' exerted
by 'Father Time' (p. 36). By the late 1920s, and probably earlier,
there was widespread belief and interest in this capacity of dream to
escape from the tyranny of time, allowing the dreamer to wander
freely and apparently at random in the past, or even in the future.
Evidence of this appears in the publication of J.W. Dunne's *An
Experiment with Time* in 1927. From his experience of several
dreams which seemed to predict the future, Dunne elaborated a
whole theory of the existence of a fourth dimension, free from the
ordinary passage of time. It could be entered in dream or visionary
states, allowing visits to things past or yet to come. Dunne's work
was sharply satirized by Wyndham Lewis, but it was widely re-
spected elsewhere at the time.[10] Dunne was invited to speak at
Oxford by the philosopher A.J. Ayer; Joyce knew and seems to have
admired his ideas; and *An Experiment with Time* was popular enough
to remain in print almost sixty years after its first publication.

Sixty or more years after the first publication of *Time and Western
Man*, Lewis's criticism remains a fascinating assessment – too often
overlooked by later commentators – of the new habits of mind
appearing in his period. Lewis's judgements carry the authority of a
contemporary eye-witness, an artist and novelist at work in the age
he describes, and they are also extraordinarily eclectic in examining this age, ranging far beyond literature and philosophy. At one
stage, for example, *Time and Western Man* talks of 'the association
of Einstein with Miss Stein, of Swann and Stein, of Bergson and
Bloom, of Miss Loos, Charlie Chaplin and Whitehead' (p. 218).
Yet the immediacy of Lewis's contact with his age, and in some
ways his eclecticism, also set some limits to the validity of his
conclusions. Discussing his own priorities, particularly as a painter,
Lewis talks of a preference for anything 'nobly defined and exact,
as opposed to that which is fluid', and for the 'definition and logical
integrity that, as a graphic artist, I require'.[11] Contrary to this
requirement, he saw the art and writing of his time apparently
dissolving into streams of consciousness or in various other ways
denying definition and exactness, temporal or otherwise. Not un-
naturally, Lewis was inclined to suppose that such a general disposition in the age, and one so contrary to his own, could hardly

have appeared of its own accord, but must be the result of some
powerful negative influence – a 'great orthodoxy'; almost a kind of
conspiracy. Finding 'fluidity . . . the life-blood of the philosophy of
Bergson',[12] Lewis chooses to see this influence and orthodoxy arising principally from his work. The choice is in one way an obvious
one, since Lewis does show successfully that the literature of his
age, its philosophy, and many other contemporary phenomena are
much preoccupied with new ideas of time largely analogous to
Bergson's. As Chapters 1 and 2 explained, however, such analogy
or parallelism is not a necessary or sufficient basis for assuming
causality. Lewis is too ready to turn correlation into cause, coincidence into conspiracy. Fredric Jameson provides a necessary warning about *Time and Western Man* when he remarks of it that

> as a neutral description of the originality of modern consciousness it is surely
> unexceptionable – but rather its form is fundamentally problematic. The theme
> of time is here an instrument of analysis and descriptive explanation which is
> then called upon to function as a causal hypothesis.

As Jameson suggests, *Time and Western Man* is 'unexception-
able' as a description of contemporary consciousness: Jameson
himself confirms of Lewis's period that

> contemporary consciousness . . . also modern art, and the modern sensibility in
> all its manifestations, are saturated by an original and historically new sense of
> temporality.[13]

The principal value of *Time and Western Man* is that it shows how
thoroughly a new sense of temporality did imbue the whole age,
not only in literature and philosophy but throughout 'the modern
sensibility' in all the manifestations – from Bergson to Charlie
Chaplin – which Lewis piles helter-skelter into his argument. To
explain this new temporality simply as the *result* of Bergson's
work, however, supposes that the intellectual contours of an age
derive from philosophy rather than, equally possibly, vice versa.
The popular impact of Bergson and Einstein may have been owed
not only to their genius in generating and persuading people of
totally new ideas, but to their formulation within scientific
or philosophic discourse of concepts already colouring popular
thought, or at least congenial to it. This is the view D.H. Lawrence
takes in the passage, quoted in Chapter 2, in which he remarks that

if 'everybody catches fire at the word Relativity', it is because 'there must have been something in the mere suggestion which we have been waiting for'. Likewise, Dorothy Richardson once remarked of the question of Bergson's influence

> I was never consciously aware of any specific influence . . . No doubt Bergson influenced many minds, if only by putting into words something then dawning within the human consciousness: an increased sense of the inadequacy of the clock as a time-measurer.[14]

Richardson's remarks suggest a worthwhile place for Bergson and other philosophers in the study of modernist fiction. Their work puts into words, makes explicit and directly accessible – in some of the passages quoted above, for example – priorities more implicitly informing fiction. Philosophy may not cause, but it can clarify. It may be tempting to go further and follow Lewis's conveniently complete explanation of modernist writing as simply the result of Bergson's persuasive philosophy, but it would hardly be logical to do so, even in Lewis's own terms. If there could be no *Ulysses* without the 'tiny seed' planted by Bergson, then presumably without some other seed or set of factors there would be no Bergson, either. This set of factors, however, cannot always just be looked for in other writers or philosophers in the way Lewis supposes. If the sense of temporality he saw so widely disseminated in the early years of the twentieth century was as Jameson suggests 'historically new', then it is in the new conditions of contemporary history that its origins must also be sought. Wyndham Lewis's enquiry in *Time and Western Man* needs to be extended into a still wider scrutiny of pressures on Western experience in the late nineteenth century and the first decades of the twentieth. Why should a hostility to clocks and a preference for time in the mind 'dawn within the human consciousness' and figure so widely throughout the thinking of this particular age?

## MEAN TIME

Resentment or suspicion of the clock is of course not unique to the modernist period, nor altogether new in literature. The *carpe diem* theme common in poetry for centuries, for example, partly depends on such thinking. So do many of Shakespeare's sonnets, and the celebration in *As You Like It* of the fact that 'there's no clock in the forest' (III, ii) sums up a widespread sense of the unnaturalness – even the actual hostility to nature – of the clock as a time-measurer. Like any other, however, this general sense can be focused by specific historical circumstances: by the end of the nineteenth century, several factors had coalesced to intensify and particularize it. Most obviously, the nineteenth century saw large sections of the British population move away from clock-free forests or rural labour to take up work in factories and a life in the kind of huge, complex cities which later provide the background for much modernist fiction. As the century went on, this factory work and city life created conditions increasingly unlike the more casual rhythms of the country or of agricultural labour shaped by sunrise, sunset and season. Eventually, shift-work made interchangeable even the activities of night and day. And as factory tasks were increasingly divided up among separate individuals, each completing a particular phase in the assembly of some product, machines recording every individual arrival and departure from the factory became necessary, replacing the hooters and whistles used to summon whole shifts of workers earlier in the century. By 1890 this ritual of 'clocking-in' and 'clocking-out' came to define the beginning and end of each day's work, the clock now exactly controlling each entry to and exit from the workplace.

From around the 1880s, labour during the working day was likewise increasingly controlled by what Frederick W. Taylor calls 'rules, laws, and formulae, which replace the judgement of the individual workman'. These were eventually codified by Taylor in *The Principles of Scientific Management*, published in 1911. 'Scientific management' depended on the belief that, as Taylor puts it, 'in the past the man has been first; in the future the system must be first' (pp. 22, 8). To establish systems of scientific management, time and motion studies were introduced to define exact durations for all tasks: like entry to the factory, each piece of work within it was now intensely regulated by the clock. It is this new attitude created by Taylorism and scientific management which D.H. Lawrence reflects in Gerald Crich's reorganization of the mine in *Women in Love*. Gerald's modernization creates

the great reform. Expert engineers were introduced in every department . . . New machinery was brought from America, such as the miners had never seen before, great iron men, as the cutting machines were called, and unusual appliances. The working of the pits was thoroughly changed, all the control was taken out of the hands of the miners, the butty system was abolished. Everything was run on the most accurate and delicate scientific method, educated and expert men were in control everywhere.

There was a new world, a new order, strict, terrible, inhuman . . . a great and perfect system that subjected life to pure mathematical principles. (pp. 259–60)

Strict, minute regulation of the kind Lawrence describes allowed management to treat individual workers more and more as components, mere cogs within the greater machine of the whole factory. Scientific management made them increasingly subordinate to the machinery they had to serve, and often virtually interchangeable with it. Its spread from the United States to Britain in the early years of the twentieth century played a significant part in the anxieties about the reification of humanity in a late capitalist age discussed at the end of Chapter 2 – the kind of anxieties that Leopold Bloom sums up in *Ulysses* when thinking 'Machines. Smash a man to atoms if they got him caught. Rule the world today' (p. 150), or that Lawrence reflects in *Lady Chatterley's Lover* in the comment 'soon there'll be no use for men on the face of the earth, it'll be all machines' (p. 109). The connection of such anxieties about reification with a new sense of temporality in the machine age is emphasized in the work of Karl Marx, and in 1920s commentary on it by the Hungarian Marxist critic Georg Lukács. In *History and Class Consciousness* (1923) Lukács traces 'the progressive elimination of the qualitative, human and individual attributes of the worker' in machine industry and concludes that

with the modern . . . analysis of the work-process (in Taylorism) this rational mechanisation extends right into the worker's 'soul' . . . he is a mechanical part incorporated into a mechanical system . . .

Marx puts it thus: 'Through the subordination of man to the machine the situation arises in which . . . the pendulum of the clock has become as accurate a measure of the relative activity of two workers as it is of the speed of two locomotives . . . Time is everything, man is nothing; he is at the most the incarnation of time. Quality no longer matters. Quantity alone decides everything: hour for hour, day for day ...'

Thus time sheds its qualitative, variable, flowing nature; it freezes into an exactly delimited, quantifiable continuum filled with quantifiable 'things' (the reified, mechanically objectified 'performance' of the worker, wholly separated from his total human personality). (pp. 88–90)

In language sometimes close to Bergson's – in seeing time as really variable and flowing rather than delimited and quantifiable – Lukács sums up the interrelated roles of the machine and of a commodified temporality in eliminating the human and penetrating into the very soul of the modern age.

Within such processes, the clock can be seen occupying a unique position – as a symbolic as well as an actual focus for concern. Entirely regulating working life, it functioned as a crucial agent in the new rule of the machine, but it also often provides in literature an emblem or metaphor for the results of such increasingly stringent regulation. As human beings in the twentieth century increasingly risked taking on the mechanical nature of their new 'rulers', they could be more and more appropriately represented by the clock – an intricate, ever-moving machine with a face and hands. In *Women in Love*, Gudrun turns immediately to this metaphor to sum up her horror both of the industrial master, Gerald, and of the men he has subordinated to his will:

> the wheels within wheels of people, it makes one's head tick like a clock, with a very madness of dead mechanical monotony and meaninglessness . . .

> Let them turn into mechanisms . . . perfect parts of a great machine . . . the miner, with a thousand wheels, and then the electrician, with three thousand, and the underground manager, with twenty thousand, and the general manager with a hundred thousand little wheels working away to complete his make-up, and then Gerald, with a million wheels and cogs and axles.

> Poor Gerald, such a lot of little wheels to his make-up! He was more intricate than a chronometer-watch. (pp. 522, 524–5)

Outside the factory, the early years of the twentieth century saw conditions of leisure made almost as firmly subject to control by the clock as those of work. Pressures on production during the First World War, concern about bad time-keeping in crucial industries, and an obvious need to avoid accidents in munitions factories led to attempts to eliminate drunkenness by controlling the opening hours of pubs through licensing laws introduced under the Defence of the Realm Act.[15] Resounding across the 'Game of Chess' section of *The Waste Land*, the pub-closing cry 'HURRY UP PLEASE IT'S TIME' – sounding almost like a warning about time itself – was still a relatively new addition to the spiritlessness of the urban landscape when T.S. Eliot published his poem in 1922.

In other ways, too, the First World War enforced new and more stringent concern with time and its measurement. Conditions of combat made exactly timed co-ordination of troop movements essential: waves of attacking soldiers required even stricter synchronization than shifts of workers. So army officers increasingly adopted the use of easily consulted wrist-watches – before the war, these had been thought an affectation, a flamboyant alternative to the leisured consultation of a fob watch. During the war such leisure ceased to exist, as did millions of the men who might have enjoyed it. Regulative apparatus bound to each wrist began to dictate the organization and timing not only of work and leisure, but of death.

Material production and military organization in the early twentieth century – the working life and death of 'the modern industrial and financial world' – thus helped make the clock master rather than servant of humanity. A particular aspect of Gudrun's fears about 'the terrible clock' indicates other factors which reached beyond factory work or the trenches of the First World War to ensure the clock's mastery of the population as a whole. Thinking of Gerald and modern industrialized man, she finds that

> she could never escape. There she was, placed before the clock-face of life. And if she turned round as in a railway station, to look at the bookstall, still she could see, with her very spine, she could see the clock, always the great white clock-face . . . the eternal, mechanical, monotonous, clock-face of time. (p. 523)

It is highly appropriate that during her chilling vision of the clock it is in a railway station that Gudrun thinks of standing. Throughout the nineteenth century, the spread of railways did at least as much as the expansion of factory-work to put the clock firmly in control of everyday life – to make time mean, and be Mean, for everyone. Until the great advance of the railways in the 1840s most British towns lived in little local time zones of their own – the time on clocks in Bristol, for example, was eleven minutes different from those in London. Strange as this now seems, it was in one way sensible and perfectly natural, since the sun and stars – markers of true or astronomical time – rise and set at different times in different parts of the British Isles. Such differences in local times, however, created the disturbing possibility that a train – at any rate one on a fairly short journey – might apparently arrive somewhere at a time before it had set out. Such confusions had to be eliminated: in general, a homogeneous, nationwide time was essential if passengers every-where were to know when to turn up for their journeys, and railway-men when to commence them. As the railway historians Jeffrey Richards and John M. MacKenzie remark,

> Trains had to leave on time for the railway system to make sense in both passenger and goods terms. For the system to work efficiently this had to be standard national time and not solar time. So God's time, or natural time, the time dictated by the sun's progress through the heavens and the countryman's age-old rhythm of life, was superseded by Man's time. (p. 94)

In some areas, such as Bristol, where the station clock had an extra hand to indicate local time as well as the time used by the railway company, God's time held out for a while. Increasingly, however, it was the railway's clocks which came to define the time for the whole population, with particular effects on the life and thinking of the age. As Richards and MacKenzie suggest, 'the life of Victorian man [came] to be programmed, conditioned, and disciplined by the railway's demand for punctuality in its customers' (p. 96). In *A la recherche du temps perdu*, Marcel likewise records that

> since railways came into existence, the necessity of not missing trains has taught us to take account of minutes, whereas among the ancient Romans . . . the notion not only of minutes but even of fixed hours barely existed. (II, p. 853)

As Marcel reflects, such 'taking account of minutes' had con-sequences for the imagination as well as the practicalities of time. He talks of the

> 1.22 train, whose hour of departure I could never read without a palpitating heart on the railway company's bills or in advertisements for circular tours: it seemed to me to cut, at a precise point in every afternoon, a delectable groove, a mysterious mark. (I, pp. 418–19)

Changes in the sense of time effected by railways in the nine-teenth century continued in various ways to influence the imagina-tion of the twentieth. Writing as late as 1934 Joyce's friend Frank Budgen suggests that where the 'social time sense' is concerned,

> discoveries of the astronomer and the mathematician have less immediate effect . . . than the electrification of the suburban lines. Light and the heavenly bodies

are doing what they always did, but the wheels of mechanical civilisation are ever accelerating. (p. 132)

In Budgen's view, in other words, railway timetables and contemporary changes in forms of transport were more responsible than the thinkers Wyndham Lewis identifies, such as Einstein, for the new sense of time in 'Western Man' – a view Budgen summarizes epigrammatically in remarking 'spacetime came in with the taximeter, which is by petrol engine out of clockwork' (p. 132).

Further changes in 'the social time sense' in the late nineteenth and early twentieth centuries resulted from further systematization of national and international time-measurement. For much of the nineteenth century, Britain's standard national time was known colloquially (and distinguished from local time) as 'Railway Time'. The 1880s saw a change in name and an increase in the influence of this national standard: evidence of interest in the new arrangement appears, for example, in Arthur Wing Pinero's *The Magistrate*, first performed in 1885. Reassuring another character about the time, Pinero's hero remarks 'Hurray! Just half-past ten. Greenwich mean, eh Guv?' (I). The comment is not only cheerfully assured, but topical. A year earlier, in 1884, as Stephen Kern explains, the Prime Meridian Congress had

establish[ed] Greenwich as the zero meridian, determined the exact length of the day, divided the earth into twenty-four time zones one hour apart, and fixed a precise beginning of the universal day. (p. 12)

Though Greenwich Mean Time thus became the standard within Britain, it was not immediately accepted world-wide. In *A la recherche du temps perdu*, Marcel records the continuing use elsewhere on the continent of Central European Time and the Eastern calendar. New forms of electronic communication, however, quickly spread Greenwich's influence. *Ulysses* shows Leopold Bloom pondering in 1904 the Dublin time-signal that 'falls at Greenwich time. It's the clock is worked by an electric wire from Dunsink' (p. 211). Just as the spread of railways made national standard times essential, still faster communications, telegraphy particularly, strongly encouraged the introduction of an international, centrally controlled, world time. As Stephen Kern explains in *The Culture of Time and Space 1880–1918*, the International Conference on Time in Paris in 1912 firmly established a world-wide, homogenized time system, centred on Greenwich, and prepared for the first world time signal to be broadcast in July 1913.

As Kern's study suggests, it was principally in the period 1880–1918 – or, more exactly, 1884 to 1913 – that the world moved from the charms and idiosyncrasies of local time-zones to a system which ensured, globally, that time and space were rationally divided, ordered and defined. This period of radical change in the world's whole sense of time, the era of the clock's final triumph in ordering life, also coincides quite exactly with the formative years of most modernist authors. Joyce and Woolf were born in 1882, and Lawrence in 1885. For anyone growing up around the 1880s, new systems of time were a subject of occasional conversation, as Pinero's play suggests, and inevitably of general interest and influence. The passage about the Dublin time-signal shows Joyce recalling this interest when he came to write *Ulysses*: a character pondering 'time ratified by Greenwich' (p. 113) in *Mrs Dalloway* suggests the same continuing awareness in the work of Virginia Woolf.

New precisions and new global powers in dividing space and time inevitably interested the modernists, but did not usually seem as agreeable or 'delectable' as Marcel finds the cutting of his afternoon into grooves by the 1.22 train. Uneasiness about the new dispensations can be traced, obliquely at least, in Conrad's *The Secret Agent*, centred on Verloc's attempt to blow up Greenwich Observatory with the help of his half-idiot brother-in-law Stevie. Verloc's sinister paymaster, Vladimir, makes clear that it is the observatory's role in defining a new world order that is to be attacked. Verloc is not supposed to be 'having a go at astronomy', but is told instead to 'go for the first meridian' since 'the whole civilised world has heard of Greenwich. The very boot-blacks in the basement of Charing Cross Station know something of it' (pp. 37, 39) – naturally enough, perhaps, since their days of labour would have been spent listening to trains rumbling overhead according to timetables based on the new universal standard of Greenwich Mean Time.

Conrad records basing the novel on true events, described in his introductory note as the

old story of the attempt to blow up the Greenwich Observatory; a blood-stained inanity of so fatuous a kind that it was impossible to fathom its origin by any reasonable or even unreasonable process of thought. For perverse unreason has its own logical processes. But that outrage could not be laid hold of mentally in any sort of way. (p. 9)

In one way, of course, *The Secret Agent* is itself an attempt to lay hold mentally of this outrage, and it is appropriate that in his introduction Conrad allows for a certain logic even in unreasonable processes of thought. Much of his fiction is concerned with attempts by reasonable, orderly figures to 'lay hold of' more unreasonable, aberrant or anarchic characters, or to discover what possible meaning or logic may be offered by them. With his 'belief in a few simple notions' – of 'fidelity to a certain standard of conduct' – Marlow tries to fathom Jim's 'subtle unsoundness' in *Lord Jim* (pp. 39, 44, 72), and Kurtz's orgiastic abandon in *Heart of Darkness*. Conflicts of this kind between reason and disorder, anarchy or the irrational are also embodied figuratively in the repeated image in Conrad's writing – perhaps most clearly presented in *Typhoon* (1903) – of the orderly microcosm of shipboard life threatened by the vast turmoil of waters around it. Set almost exclusively in London and on dry land, *The Secret Agent* considers the same sort of conflict in political and social rather than elemental terms. Conrad shows it occurring between agents of law and order such as Chief Inspector Heat and his governmental superiors, and forces ranged against them which include strange anarchist elements such as the Professor, Ossipon and Verloc, and also – in some ways – the new, bewildering complexity and anonymity of twentieth-century city life itself. In a more abstract, figurative way, the conflict extends into contrasts between, on the one hand, the rational, world-ordering and time-defining meridians which circle the globe, officially centred on Greenwich, and, on the other, Stevie's habitual, half-mad, drawing of

> circles, circles; innumerable circles, concentric, eccentric; a coruscating whirl of circles that by their tangled multitude of repeated curves, uniformity of form, and confusion of intersecting lines suggested a rendering of cosmic chaos . . .

> the pastime of drawing those coruscations of innumerable circles suggesting chaos and eternity. (pp. 45–6, 192–3)

While Stevie's explosions early in the novel – though only of fireworks – parody anarchist tactics, so his cosmic chaos of circles seems to mock Greenwich's drawing of world-circling, universally ordering lines around the globe. It certainly opposes it symbolically, and it is horribly appropriate that Stevie is destroyed, literally blown into fragments, in the course of an actual assault on the Observatory – which itself, Conrad records, 'did not show as much as the faintest crack' (p. 9). It is equally appropriate that after planning an attack on the universal clock at Greenwich Verloc dies (in the passage quoted at the start of this chapter) to the sound of 'ticking growing fast and furious', as if attacked in turn by an enraged clock.

Conrad's irony throughout *The Secret Agent* is firmly directed against Verloc and his associates, leaving little affection for him either in life or death. Stevie, however, is a different matter. He is a centre of some sympathy throughout the novel – an innocent, idealistic, if barely coherent opponent of 'injustice and oppression' (p. 18), whether exercised against poor people, cab-horses, or in general. And it is not only chaos or anarchy which his scribblings oppose against the universal system of Greenwich. Stevie's circles represent chaos but also eternity; a relic in the novel of a time without beginning, end, or division; God's time beyond the systems of man's time or Mean Time. Stevie's actual fragmentation, exactly on the first meridian, embodies figuratively in *The Secret Agent* a sense of the menace to humanity of the new system of organization and power centred on Greenwich – to borrow Lawrence's term, 'a great and perfect system that subjected life to pure mathematical principles'. As his introductory note suggests, consciously or explicitly Conrad had little liking for forces attempting to destroy this system. Yet at other levels, unconscious or figural, Conrad remains fascinated, even sympathetically interested in such forces. He would hardly, otherwise, have spent a whole novel trying to 'lay hold of mentally' what he took to be beyond reason; or examined so frequently in his fiction as a whole conflicts of reason with its opposite; or made of Stevie, the character most given to unreasonable processes of thought, his most sympathetic figure in *The Secret Agent*. Like Mrs Verloc after the murder of her husband, and more secretly than overtly, Conrad's novel looks with 'inquiring mistrust' at the clock and the power it had recently come to exercise so widely over modern life.

Perhaps Conrad was particularly disposed to such mistrust, some time before most of the modernists, as a result of enforced, extended reliance on Greenwich-based co-ordinates and chronometry during his early life as a seaman. Captain Brierly's suicide in *Lord Jim*, immediately after charting so carefully position, date and time, may be emblematic of some of the tensions involved: rather like Gerald in *Women in Love*, Brierly is a figure who eventually finds that the exacting rationalizations of modern life cannot be humanly sustained. Conrad's interest in Greenwich can at any rate be related to the 'inquiring mistrust' with which some of his fiction looks at the spread of empire at the end of the nineteenth century. The critic Edward Said describes imperialism as 'an act of geographical violence through which virtually every space in the world is explored, charted, and finally brought under control'.[16] Brought about largely by commercial and political interests at the time, the Prime Meridian Congress constituted just such an act of 'geographical violence', the meridians centred on Greenwich throwing across the world a grid insidiously confirming its economic and political domination from London – described in *The Secret Agent* as 'the very centre of the Empire on which the sun never sets' (p. 174). Significantly, the novel in which Conrad most sharply criticizes imperialism, *Heart of Darkness*, opens near London just at the moment the sun is setting over the Thames.

Other modernist writers shared Conrad's scepticism about empire: more generally, as suggested earlier, they were often sceptical of ordinary reason and what could be, in Conrad's terms, 'laid hold of mentally', or at any rate by means of the intellect. Such scepticism made them unlikely to welcome Greenwich's new systems and rationalizations, however sensible these seemed to anyone from railway travellers to explorers or scientists. Quoted at the end of Chapter 2, Lawrence's short story 'The Fox' shows his hero finding 'a network of English hedges netting the view', leaving England 'little and tight'. After the Prime Meridian Congress, a network of imaginary lines also spread far beyond England, invisibly netting and tightening control of the whole world – further encouragement to the movement undertaken by modernism, discussed in Chapter 2, from a restrictive external reality to the freer, private spaces of the mind.

Modernism also had to seek a freer temporality. The new systems left time as fragmented as space, the 'age old rhythms of life and the sun's progress through the sky' dissected as firmly as Marcel's afternoon is bisected by the 1.22 train, and much more universally and inescapably. Such divisions and dissections, along with the 'rules, laws, and formulae' which Taylor's scientific management erected around them, confronted the early twentieth

century with a sense that 'Time is everything' which was historically quite new, as Fredric Jameson suggests. More than ever
before, time could be exactly and officially measured, treated as a
quantity or commodity which could be bought and sold for wages,
and used to regulate with minute precision the movements of
workers or machines. No wonder the kind of chronometer used to
reward Captain Brierly in *Lord Jim*, or Captain Mitchell in
*Nostromo* – or a cheaper equivalent – had become by the end of
the nineteenth century the standard retiral present for faithful
employees. Such instruments celebrated the ingenious mechanical
precision achieved by the machine age and also counted the commodity most recently and successfully brought under its control.
They were even emblematic of the likely nature of the employees
so rewarded – reified and drained of vitality, reduced, in Gudrun's
assessment to 'so many little wheels', by prolonged servitude to the
modern industrial and financial world. A further summary image
of such servitude occurs not in fiction but in film – in the scene in
*Modern Times* (1936) which shows Charlie Chaplin so trapped by
intricate cogs and wheels of industrial machinery it is as if he were
being mangled by the workings of a monstrous clock.

No wonder D.H. Lawrence found that by the 1920s 'the mere
suggestion' of Relativity was one which his contemporaries had all
been waiting for. An age so subject to new rules, laws, formulae
and precisions in its everyday life was naturally ready to 'catch fire'
at something which offered to dissolve the whole basis on which
such rules were made, making time once again relative, local, idiosyncratic, rather than rigidly exact. Along with much of the
philosophy of the time, modernist writing shares in this sort of
reaction against new systematizations of life – in Mean Time,
clocking in for factory work, and synchronized death in the
trenches. Chapter 2 suggested that modernism's location of narrative within consciousness attempted to sustain a full sense of individuality within a domain beyond the grasp of 'the modern
industrial and financial world'. Modernism's disposition against
time on the clock, and its structuring of narrative to reject it in
favour of time in the mind, can be similarly construed – in Fredric
Jameson's terms, as a further 'utopian compensation' for 'the logic
and dynamics of late capitalism'. When confronted by 'true perception of . . . peril', Conrad's characters drop the clock 'like a hot
potato'. Recognizing consciously or unconsciously the growing

peril of 'great and perfect systems' – of 'rules, laws, and formulae' in a complex late industrial age – modernist writing likewise drops the clock, or, like Lawrence in *The Plumed Serpent*, seeks a domain in which

> the clock didn't go. Time . . . fell off, the days walked naked and timeless, in the old, uncounted manner of the past. The strange, old, uncounted, unregistered, unreckoning days . . . the striking of the hours had ceased. (p. 288)

Moving away from serial chronology, modernism recreates in a past recovered in memory, in streams of consciousness, or in a time in the mind otherwise established in the ways discussed, some of the organic continuity – the 'uncounted, unregistered, unreckoned days' – which had been divided and dissected out of existence in contemporary public life. The 'temporal autonomy' Joyce creates at the end of *Ulysses*, or Proust throughout *A la recherche du temps perdu*, shows modernism freeing narrative as far as possible from time on the clock in an era – and as a *result* of an era – which had used the clock to make time less than ever free. Similarities in the work of Bergson, Joyce, Woolf and the other figures discussed above did not necessarily arise, as Wyndham Lewis claimed, from influence or mutual relations of cause and effect. They can be seen as the consequence of an age whose new, highly specific, sense of temporality inevitably created reactions of a comparable nature in a variety of areas of contemporary art and life.

## FRAGMENT OR FLOW

Modernist fiction's 'temporal autonomy' and reshaping of structures and styles may free narrative as far as possible from time on the clock, but such freedom could neither be absolute nor altogether continuously sustained. The old clock ticked on within or beneath modernism's new structures. This leaves in modernist literature a conflicting, double awareness; of two separate, even antithetical views of time and life – a double awareness shared by other phases of contemporary culture, and in some ways by the age as a whole. Stephen Kern sums up dual allegiances in the period he examines when he remarks that 'the introduction of World Standard Time had an enormous impact on communication, industry, war, and the everyday life of the masses' – but adds that a further feature of the age was

> the assault on a universal, unchanging, and irreversible public time . . . the metaphysical foundation of a broad cultural challenge to traditional notions about the nature of the world and man's place in it. (pp. 313–14)

Developments in contemporary science provide good examples of the contradictory movements Kern indicates. Einstein's ideas, denying the existence of an absolute time – 'the time of physicists' – were finally formulated in his General Theory of Relativity in 1916. The kind of thinking on which they were based, however, originated some time before, at least as early as Ernst Mach's suggestion that the idea of absolute, universal time and space, outlined by Isaac Newton in the late seventeenth century, was no more than an 'idle metaphysical conception'.[17] Mach's claim was made in *The Science of Mechanics*, published in 1883. The period in which, as the last section discussed, international congresses were determining Prime Meridians and firmer than ever ways of measuring universal time – from 1884 to 1913 – therefore coincides almost exactly with the period – 1883 to 1916 – during which science and mathematics dissolved time more and more towards indefiniteness or even non-existence. *The Times* for 7 November 1919 offers a perfect indication of the simultaneous, antithetical imperatives which had developed in thinking about time by the end of the First World War. A column on the right of page 12 is headlined 'Revolution in Science. New Theory of the Universe. Newtonian Ideas Overthrown'. It outlines the challenge to conventional ideas of space and time developed in Einstein's theories, whose confirmation had been announced at a meeting of the Royal Society the previous evening. Meanwhile the extreme left-hand column of page 12 explains in detail how the entire country is to be simultaneously immobilized – trains, factories, traffic, even pedestrians, arrested in mid-stride – at precisely 11 a.m., Greenwich Mean Time, on the 11th of November, at the request of the King, to mark the first anniversary of the armistice at the end of the war. Just as time measured by the clock was finally being denied any absolute significance by scientists, it was being employed more uniformly and absolutely than ever to rule ordinary life.

Other factors in contemporary life confirmed such contradictions in thinking about time. New technologies of communication, for example, required increasing systematization of time in public life, but also created for it an increasing fluidity and amorphousness within private experience. Telephones, telegraphy and rapid transport by road, rail, or eventually air, all required firm, standardized time-systems for their effective operation. By performing almost immediately tasks or journeys previously hugely prolonged they also, however, seemed to deny fairly completely the power of time in life. In *A la recherche du temps perdu*, Marcel records with admiration the 'instantaneous speed' (III, p. 96) of the telephone. He also suggests that 'distances are only the relation of space to time and vary with it' (II, p. 1029), adding that they had been 'habitually shortened by speed . . . today' (III, p. 413). At many other points, *A la recherche du temps perdu* further praises the ability of new forms of transport, cars in particular, to undermine and reshape the old, firm assumptions about distance, time and space.[18] As Chapter 1 discussed, these were changes which seemed particularly significant to the Futurist F.T. Marinetti – the basis for his conclusion in 'The Founding and Manifesto of Futurism' (1909) that 'Time and Space died yesterday . . . because we have created eternal, omnipresent speed'.

The continuing power of time, as well as of attempts to escape it, was also more evident in contemporary philosophy than Wyndham Lewis suggests in *Time and Western Man*. Distress about the apparent popularity of ideas of time's flexibility, fluidity or non-existence led Lewis to exaggerate the uniformity of support for them in contemporary philosophy. Views quite contrary to Bergson's were hardly unheard of at the time. Although Nietzsche often seems close to Bergson, there are times when he is very far from seeing mental processes as stream-like – for example, when suggesting that 'every successive phenomenon in consciousness is completely atomistic'. Even among philosophers more consistently close to Bergson, ideas of the fluidity of time and the incompetence of the clock figure as a matter of debate rather than certainty. One symptom of this is the regularity with which contemporary philosophy re-examines the problems raised by Zeno of Elea. Like some of Marcel's musings in *A la recherche du temps perdu*, Zeno's paradoxes question relations of distance, time and space, and the divisibleness or continuity of each medium. The Eleatic paradoxes suggest, for example, that a flying arrow cannot really be supposed to traverse space at all, since at any specific moment it must be imagined static, frozen in mid-flight at a single point. Such paradoxes are examined at one stage or another in the work of Nietzsche, Bergson, A.N. Whitehead, Bertrand Russell and Samuel Alexander as well as Wyndham Lewis himself. Naturally, each of them uses Zeno to advance his own point of view: Nietzsche, for example, to emphasize further the unbridgeable gap between life and knowledge, reality and mind; Bergson to stress the obvious fallacies created by conceiving time as divisible or made up of individual parts.

Concepts of reality similarly divided between the frozen and the fluid, fragmentation and continuity, also preoccupied mathematics and physics in the last decades of the nineteenth century and the early part of the twentieth. Mathematical calculus, for example, depends on Zeno-like techniques of imagining a moving body immobilized, for purposes of computation, by subdividing the space and time through which it travels. The theoretical grounding of calculus developed rapidly in the early years of the twentieth century, as did its use. Silvanus R. Thomson's guide, *Calculus Made Easy*, for example, went through fourteen printings between 1900 and 1922 – though possibly only because ballistics and the study of the flight-path of projectiles, which calculus facilitates, were made a priority by the First World War.

In physics, by 1887 much experimental evidence had accumulated to support James Clerk Maxwell's view of radiation as continuous and wave-like in form. From then on, however, anomalies in experiment and observation led to new theories suggesting that radiation and energy exist primarily in quanta – as particles; as individual, separate units. The award of the Nobel Prize to Max Planck in 1918 confirmed the general acceptance of this new idea by that date. Writing two years later, Einstein's acquaintance Alexander Moszkowski suggested the wider relevance of the wave-particle debate within the general outlook of the age:

> The absolute continuity of events was one of the generally accepted canons of thought . . . but deep down in the consciousness of man there has always been an opposition to it, and when the French philosopher Henri Bergson set out to break up this line of continuity by metaphysical means in ascribing to human knowledge an intermittent, cinematographic character he . . . made no new 'discovery', he felt his way intuitively into a new field of knowledge and recognised the time was ripe for the real discovery. This was actually presented to us in our day by the eminent

physicist Max Planck, the winner of the Nobel Prize for Physics in 1919, in the form of his 'Quantum Theory' . . . a discontinuous, intermittent sequence, an atomistic structure, was proved by means of the weapons of exact science, to be true of energies which, according to current belief, were expected to be radiated regularly and connectedly. This was probably not a case of the accidental coincidence of a new philosophical view with the results of reasoning from physical grounds, but a demand of time, exacting that the claims of a new principle of thought be recognised. (pp. 91–2)[19]

Moszkowski usefully confirms how widely his age was engaged with conflicts between continuity and intermittency, though direct correlations between Bergson and Planck are less clear than he implies. Moszkowski partly misreads Bergson, who discussed but certainly did not 'break up the line of continuity', or 'the absolute continuity of events', by metaphysical or any other means. On the contrary, he thoroughly supported the idea of continuity, but complained that the nature of knowledge left little opportunity for its proper appreciation. Typically of his philosophy, Bergson's discussion of knowledge indicates that the intellect impedes true contact with experience rather than assisting it. In *Creative Evolution* (*L'Evolution Créatrice*, 1907), he warns that

instead of attaching ourselves to the inner becoming of things . . . we take snapshots, as it were of the passing reality . . . perception, intellection, language . . . set going a kind of cinematograph inside us . . . the *mechanism of our ordinary knowledge is of a cinematographic kind.* (pp. 322–3)

Knowledge, for Bergson, distorts the continuous evolution of life, freezing it into static, conveniently graspable units, single images plucked from the stream of time.

Bergson explains at some length in *Creative Evolution* how the cinematograph creates an impression of continuous movement out of what is actually a series of static images. This explanation was probably necessary not only for philosophic purposes, but on account of the novelty and likely unfamiliarity of the apparatus he uses for his metaphor. The cinematograph had only quite recently reached a fully effective stage in a development reaching back at least as far as the 1870s, when Eadweard Muybridge had recorded multiple images of a galloping horse, triggering each of a series of cameras in its passing. In the 1880s, E.J. Marey's 'chronophotography' used rapidly successive exposures to create a composite image expressive of movement. By the later nineteenth century, such techniques were extended into the machinery of popular entertainment – 'bioscopes', for example, or the 'Mutoscope pictures . . . for men only. Peeping Tom . . . Do they snapshot those girls or is it all a fake?' which Bloom remembers in *Ulysses* (p. 480). These used a series of photographs falling rapidly on top of each other to create the impression of motion out of still pictures. But it was only with the work of the Lumière brothers in 1896 that the cinematograph evolved into the form Bergson refers to – hardly long enough before his lectures on 'the mechanics of our ordinary knowledge', at the Collège de France in 1902, for him to be sure his audience would be quite familiar with the new invention.

The rapid development of cinema in the early twentieth century can be seen as significant for modernism in a number of ways. Cinema probably contributed more than other media to the popular, mass culture from which modernism may have sought to differentiate itself (see Chapter 4), though cinematic techniques such as montage – juxtaposition of disconnected images or narrative strands – may nevertheless have influenced the structure of some modernist novels. Joyce, in particular, gained an early familiarity with films and their techniques from his involvement in opening the first cinema in Dublin in 1909. Concentration within inner consciousness in his and other modernists' work may reflect a recognition that film could be more effective than written narrative in recording external reality, and that the novel should seek some of its material elsewhere, in areas the camera could not so easily reach. At any rate, whatever the later influence of film on modernist fiction, the invention of the cinematograph – almost simultaneously in France and the United States – can be seen as significant in itself for the modernist age; as a further manifestation of 'the demands of the time'. An age torn between envisaging reality as fragmentary and as continuous naturally welcomed, perhaps even inspired, a technology able to create the impression of continuous movement out of what were actually separate, individual images. The cinematograph and the mechanics of its operation certainly quickly caught the imagination of artists and writers as well as philosophers, though their interest was sometimes tempered with suspicion. The Italian Futurists were generally excited by the new technologies, but one of their number, Anton Bragaglia, complained rather like Bergson that cinematography . . . merely reconstructs fragments of reality, already coldly broken up, in the same way as the hand of a chronometer deals with time even though this flows in a continuous and constant stream.

Bragaglia went on to work out a new technique of his own, 'Photo-dynamism' – not a series of static images but a sort of time-exposure creating a blurred picture suggestive of movement. Bragaglia explains that

chronophotography could be compared with a clock on the face of which only the quarter-hours are marked, cinematography to one on which the minutes too are indicated, and Photodynamism to a third on which are marked not only the seconds, but also the *intermovemental* fractions existing in the passages between seconds.

Other Futurists were more content to exploit the tactics of chrono-photography or cinematography. In paintings such as 'Dynamism of a Dog on a Leash' (1912) or 'Little Girl Running on a Balcony' (1912), for example, Giacomo Balla follows Marey's work, using multiple, superimposed images to suggest the dynamics of a moving object.[20]

Among contemporary novelists, Proust shows himself as interested as Bergson in the mechanics and metaphoric potential of cinematography and of earlier stages in its development. Discussing in the opening section of *A la recherche du temps perdu* the overall effect of 'shifting gusts of memory', Marcel suggests that he

did not distinguish the various suppositions of which it was composed any more than, when we watch a horse running, we isolate the successive positions of its body as they appear upon a bioscope. (I, p. 7)

Later, Proust further investigates a fragmentary quality underlying the apparent continuity of life and experience. Though Marcel suggests that 'Nothing is further from what we have really perceived than the vision that the cinematograph presents' (III, p. 917), after the death of his lover Albertine he recalls her in cinematographic, almost chronophotographic terms:

In order to enter into us, another person must first have assumed the form, have adapted himself to the framework of time; appearing to us only in a succession of momentary flashes, he has never been able to reveal to us more than one aspect of himself at a time, to present us with more than a single photograph of himself. A great weakness no doubt for a person, to consist merely of a collection of moments

... he is a product of memory ... this moment which it has recorded endures still, lives still, and with it the person whose form is outlined in it. And moreover, this disintegration does not only make the dead one live, it multiplies him or her. In order to be consoled I would have to forget, not one, but innumerable Albertines ...

It was not Albertine alone who was a succession of moments, it was also myself ... I was not one man only, but as it were the march-past of a composite army. (III, pp. 487, 499)

Marcel outlines a similar view of the emotions in general:

What we suppose to be our love or our jealousy is never a single, continuous and indivisible passion. It is composed of an infinity of successive loves, of different jealousies, each of which is ephemeral, although by their uninterrupted multiplicity they give us the impression of continuity, the illusion of unity. (I, p. 404)

The mechanics of cinematography, of multiple stases giving the impression of continuity, also provide a summary metaphor for some of Wyndham Lewis's conclusions. As an image of contemporary thinking about time, he discusses in *Time and Western Man* the idea of a

domestic cinematograph ... The mechanical photographic reality ... somewhat that sense of things laid out side by side, of the unreality of time, and yet of its paramount importance. (p. 266)

Lewis was impressed by the Italian Futurists at an early stage of his career, and obviously, as *Time and Western Man* lengthily explains, generally disposed against any idea of time as fluidly continuous. His own early fiction accordingly creates an innovative prose style which does lay things out side by side, creating a 'succession of moments', a series of static images diminishing the sense of time's flowing. This is immediately apparent in the striking opening paragraphs of Lewis's first published novel, *Tarr* (1918):

Paris hints of sacrifice.=But here we deal with that large dusty facet known to indulgent and congruous kind ...
Inconceivably generous and naive faces haunt the Knackfus Quarter.=We are not however in a Selim or Vitagraph camp (though 'guns' tap rhythmically the buttocks).=Art is being studied.=Art is the smell of oil paint, Henri Murger's 'Vie de Bohème', corduroy trousers, the operatic Italian model. But the poetry, above all, of linseed oil and turpentine.

The Knackfus Quarter is given up to Art.= Letters and other things are round the corner.=Its rent is half paid by America.[21]

Lewis's invention of the curious, emphatic punctuation mark '.=' sharply separates his sentences, framing them as discrete, autonomous units. Such tactics do in a way make *Tarr* into a 'domestic cinematograph' of the kind described in *Time and Western Man*. Lewis probably began writing *Tarr* as early as 1909 and – like Bergson in 1902 – might have had the mechanics of the recently-invented cinematograph in mind. References in these cryptic opening paragraphs to Selim and Vitagraph help suggest this – Selig and Vitagraph were early, pioneering cinema production companies. At any rate, consistently with antipathies to the 'time-school' expressed in *Time and Western Man*, and to Joyce as a particular exemplar of it, Lewis's early writing moves as far as possible from any idea of time as stream-like. So strangely and heavily punctuated, the prose of *Tarr* offers an interestingly complete contrast to the unpunctuated stream of Molly's consciousness at the end of *Ulysses*.

Contrasts and antipathies of this kind continue to figure in Lewis's later career – often as part of a self-proclaimed persona as 'The Enemy' which he sustains throughout the huge volumes published in the 1920s and early 1930s, *The Art of Being Ruled* (1926), *Paleface* (1929) and *Men Without Art* (1934), as well *Time and Western Man*. Criticism of contemporary culture in these volumes – of the modernist age as a whole – also extends into much of his fiction at this time. *The Childermass* (1928) contains satiric representations of Joyce, Bergson and Gertrude Stein, and its style expands into huge, parodic excess some of the linguistic experiment and temporal fluidity of modernist writing. The satire of *The Apes of God* (1930) focuses more generally on contemporary art and artists – figures whose behaviour, speech and appearance Lewis mocks and caricatures by means of an 'external method', as he calls it, largely exclusive of attention to inner consciousness. Such tactics are consistent with the conclusion his hero reaches in *Tarr* – that

Anything living, quick and changing, is bad art, always . . . No restless, quick, flame-like ego is imagined for the *inside* of it. It has no inside. This is another condition of art; *to have no inside*. (p. 295)

These priorities also shape *Tarr* itself, resistant to temporal fluidity or the 'quick and changing' in its heavily punctuated prose, and generally attentive to characters' appearance and behaviour rather than their inner thoughts. Such writing obviously opposes many of the new tactics and emphases of modernist fiction. As he might have wished in his role as the 'Enemy' of his age, Lewis provides in practice as well as theory, in creative as well as critical writing, a kind of inverted or reversed, mirror image of modernist innovation, highlighting in antitheses many of the controlling assumptions and preferences of his age. *Tarr* and the closing chapter of *Ulysses*, in particular, offer a paradigmatic set of contrasts between inner and external methods of representing character, as well as between conflicting conclusions about the divisibility or stream-like continuity of time.

Not all of *Ulysses*, of course, is written in the style of Molly's concluding soliloquy. Much as this section shows time as a stream – or even, in the end, time denied or transcended – the clock and the divisions of its hours by no means disappear from the novel as a whole. In the early pages of *Ulysses*,

> the bells of George's church . . . tolled the hour: loud dark iron.
> *Heigho! Heigho!*
> *Heigho! Heigho!*
> *Heigho! Heigho!*

and

> the sound of the peal of the hour of the night by the chime of the bells in the church of Saint George

recurs towards the end (pp. 85, 826). Between, across the 'flowing . . . stream of life' (p. 193), there often falls the iron voice of the clock. Even Molly keeps consulting the 'unearthly hour' (p. 930) as she lies awake at the end. In this way, *Ulysses* is not just a stream of consciousness, but a 'dance of the hours . . . morning hours, noon, then evening coming on, then night hours' (p. 87). Other aspects of the novel add further to a sense of discontinuity as much as of fluidity. Joyce's plans for *Ulysses* indicate a separate hour of the day for each chapter, and also – among many other distinguishing aspects – often specify a different style. Such stylistic differences ensure that however stream-like individual sections of *Ulysses* seem, the novel, overall, reads very discontinuously. Discussing Joyce's work, the critic Hugh Kenner rightly emphasizes 'the pains he takes to impede the notion of linear narrative: *Ulysses* is as discontinuous a work as its author can manage'.[22] Passing between Chapters 13, 'Nausicaa', and 14, 'Oxen of the Sun', for example, is almost like passing between novels by different writers, and some of the other styles used in individual chapters are equally sharply contrasted. Even the transcription of consciousness within them is not always as stream-like as in the final chapter. Much of Bloom's inner life takes the form of telegrammatic, fragmentary sentences – 'Cup of tea soon. Good. Mouth dry.' (p. 65) – presenting thought as more atomistic than fluid. Such sections and the radical shifts in style (further discussed in Chapter 4), create in *Ulysses* as much a sense of fractured multi-facetedness as of seamless, homogeneous flow.

Other modernist fiction exhibits a similar duality of allegiance. Dorothy Richardson's narrative in *Pilgrimage* (1915–67), however fluently it moves into the unfolding thoughts of Miriam Henderson, also remains at times sharply fractured. Large gaps in the text's layout on the page are used to indicate transitions of time or locale, and are all the more marked since conventional exposition – explaining changes of time or place between different scenes, or offering brief summaries of intervening events – is generally missing from *Pilgrimage*. Chapter divisions occur even more arbitrarily in Proust, who passes over natural breaks in his story in favour of extending chapters at great length, then ending them more or less in the middle of episodes.

Division and continuity likewise compete in Virginia Woolf's construction of *The Waves* (1931), which alternates between characters' freely associative thoughts or memories and sections which intrude upon them to reflect the passage of time throughout a single day in the natural world. Such distinctions between fluidity and division, atom and flux, preoccupy Woolf throughout her writing. She asks in her diary

is life very solid or shifting? I am haunted by the two contradictions. This has gone on for ever; will last for ever; goes down to the bottom of the world – this moment I stand on. Also it is transitory, flying, diaphanous. I shall pass like a cloud on the waves. Perhaps it may be that though we change, one flying after another, so quick, so quick, yet we are somehow successive and continuous we human beings. (*A Writer's Diary*, p. 140)

Woolf's 'Modern Fiction' essay likewise considers relations between the successive and the continuous – between 'myriad impressions . . . an incessant shower of innumerable atoms' and the 'luminous halo' into which they seem to form themselves. Mrs Ramsay ponders in *To the Lighthouse* the 'little separate incidents which one lived one by one' and which – almost in a wave-particle duality of her own – she then thinks of as 'curled and whole like a wave' (p. 55). *To the Lighthouse* further contrasts the intuitive wholeness of Mrs Ramsay's mind with the 'little separate incidents' of her husband's. Mr Ramsay creates a whole alphabet of separate philosophical concepts, running from A to Z, or sometimes A to Q – another device of 'the masculine intelligence, which ran up and down, crossed this way and that, like iron girders spanning the swaying fabric' (p. 122). Across the 'swaying fabric' of the novel itself, the 'eternal passing and flowing' (p. 183) of its characters' thoughts and memories, there falls both the beam of the lighthouse, with its clock-like rhythm of recurrence, and the shadow of time and history, intruding in the middle section of the novel, 'Time Passes', to shatter the hopes and trouble the memories outlined in the first and third parts.

Time's passage intrudes equally divisively and persistently into *Mrs Dalloway*, originally named *The Hours*. The 'irrevocable . . . leaden circles' (p. 6) of Big Ben's chimes fall across the novel's fabric of thoughts as firmly as the 'loud dark iron' of the clock in *Ulysses*. *Mrs Dalloway* frequently shows how much harder than at present (even in an age of squeaky digital watches) time's passage must have been to ignore in the early years of the twentieth century, when so many clocks, public or private, routinely chimed. 'Flooding' characters' minds, sometimes between single lines of conversation, the deafening intrusion of Big Ben's chime is backed up by an extraordinary number of other vociferous clocks in *Mrs Dalloway* – forcing characters to consider, for example, how

Shredding and slicing, dividing and subdividing, the clocks of Harley Street nibbled at the June day, counselled submission, upheld authority, and pointed out in chorus the supreme advantages of a sense of proportion, until the mound of time was so far diminished that a commercial clock, suspended above a shop in Oxford Street, announced genially and fraternally, as if it were a pleasure to Messrs Rigby and Lowndes to give the information gratis, that it was half-past one.

Looking up, it appeared that each letter of their names stood for one of the hours; subconsciously one was grateful to Rigby and Lowndes for giving one

time ratified by Greenwich; and this gratitude . . . naturally took the form later
of buying off Rigby and Lowndes socks or shoes. (pp. 113–14)

Woolf's view of 'the clocks of Harley Street' is in several ways
exemplary – first of all, of the new sense, in the early twentieth
century, of a 'time ratified by Greenwich' and also closely connected
with commerce – of time commodified and turned into saleable
socks and shoes, in fact. The passage is also typical of Bergson's – or
other – views of time in the mind as something whole or continuous;
time as a 'mound', but one which is shredded and divided up by time
on the clock. Such distinctions underlie much of Woolf's view of
time in the rest of her writing. They also appear, for example, in the
passage from *Orlando* quoted at the start of this chapter, or in
Bernard's conclusion in *The Waves* that, in a kind of separate world,
there is an 'unlimited time of the mind, which stretches in a flash
from Shakespeare to ourselves'. He adds, however, that when 'suddenly one hears a clock tick. We who had been immersed in this
world became aware of another. It is painful' (p. 235).

Such 'pain', such tension between 'worlds' separated by different concepts of time, appears not only in Woolf's writing, and in
modernist fiction generally, but also in modernist poetry. Awareness of distinct worlds, or ways of seeing the world, are highlighted
and contrasted with particular clarity in T.S. Eliot's 'Rhapsody on
a Windy Night'. In passing a succession of bright streetlamps, the
speaker establishes a regular, drum-like rhythm, which includes
precise recording of the hour of the night, and the voice of the
lamp itself, often directing attention to the more reified, mechanical aspects of humanity depicted in the poem. Between the lamps,
darker 'reaches of the street' are infused with the subtler illumination of the moon, helping to 'dissolve . . . clear relations . . . divisions and precisions', partly by stirring the memory and the
subconscious into throwing up throngs of imaginative images.
Chapter 2 suggested 'Rhapsody on a Windy Night' exemplifies
modernist anxieties about reification: the poem's different areas,
different illuminations and different priorities are also paradigmatic of other – related – tensions and antitheses central to art and
literature in the early twentieth century. On the one hand, there is
precise, orderly, proportioned, intellectual division and categoriza-
tion of life; life viewed as a 'series of gig-lamps' – or street lamps –
'symmetrically arranged'. On the other hand, there is a preference

for darker, less measured entry into memory, intuition, movement away from exactness – measured by the clock or otherwise – and even away from the waking consciousness towards deeper, more inward reaches of the mind.

Though Wyndham Lewis and other commentators, at the time and since, rightly see modernism principally favouring the latter set of priorities, the other side could not be and never was ignored. 'Rhapsody on a Windy Night' wholly favours neither set of the possibilities it outlines, but simply presents and contrasts them. Even writers apparently following Bergson in favouring 'time in the mind' could not ignore 'time on the clock', and indeed became – like Woolf in *Mrs Dalloway* – all the more painfully aware of it because of their own antithetical disposition. However much 'Zeit's sumonserving' (p. 78), as Joyce calls it in *Finnegans Wake*, might have been disliked, especially now that it was equipped with all the authority of Mean Time and World Standard Time, it remained stubbornly a part of life. Even while complaining in *Women in Love* about 'the terrible bondage of this tick-tack of time . . . oh God . . . too awful to contemplate', Gudrun acknowledges that 'there was no escape from it, no escape' (p. 522). Though Quentin Compson twists off the hands of his watch in *The Sound and the Fury*, 'the watch ticked on . . . the blank dial with little wheels clicking and clicking behind it' (p. 76).

Critics have long pointed to the stream of consciousness, yet also to representations of a fragmentary, disjointed quality in modern life, as characteristic of modernism's innovative view of the world. Though this seems contradictory, the contradiction is not in the criticism but in the phenomenon itself. Michael Levenson talks of 'the modernist urge towards dualistic opposition and radical polarities' (1984, p. ix): one of the best examples of this is in modernism's contrasts or reconciliations between fragment and flow, between atom and wave, between the divisions of the clock and the continuity of consciousness. Such antitheses and tensions not only run through and structure modernist fiction, but, with unusual intensity, the whole age in which it was written, evident in it from Bergson to Bloom, as Wyndham Lewis might have said, and from quantum theory to cinematograph. Another factor contributed to them, not so much in daily life and the measurement of its passage, but in the wider sense of the evolution of history itself. That factor was the age's greatest crisis, the First World War.

CRACKS AND CHASMS: TIME AND THE WESTERN FRONT

The effects of the war on contemporary life – and writing – were immense and inescapable. J.B. Priestley, himself a combatant in the trenches, remarks that

> No intelligent and sensitive European – and writers can hardly succeed without intelligence and sensitivity – could escape the terrible impact of these four years . . . the war was there, all around them. (p. 322)

Destruction, loss and sorrow seemed to enter the world on a scale unknown before, the war creating 'horrors that make the old tragedies seem no more than nursery shows' as Rebecca West puts it in *The Return of the Soldier* (p. 63). Sigmund Freud worked out his principle of *thanatos*, the death wish, during the war and believed that his contemporaries might never again see a joyous world. He even thought it possible that the human race might be replaced by a more tractable species – an idea that 'man is a mistake, he must go' which D.H. Lawrence also ponders in *Women in Love* (p. 142), written at the time of the war. Given Freud's views, it is ironic that his reputation was greatly enhanced by the war, after the application of some of his principles to treatment of its shell-shocked victims.

One such victim, Septimus Warren Smith functions in *Mrs Dalloway* partly as a symbol of a whole society, non-combatants included, still in a state of some shock even years after the war was over. The novel remarks of Septimus's state

> such things happen to everyone. Everyone has friends who were killed in the War . . .

> this late age of world's experience had bred in them all, all men and women, a well of tears. (pp. 74, 12)

Though never mentioned directly, this late experience is in a way even more strongly marked in Woolf's *Jacob's Room* (1922), from the moment the protagonist's name, Jacob Flanders, begins to resound in the novel its anticipatory echo of the geography of the trenches. Named as a figure of doom, Jacob is destined to leave behind the empty room towards which all the desires and memories in the novel are fruitlessly directed. The tormenting emotional vacuum left among those who loved him typifies an experience of the 1920s generally – of hollow men and women surviving in a sad decade. D.H. Lawrence also points out how deep and long the war's emotional scars remained in the years that followed it. In *Lady Chatterley's Lover* (1928) he talks of

> the bruise of the war . . . creating the great ache of unrest, and stupor of discontent. The bruise was deep, deep, deep . . . the bruise of the false inhuman war. It would take many years for the living blood of the generations to dissolve the vast black clot of bruised blood, deep inside their souls and bodies. (p. 52)

Fiction always offers opportunities to recreate or reinhabit the past imaginatively, and is often strongly shaped by nostalgia. The war, however, made memory and nostalgia more than usually important for the modernists. The ache of unrest in the years after 1914 offered a particular incentive to let down ropes of memory into more orderly earlier times, untroubled by the explosions of contemporary history. Writers in the 1920s had reason to look at the war with what Ford Madox Ford might have described as a wish to 'cut it out and join time up' – to find ways of reconnecting the present with a pre-war Edwardian period offering the coherence and security contemporary life lacked. Chapter 2 suggested the uncongenial public world of the 1920s encouraged withdrawal into the private domain of the individual mind: withdrawal into memory existed concurrently with this urge. When considered in retrospect during the 1920s, or indeed many later phases of the twentieth century, the pre-war years seemed, or could be made to seem, an especially splendid age – even after 1910, when Virginia Woolf thought 'human character changed'. Richard Aldington talks in *Death of a Hero* of 'the feeling of tranquil security which existed, the almost smug optimism of our lives' (p. 199) at this time. In his open *Letter to Mrs. Virginia Woolf* (1932) Peter Quennell invites his readers to remember

> the placid pre-war universe – how tranquil and how olympian it must have been! Was the pound really worth twenty shillings, and were there parties every night and hansom cabs? . . . then the War to End Wars and so good-bye. (p. 17)

Confronted by an imminent second war in *Coming up for Air* (1939), George Orwell looks back all the more fondly on the years before the first:

'before the war'? I *am* sentimental about it . . . It's quite true that if you look back on any special period of time you tend to remember the pleasant bits . . . But it's also true that people then had something that we haven't got now.

What? . . . It isn't that life was softer then than now. Actually it was harsher. People on the whole worked harder, lived less comfortably, and died more painfully. The farm hands worked frightful hours for fourteen shillings a week and ended up as worn-out cripples with a five-shilling old age pension . . . And yet what was it that people had in those days? A feeling of security, even when they weren't secure. More exactly, it was a feeling of continuity . . . things would go on as they'd known them . . . a settled period, a period when civilization seems to stand on its four legs like an elephant . . . their way of life would continue . . . they thought it was eternity. (pp. 106–9)

Sentimentally or otherwise, modernism looks back to recover in fiction what had vanished in fact. Rebecca West's *The Return of the Soldier* offers a kind of paradigm of this tendency, its hero's response to shell-shock in 1916 taking the form of complete mental reversion to a happier life fifteen years earlier, long before the war began. Figuratively, many modernist novels make much the same move. Written between 1914 and 1922, *Ulysses* meticulously recreates the life and geography of Dublin in 1904, partly destroyed in the Easter Rising of 1916. In the first section of *To the Lighthouse*, Woolf recreates one of the long summer afternoons of the 'placid pre-war universe', with the Ramsay family secure in their assumption that 'things would go on as they'd known them'. Ford Madox Ford looks back ironically at the start of *Parade's End* to the belief that 'a war is impossible' (p. 20), and regretfully to the 'perfectly appointed . . . luxuriant, regulated . . . admirable' pre-war world (p. 3). Its decay and loss is charted in the thousand pages that follow. As his title *A la recherche du temps perdu* ('In Search of Lost Time') emphasizes, Proust seeks in memory experiences now irrecoverable in any other way. The landscape of his childhood which Marcel so fondly and frequently recalls has in reality been utterly obliterated by the battles of the First World War. As a letter from Gilberte informs him, it is now a

ravaged countryside, where vast battles are fought to gain posession of some path, some slope which you once loved . . . they have become for ever a part of history . . . The battle of Méséglise lasted for more than eight months; the Germans lost in it more than six hundred thousand men. (III, p. 778)

In the process of writing, Proust changed the location of *A la recherche du temps perdu*, setting its childhood scenes in what became the battlefields of the First World War in order to emphasize how completely times recalled in its early stages had vanished. Rather like his contemporary Alain-Fournier, in *The Lost Domain* (*Le Grand Meaulnes*, 1913), Proust shows that in the French context as much as the British, the years before the war seemed a *belle époque*, of alluring tranquillity, but a lost domain only art or memory could re-enter. As Proust remarks, the years before the war had become an

> epoch from which it is now the convention to say that we are separated by centuries – for the philosophers of the war have spread the doctrine that all links with the past are broken. (III, p. 811)

In a letter written only four days after the war began, Henry James already describes the past as 'disconnected and fabulous, fatuous, fantastic, belonging to another life and another planet' (p. 402): looking back from the end of the 1920s Richard Aldington likewise remarks in *Death of a Hero* that 'pre-war seems like pre-history' (p. 199).

Stephen Kern confirms how far this sense of disjuncture from a lost past affected the post-war period. He remarks that 'the restlessness . . . of the "lost generation"' in the 1920s resulted from a desire for '*temps perdu*' and from a frustrated wish for 'reintegration in the flow of time' (p. 298). As Kern suggests, the ache of unrest in the 1920s arose not simply from an unrealizable, nostalgic wish somehow to re-enter earlier, happier times, but from uneasiness with the sense of time itself. The war's enormous violence not only swept away a style of life, a *belle époque*: it extinguished a form of thinking, a sense of integration in the flow of time. It destroyed a 'feeling of continuity' which Orwell particularly ascribes to the Edwardian age, but which had actually existed, influentially, for much longer. A sense of some security within history, and a belief in the attractive qualities of the future to which it probably led, had sustained a good deal of thinking – and fiction – throughout much of the Victorian period. Rapid developments in science and technology, as well as a long period of relative peace and advancing imperial power for Britain, sometimes allowed belief in material progress to replace declining religious faith in the later nineteenth century. Some of the thinkers who most seriously challenged religious belief still held strongly to ideas of a progress ordained not divinely but nevertheless logically and naturally. Charles Darwin, for example, outlined processes of natural selection which he saw leading step by step, over millennia, to the evolution of creatures best adjusted to their environment and fittest for survival in it.

Though not necessarily demonstrating the idea of the 'survival of the fittest',[23] Victorian fiction often follows characters who do progress through time to realize their own potential, and fit in with society, as fully as possible. This process is central to the *Bildungsroman* form, following individual life sequentially through its day-by-day, year-by-year evolution. Within and beyond the *Bildungsroman* form, as Virginia Woolf remarks, 'peace and prosperity were influences that gave the nineteenth-century writers a family likeness'.[24] As she goes on to suggest, part of this likeness was their shared assumption of the meaningfulness of history, public or personal; of the coherence of development through time. The survival of this assumption in the early years of the twentieth century is suggested, for example, by H.G. Wells (a firm believer in utopian progress through technology) choosing for his 1910 novel the title *The History of Mr Polly*. Relative stability in political history encourages faith in the possibility of stability in private life, and in fiction. In what Orwell calls 'a settled period, when civilisation stands on its four legs like an elephant' straightforward progress in time naturally offers a structuring basis for fiction. Victorian or Edwardian novels certainly show moral, emotional or other problems disturbing private or social life, but they also, almost always, offer and fulfil the promise that these problems will be ordered and resolved – coherently, if not necessarily happily – in the end.

The First World War changed all that. After its outbreak, H.G. Wells abandoned his utopianism and turned to writing a history of the world, as if attempting to recreate in a text an orderliness otherwise missing from public events, or seeking in the past some explanation of how present hopes could have been so dashed. The philosophies of time which Wyndham Lewis saw proliferating in the 1920s, and added to in his own work, may sometimes have resulted from a comparable response to the shock of the war. Such a radical break in the life of 'Western Man' demanded reconsideration of what principles of evolution or of coherent life in time, if any, could be thought to remain valid. Oswald Spengler's work is symptomatic of this new phase of uncertainty. His huge

study, *The Decline of the West* (*Der Untergang des Abendlandes,*
1918–22) establishes from its title onwards a flat contradiction to
any surviving faith in progress. Within a day of the war's outbreak,
Henry James saw how completely it had invalidated such faiths. In
a letter written on 5 August 1914 he remarks of the war that

> the plunge of civilisation into this abyss of blood and darkness . . . is a thing that
> so gives away the whole long age during which we have supposed the world to
> be, with whatever abatement, gradually bettering.

Later letters talk of the war as 'this wreck of our belief that
through the long years we had seen civilization grow' and describe
its 'violence of rupture with the past' as 'a breach . . . with the
course of history'. The war not only destroyed ideas of progress,
but almost the idea of history itself, certainly as a coherent
'course'. James remarks of its outbreak that

> one of the effects of this colossal convulsion is that all connection with every-
> thing of every kind that has gone before seems to have been broken short off in
> a night.

By September 1914, in the war's second month, Wyndham Lewis
was likewise suggesting that 'we have got clean out of history . . . we
are not to-day living in history'.[25] In his study *The Great War and
Modern Memory* (1979), Paul Fussell similarly concludes that 1914
may have been virtually the last moment when events could be

> conceived as taking place within a seamless, purposeful 'history' involving a
> coherent stream of time running from past through present to future. (p. 21)

Rupturing the sense of the stream of time in this way, the First
World War added powerfully to the tendencies discussed in the
last section to conceive time as divided or fractured rather than –
or sometimes as well as – seamlessly flowing. Modernist writing
repeatedly figures the war in a divisive, cutting role, slicing across
time and history as sharply, as absolutely, as the trenches cut
across space on the battlefields, severing the map of modern
Europe. D.H. Lawrence opens *Lady Chatterley's Lover* by remarking that 'The cataclysm has happened . . . there is now no
smooth road into the future' (p. 5). Using almost the same image,
Virginia Woolf remarks that in 1914, 'suddenly, like a chasm in a

smooth road, the war came' and 'cut into' contemporary lives.[26] In *Parade's End*, Ford Madox Ford similarly describes the war as a 'crack across the table of History' (p. 510). Like Proust, in his First World War novel *All Our Yesterdays* (1930) H.M. Tomlinson writes of looking back into a lost pre-war landscape and finding 'a summer dubious with its immemorial aspect of continuity, yet suggesting bleakly a subtle yet disastrous interruption in the life of the earth' (p. 364). In *Death of a Hero*, Richard Aldington describes trench combat as a 'timeless confusion' which 'made a cut in . . . life and personality' (p. 323). He adds that in general 'adult lives were cut sharply into three sections – pre-war, war, and post-war' (p. 199).

This cutting of life into three sections is clearly reflected in the tripartite structure of *To the Lighthouse*. The novel begins on a summer's day with a strong aspect of continuity, an almost untroubled expectation of continuing holiday time. Woolf moves on to show in the short, sharp middle section the disastrous interruption which cuts into or destroys altogether the lives of Mrs Ramsay and several of the figures central to the first part. *To the Lighthouse* ends with a third section in which there sometimes seems little left except a looking back on lost time, to the sound of forlorn voices crying 'Mrs Ramsay! Mrs Ramsay!' (p. 229) across the 'field of death' (p. 206) of the war. The middle section is the clearest, saddest indication in modernist fiction of the effects of a time emphatically not in the mind, but part of a world which as Chapter 2 explained offers the mind no reflection, echo or sympathy for itself in a landscape irretrievably stained and broken by the war. Human disasters scarcely impinge on such a world: like his mother's, Andrew Ramsay's death merits only a casual parenthesis:

[A shell exploded. Twenty or thirty young men were blown up in France, among them Andrew Ramsay, whose death, mercifully, was instantaneous.] (p. 152)

Laying such cracks and chasms across the previously 'smooth road' of history, the war also dictates the structure and sentiments of other modernist novels, though in ways sometimes less immediately visible than in *To the Lighthouse*. Some of these can be illustrated by looking in detail at the development of D.H. Lawrence's project, *The Sisters*. In the course of his writing during the First World War, Lawrence decided to split this long projected novel into two separate works, *The Rainbow* (1915) and *Women in*

*Love*, eventually published in 1921. Differences in tone, structure and vision between the two finished novels are worth examining at length for their exemplification of the effects of the war, and of other pressures which dictated modernism's evolution from Victorian fiction.

The opening of *The Rainbow* shows the steady, almost timeless conditions of the Brangwen family, adapted as much to the cyclic life of the seasons as to forward progress in time or history:

> The Brangwens had lived for generations on the Marsh Farm . . . they felt the rush of the sap in spring, they knew the wave which cannot halt, but every year throws forward the seed to begetting, and, falling back, leaves the young-born on the earth. They knew the intercourse between heaven and earth, sunshine drawn into the breast and bowels, the rain sucked up in the daytime, nakedness that comes under the wind in autumn, showing the birds' nests no longer worth hiding. Their life and interrelations were such; feeling the pulse and body of the soil. (pp. 7–8)

In examining 'Forms of Time and Chronotope in the Novel', Mikhail Bakhtin sums up the characteristics of this 'agricultural stage in the development of human society'. He considers that at this stage

> Time is collective, that is, it is differentiated and measured only by the events of *collective* life . . .

> Human life and nature are perceived in the same categories. The seasons of the year, ages, nights and days (and their subcategories), copulation (marriage), pregnancy, ripening, old age and death: all these categorical images serve equally well to plot the course of an individual life and the life of nature (in its agricultural aspect) . . . Time here is sunk deeply in the earth, implanted in it and ripening in it. Time in its course binds together the earth and the labouring hand of man . . .
> The mark of cyclicity, and consequently of cyclical repetitiveness, is imprinted on all events occurring in this type of time. Time's forward impulse is limited by the cycle. (pp. 206, 208, 210)[27]

This 'immanent unity' (p. 217) of individual life, society and nature does not last, however. 'The time of personal, everyday family occasions' becomes

> individualized and separated out from the time of the collective historical life of the social whole, at a time when there emerged one scale for measuring the events of a *personal* life and another for measuring the events of *history*. (p. 208)

*The Rainbow* charts this process of gradual fragmentation in the organic, agricultural community; the gradual emergence of a life experience oriented around an individual who is increasingly separated from nature and from the full unity of a society. The apparently immutable, integral continuity of the Brangwens' life – an immemorial quality emphasized, early in *The Rainbow*, by the Biblical vocabulary and rhythms of Lawrence's prose – is first of all ruptured by the effects of the Industrial Revolution:

> About 1840, a canal was constructed across the meadows of the Marsh Farm, connecting the newly-opened collieries of the Erewash Valley. A high embankment travelled along the fields to carry the canal . . .
>
> Then, a short time afterwards, a colliery was sunk on the other side of the canal, and in a while the Midland Railway came down the valley . . .
>
> The Brangwens were astonished by all this commotion around them. The building of a canal across their land made them strangers in their own place, this raw bank of earth shutting them off disconcerted them. As they worked in the fields, from beyond the now familiar embankment came the rhythmic run of the winding engines . . . Then the shrill whistle of the trains re-echoed through the heart, with fearsome pleasure, announcing the far-off come near and imminent . . .
>
> The farmers of the land met the blackened colliers trooping from the pit-mouth. As they gathered the harvest, the west wind brought a faint, sulphurous smell of pit-refuse burning. As they pulled the turnips in November, the sharp clink-clink-clink-clink-clink of empty trucks shunting on the line, vibrated in their hearts with the fact of other activity going on beyond them. (pp. 11–13)

Throughout the novel, the canal is called, appropriately, 'the Cut'. It cuts off the Brangwens, in space, from a part of their land: along with the other effects of the Industrial Revolution and the encroaching machine age, it also cuts them off in time, separating them from the older, settled continuities of life in nature. This is emphasized when the Cut destroys one of the last survivors from the old life, Tom Brangwen, who drowns when it overflows and floods the land. The new rhythms of the engine, the shriek of whistles announcing the far-off come near and imminent, force the other Brangwens to look beyond their old life at a world of history now developing beyond the reach of their old existence. Change increasingly impinges upon their lives. Each succeeding generation moves on into new sets of circumstances, rather than – in the old, natural, cyclic rhythm – only reliving the experience of its predecessors.

Some possibilities nevertheless remain for seeing human life and nature whole and unified, and for remaining in touch with the old, cyclic movement of time – 'still it was there, even if it were faint and inadequate. The cycle of creation still wheeled in the Church year' (p. 280). The year still moves through its seasons, and its religious festivals, Christmas and Easter, with all the strange awe and wonder which Lawrence shows surrounding them. Lawrence also shows traces of a cyclic movement within human affairs, of recurrence and continuity despite change. Portraying three generations of Brangwens, *The Rainbow* shows each encountering new challenges, but within some of the same basic, recurrent patterns of marriage and procreation, and often with substantial repetition of the moods and attitudes associated with each.

Yet these patterns, too, grow insecure and unsettled in the end. The last of the Brangwens Lawrence considers, Ursula, remains – at least at the end of *The Rainbow* – outside the established cycles. The concluding phase of the novel finds her uncertain and alone, her relationship with a lover having ended unfulfilled, and with a miscarriage after it has been broken off. She experiences the painful necessity of forging an individual existence independently of shared values and sustaining community. At the moment of her deepest depression, close to the end of the novel, she remarks, 'in an ache of utter weariness',

I have no father nor mother nor lover, I have no allocated place in the world of things, I do not belong to Beldover nor to Nottingham nor to England nor to this world, they none of them exist, I am trammeled and entangled in them, but they are all unreal. (p. 493)

Unlike members of any earlier generation in *The Rainbow*, Ursula is eventually lost, alone and unsure of anything except her own subjective sensations. Her experience at this point provides a final term in Lawrence's tracing, from around 1840 to the early years of the twentieth century, a process of ejection from a secure society and a 'collective historical life': *The Rainbow* helps locate, as a consequence of demographic shifts after the Industrial Revolution, a transition towards modernism's frequent concentration on individuals largely detached from a supportive social sphere. Ursula's life and situation towards the end of the novel share many of the stresses characteristically examined in modernist and later twentieth-century fiction, following the lives of isolated, alienated protagonists; out-siders in a confusing world; individuals lonely and anonymous even in huge, crowded cities.

Ursula's utter weariness, however, does not quite end the novel. Instead, at the moment of her maximum loneliness and distress, Law-rence once again re-establishes a kind of unity between individual, nature and society. Once again, human life and nature are 'perceived in the same category' – at least at a level of vision and hope, if not in the raw real world which Ursula finds so uncomfortable:

> And again, to her feverish brain, came the vivid reality of acorns in February lying on the floor of a wood with their shells burst and discarded and the kernel issued naked to put itself forth. She was the naked, clear kernel thrusting forth the clear, powerful shoot, and the world was a bygone winter, discarded . . . whilst the kernel was free and naked and striving to take new root, to create a new knowledge of Eternity in the flux of Time. (p. 493)

Ursula's vision relocates her in an organic space of Eternity, of cyclic recurrence and natural growth beyond the destructive forward movement of historical time hitherto shown in the novel. This op-timism – almost mysticism – Lawrence extends into hopes of a 'new germination' for Ursula's society as a whole. These hopes largely depend upon belief in the redeeming power of relationships, em-phasized throughout the novel by symbolism attached to rainbows and arching shapes of all kinds. These represent the potential for mutual equilibration, secure support and joy, which can be achieved in balanced, complete union of man and woman. Summed up in her final vision of a rainbow, this potential offers Ursula a promise of redemption from the dreary tide of industrialization which has flooded across the countryside and her family's land:

> She saw the stiffened bodies of the colliers, which seemed already enclosed in a coffin, she saw their unchanging eyes, the eyes of those who are buried alive: she saw the hard, cutting edges of the new houses, which seemed to spread over the hillside in their insentient triumph, a triumph of horrible, amorphous angles and straight lines . . .
>
> And then, in the blowing clouds, she saw a band of faint iridescence colouring in faint colours a portion of the hill. And forgetting, startled, she looked for the hovering colour and saw a rainbow forming itself . . .
>
> And the rainbow stood on the earth. She knew that the sordid people who crept hard-scaled and separate on the face of the world's corruption were living

still, that the rainbow was arched in their blood and would quiver to life in their spirit, that they would cast off their horny covering of disintegration, that new, clean, naked bodies would issue to a new germination ... She saw in the rainbow the earth's new architecture, the old, brittle corruption of houses and factories swept away. (pp. 495–6)

The miners, entombed in their industrial thraldom, or the scaly, empty shells of people – the hollow men Lawrence later examines in the figures of Gerald Crich or Clifford Chatterley – all seem redeemable in *The Rainbow* by this 'new germination', able to restore the spirit and nature of a whole civilization from its ravaging by the modern machine age.

No such optimism or redeeming mysticism appears in *Women in Love*, which shows a society, and many individual lives, disintegral to an extent beyond the power or promise of any relationship or rainbow to redeem. In Gudrun and Gerald, physical attraction and passion function largely destructively. Birkin and Ursula's relationship and marriage, far from having any wider effect on the society around them, is mostly an act of individual refuge and escape, and they are tempted to flee altogether (as Lawrence himself did, later in life) from a drab, declining, industrialized Britain to a less sullied civilization elsewhere. Like many modernist authors and their characters – Ursula at her worst moments in *The Rainbow* – they feel alien from any sense of community, considering in their own way the possibility that they 'do not belong to Beldover, nor to Nottingham, nor to England'. Though Gerald's death forces them to return to England in the end, any possibility of 'new germination' even within their private relationship is questioned by Birkin's ultimate denial that Ursula is really enough for him. Such questioning leaves the nature and future of their relationship uncertain, and the ending of the novel unresolved.

A disintegral, uncertain quality in the characters' lives, throughout *Women in Love*, is stressed and reduplicated by the disintegral aspect of the novel's structure. Much more than *The Rainbow*, *Women in Love* acts on Lawrence's claim 'I don't want a plot' and his warning

don't look for the development of the novel to follow the lines of central characters; the characters fall into the force of some other rhythmic form.[28]

This 'rhythmic form' abandons straightforward, consecutive progress. Individual chapters exemplify `a range of what Lawrence might have called 'allotropic states'[29] in his central characters, rather than always showing how such states follow from or logically relate to each other. As the critic Frank Kermode remarks, *Women in Love* is not, like *The Rainbow*, 'a novel of extended arcs' but instead 'proceeds by awful discontinuous leaps' (pp. 63–4). Though some chapters do follow directly and clearly from others, many begin only with a mention of habitual action, or some other inspecific indication of time – 'A School Day'; 'Every Year'; 'One morning'; 'One day at this time' and so on. Especially in its early stages, *Women in Love* seems almost like a collection of short stories about the same group of characters, rather than a conventional novel about them. This fragmented narrative makes *Women in Love* as different from *The Rainbow* structurally as it is in vision. *The Rainbow* is a connected, chronological novel, showing events following one another more or less in causal sequence, one set of family circumstances setting off consequences and emotional patterns which Lawrence traces into the next generation. In this way at least, *The Rainbow* is closer to conventional fiction than its successor, sometimes resembling the kind of chronicle or saga of family life which was popular in the Victorian period and continued to be written in the early twentieth century by authors such as John Galsworthy. In showing Ursula's anguished exile from supporting society Lawrence moves in the end towards an open, alienated modernist vision, but the novel's optimistic conclusion postpones full consideration of this state, and leaves *The Rainbow* fairly firmly and satisfactorily resolved at the end. The implications of Ursula's kind of autonomy and isolation are examined throughout *Women in Love*, which not only ends unresolved, but challenges the very possibility of convincing or satisfactory resolution, in life or in the novel. Birkin's scepticism about marriage questions both a social institution and a literary one: marriage, at least until the uncertainties of the twentieth century, provides one of the standard – usually comedic – conclusions of narrative.

Radically different in structure, vision and conclusion, *Women in Love* is only 'more or less a sequel' to *The Rainbow*, as Lawrence himself admits.[30] Small but inescapable clues in the later novel help account for its difference from its predecessor. These are apparent in the description of the corpses at the end of the 'Water Party' chapter (p. 212), found lying sodden in 'horrible raw banks of clay . . . raw rottenish water' – like bodies on the flooded battlefields of the war – and in Birkin's earlier conclusion that

> What people want is hate – hate and nothing but hate. And in the name of righteousness and love, they get it. They distil themselves with nitro-glycerine. (p. 141)

A more certain hint is given towards the end of the novel when Birkin looks at Gerald's corpse, after his death in the snow:

> 'I didn't want it to be like this – I didn't want it to be like this,' he cried to himself. Ursula could but think of the Kaiser's: '*Ich habe es nicht gewollt.*' She looked almost with horror on Birkin . . . he watched the cold, mute, material face. (p. 539)

Ursula recalls here the disillusioned remark made by Kaiser Wilhelm II about the First World War.[31] In a letter of 1917, Lawrence confirms this connection between *Women in Love* and the destructiveness of contemporary history, indicating factors which coloured his imagination while he worked on *Women in Love* in the years following the publication of *The Rainbow* in 1915:

> About *The Rainbow*: it was all written before the war, though revised during Sept. and Oct. 1914. I don't think the war had much to do with it – I don't think the war altered it, from its pre-war statement . . . alas, in the world of Europe I see no Rainbow. I believe the deluge of iron rain will destroy the world here, utterly . . .
>
> There is another novel, sequel to *The Rainbow*, called *Women in Love* . . . This actually does contain the results in one's soul of the war: it is purely destructive, not like *The Rainbow*, destructive-consummating.[32]

Lawrence himself thus judges that the shadow cast upon his imagination by the war accounts for differences between *The Rainbow* and *Women in Love*. The war provides the final, catastrophic term to an increasingly disturbing phase of history, traced in the two novels from the aftermath of the Industrial Revolution in the 1840s. This phase begins with organic community; with 'time sunk deeply in the earth' and 'human life and nature in the same categories'. It leads on through the supposedly progressive history of the

Victorian period. It ends with the cataclysm of the machine age, with humanity reduced to mere material, to be diluted with high explosives and left as 'flesh turned to atoms which drove before the wind', as Virginia Woolf writes in *To the Lighthouse* (p. 150). The first 'cut' across landscape and history made by the Industrial Revolution thus initiates a period terminated by a second – by the crack, cut or chasm in the life of the times made by the trenches of the First World War. The first cut still leaves it just possible, in *The Rainbow*, to find 'a rhythm of eternity in a ragged, inconsequential life' (p. 280); 'God's time' or natural time still tenuously existing in the cycles of events wheeling in the seasons and the church year. After the second cut, in *Women in Love*, Gerald finds

> his eternal and his infinite in the pure machine-principle . . . complex, infinitely repeated motion, like the spinning of a wheel . . . this is the God-motion . . . and the whole productive will of man was the Godhead. (pp. 256–7)

Time passes from God or nature to the possession of the machine; from the wheeling seasons to the spinning of a factory wheel; from the sun and stars to the laws and formulae which rule the age of Frederick W. Taylor – the age of Man's time, of Mean Time, of 'the logic and dynamics of late capitalism'.

Such transformations in views of history and the life in time in Lawrence's two novels are representative of wider changes in the thinking of his age. Differences between *The Rainbow* and *Women in Love* are likewise paradigmatic of structural and other changes which distinguish modernist from Victorian or Edwardian fiction. Still holding to some sense of organic community and to the possibility of the individual's integration in society, *The Rainbow* retains an organic, developmental form, an arrangement of events in coherent and progressive historical sequence. In *Women in Love*, fragmentation and disintegration, accepted as fundamental in modern society, are also installed in Lawrence's disconnected form of fictional construction. More generally apparent in fiction at the time, such changes are summed up, as aptly as anywhere, by the Italian novelist Italo Calvino. He remarks of the development of the novel:

> Long novels written today are perhaps a contradiction: the dimension of time has been shattered . . . We can rediscover the continuity of time only in the

novels of that period when time no longer seemed stopped and did not yet seem
to have exploded, a period that lasted no more than a hundred years.[33]

Before the Industrial Revolution, in the sort of immemorial agricultural life the Brangwens once enjoyed on the Marsh, time did
seem to have stopped, or at any rate to be at least as much cyclic
as progressive. While change and development dominated
the nineteenth century, long, sequential novels rested easily on
what seemed the continuing forward progress of history. With ,
the First World War, the dimension of time finally cracked, shat-
tered or exploded, leaving it 'one livid final flame', and history
itself, as Stephen Dedalus also suggests in *Ulysses*, 'a nightmare'
(pp. 28, 42).

Writing about *Ulysses* in 1923, T.S. Eliot talks – rather like
Calvino – of the genre of the novel as the expression of an age
which had not 'lost all form'. What Eliot calls the 'futility and
anarchy which is contemporary history' left the novel 'a form
which will no longer serve'.[34] Given history as nightmare, futility
or anarchy, and time as a livid final flame or the 'terrible bondage'
Gudrun finds it in *Women in Love*, novelists by the 1920s could no
longer find form and structure for their fiction simply in 'life as a
series'. Two other possibilities remained. Narrative could in
various ways reproduce the fragmented, discontinuous aspect of
contemporary history – to some extent the option chosen by
Lawrence in *Women in Love*, or by Aldous Huxley in the fractured, contrasted narratives juxtaposed in *Point Counter Point*
(1928). Or fiction could try to smooth over or escape from the
cracks and chasms in contemporary life through streams of consciousness, recovered memories, and loops in time. If time in the
world became intolerable, in other words, narrative could cele-
brate and expand upon its capacity for 'temporal autonomy', creating an independent imaginative dimension of 'Time ruled,
captured, bewitched, surreptitiously subverted'. Or ruled and subverted, at any rate, as far as possible: as the last section suggested,
since the ticking of the world's Mean times could never entirely be
ignored, modernist fiction is most often divided between the fluid
and the fragmentary.

Though movements into time subverted or time in the mind are
visible throughout modernist novels, in several cases – such as
*Ulysses* – they are most clearly marked at the end. Conclusions of

modernist texts often provide a point of maximum contrast with Victorian fiction. The latter finds points of stability or resolution within social or individual life, and brings the story firmly to a close – most often in marriage, if it is to end happily, or in death, if it is tragic. Modernist fiction more often ends in openness and uncertainty. In a disintegral society, as in *Women in Love*, marriage scarcely provides a securely stable conclusion. Even the conclusiveness of death diminishes in the early twentieth century. In *To the Lighthouse*, the perfunctory recording of the killing of Andrew Ramsay, along with twenty or thirty other young men, suggests that the scale of slaughter in the First World War hardly left death with sufficient significance or decency to resolve or conclude anything. Faced by this unresolvable turbulence in contemporary social and historical experience, modernist fiction's endings are often forced to move altogether beyond it in one way or another, towards vision rather than reality. Individual marriages or relations may fail, but there is still scope for ecstatic vision of their potential, or visionary memory of their ecstasies, at the end of *The Rainbow* or *Ulysses*. This need for the visionary or transcendent, however – though a consequence of the 'futility and anarchy which is contemporary history' – also relates to a more general modernist characteristic: its direct concern with imaginative vision or art themselves. This frequent modernist interest is further considered in the next chapter.

— 4 —

# *ART*

Real life, life at last laid bare and illuminated – the only life which in
consequence can be said to be really lived – is literature.
(Marcel Proust, *A la recherche du temps perdu*, III, p. 931)

Art and Life were to them the Reality and the Unreality. 'Of course,'
said Gudrun, 'life doesn't *really* matter – it is one's art which is central.'
(D.H. Lawrence, *Women in Love*, p. 504)

## ART AND THE NOVEL

Art and literature may not appear as the *only* 'real life' in modernist fiction, but they do figure frequently as subjects of substantial
interest. *Women in Love*, for example, itself demonstrates some of
Gudrun's conclusions about the importance of art. The shaping of
reality into models or pictures is an activity examined from the
very first lines of the novel, which describe Ursula embroidering
while Gudrun sketches. Art is also central to the 'Crème de
Menthe' and 'Totem' chapters, in which Gerald discusses and
broods over the statuettes which he finds in Halliday's London flat.
Later, Gudrun's attraction for Loerke – finally, fatally excluding
Gerald from her life – is shown growing up largely through discussions of Loerke's sculpture and other conversations, such as the
one quoted above, about art in general.

Discussions of this sort reappear elsewhere in Lawrence's novels
and throughout modernist fiction generally. In Lawrence's *Sons
and Lovers* (1913), Paul Morel believes firmly in the importance of
his drawing and painting, and sometimes talks over its styles and
aims at length with his girlfriend Miriam. Painting is the profession
of Wyndham Lewis's hero in *Tarr* (1918) – his name a near-

anagram of art – and a regular subject of arguments with girl-friends and others. Like Joyce's Stephen Dedalus in *A Portrait of the Artist as a Young Man* (1916), May Sinclair's heroine in *Mary Olivier* (1919) often ponders or discusses art and writing, each of which seems to offer some escape from a constraining society. Such interests also figure in Dorothy Richardson's *Pilgrimage* (1915–67), which records at an early stage Miriam Henderson's feeling that 'she wanted to "write a book"' (I, p. 80). In Woolf's *The Waves* (1931), Bernard more or less shares this urge, finding it necessary to spend a lifetime making 'phrases and phrases' (p. 25) and reflecting on their nature and worth. Similar reflections on what Marcel calls 'the way in which artistic impressions are formed' and on 'the perspective of imagination and art' (I, p. 544; III, p. 50) appear at some stages on almost every page of Proust's *A la recherche du temps perdu* (1913–27). Marcel's acquaintance with a novelist, Bergotte, as well as the painter Elstir and the composer Vinteuil, ensures that such issues are examined widely and in relation to a range of artistic forms. A range of artistic issues, artists and writers – sometimes fictional portraits of modernist novelists such as Lawrence – also appears in Aldous Huxley's *Point Counter Point* (1928), and in *The Apes of God* (1930), in which Wyndham Lewis famously, or notoriously, caricatures several highly recognizable individuals from artistic and literary circles in contemporary London.

Such frequent, substantial discussion of art and writing, within the novel, in one way reflects a wider debate growing up in the early twentieth century about the role of the novel *as* art; as a literary genre with structural and aesthetic principles of its own. This begins with Henry James, one of whose complaints about the state of the novel was that such thinking ought to have begun much sooner. Discussing fiction in 1914, James pointed to 'the scant degree in which that field has ever had to reckon with criticism'. James had long complained that the novel's lack of what he calls 'a theory, a conviction, a consciousness of itself behind it' left

> a comfortable good-humoured feeling about that the novel is a novel, as a pudding is a pudding, and that your only business with it could be to swallow it.[1]

This uncritical 'swallowing', however, had already begun to be challenged, by 1914, by the many prefaces James wrote for his own fiction, setting out his priorities in form and style. James was virtually the first novelist writing in English to articulate a strong critical position around the practice of his fiction, making him one of the first theoreticians of the novel of any sort. Other critics and commentators soon appeared to expand on his ideas. Percy Lubbock's *The Craft of Fiction* (1921) offers 'a theory, a conviction' based fairly firmly around James's reasoning, and other critics and writers – such as Elizabeth Drew, John Carruthers, Gerald Bullett, Edwin Muir and Edith Wharton – continued to produce substantial studies of fiction throughout the 1920s: some of these are referred to in Chapter 2. Several modernist authors also followed James in discussing the theory and practice of novel-writing. D.H. Lawrence and Virginia Woolf frequently wrote essays on fiction, sometimes advocating for it the kind of firmer aesthetic favoured by James. Woolf, for example, held a 'grudge against novelists . . . that they select nothing'[2] and felt that all literature should aspire to the density of poetry. Such ideas informed a critical output extensive enough to have made Woolf at some stages almost as influential a writer on fiction – especially in her celebrated arguments with Arnold Bennett – as she was as a writer of fiction. Wyndham Lewis certainly made himself into more of a critic and commentator than a novelist in the 1920s, when volumes such as *The Art of Being Ruled* (1926) and *Time and Western Man* (1927) far outstripped his writing of fiction.

From the scant beginnings indicated by James, the early decades of the twentieth century – and the 1920s in particular – were thus a period in which the novel rapidly acquired a theory and a framework for critical debate, and a new awareness of its status as art and not 'pudding'. As critics such as Peter Keating have shown, this new awareness also resulted from more flexible conditions of publishing and the great increase in literacy, and hence the size of the reading public, in the late nineteenth and early twentieth centuries. This overall expansion made it financially possible for novels to address minority tastes or specific sections within the fiction-reading public rather than trying more or less to reach it all. From the time of James, authors found it more feasible than hitherto – and often more desirable – to concentrate not only on the likely popular appeal of their work, but on its status as an artistic form. As novels came to be written and valued more and more as art, so art came to be more valued and discussed in novels.

Another symptom of this shift in values and interests – and of the increasing centrality of art in fiction generally – appears in a gradual change away from the *Bildungsroman* and towards the *Künstlerroman* – the novel which follows growth towards maturity as an artist rather than only as an individual. In the early years of the century the *Bildungsroman* remained a popular, frequently used form – in novels such as Compton Mackenzie's *Sinister Street* (1913–14), Somerset Maugham's *Of Human Bondage* (1915), Arnold Bennett's *Clayhanger* series (1910–18), or D.H. Lawrence's *Sons and Lovers*. Each of these novels, however, has a hero with some artistic interests or pretensions, and in *Sons and Lovers*, in particular, Lawrence shows Paul Morel's concern with art as a significant part of his more general progress towards adulthood and away from the influence of his family.

For modernist authors, growth came to be considered more and more exclusively in terms of artistic rather than personal maturity. Modernist fiction often concentrates on characters who move towards a point at which – however orderly or otherwise their actual lives – they can at least make of their experience something coherent in terms of vision, if not always in fact. This movement dominates *A la recherche du temps perdu*. Proust's narrator Marcel announces in its first volume that he 'wished some day to become a writer' (I, p. 188), and he subsequently presents and discusses the many stages through which his ambition is realized and he finally discovers means whereby 'a life ... can be realised within the confines of a book' (III, p. 1088). In a sense, the novel shows Marcel chasing his own tale: it follows his development to the point at which he is finally able to write the narrative in which he appears – able at last to recover in art all the times he has in reality lost in the past. Similar processes of development, and comparable discussions of art and its principles, run through Joyce's *A Portrait of the Artist as a Young Man*. Joyce's change from his original title, *Stephen Hero*, indicates an increased emphasis on art since the draft novel was begun early in the century. Stephen Dedalus's name indicates from the start that he will become a fabulous artificer: throughout, Joyce follows the thinking through which – particularly in his lengthy artistic conversations with Lynch – he works out a 'theory of esthetic' (p. 214) of his own. By the end, Stephen can declare himself ready to encounter for the millionth time the reality of experience and to forge in the smithy of my soul the uncreated conscience of my race. (p. 253)

Certain stages in Stephen's development indicate another factor which encouraged early twentieth-century fiction's growing interest in the orders of art. Chapter 3 pointed out that by the late nineteenth century religious belief had been partly replaced by faith in the potentials of science and technologic progress. Art also provided a kind of substitute faith or system of values at this time. Especially in the 1890s – and in the case of Oscar Wilde in particular – aestheticism and the doctrine of art-for-art's sake offered an alternative code of conduct, a substitute for conventional morality. Stephen's experience partly reflects this shift from the spiritual to the aesthetic. However much his name may propel his flight from the reality of experience into the realms of art, his first steps are towards a different transcendence of the immediate world, not in art but in religion. It takes some time and anguish before he rejects the 'grave and ordered and passionless . . . the inhuman voice that had called him to the pale service of the altar' (pp. 160, 170) in favour of working in the

name of the fabulous artificer . . . the artist forging anew in his workshop out of the sluggish matter of the earth a new soaring impalpable imperishable being. (p. 169)

Though eventually reaching a conclusion in favour of art rather than religion, the terms in which Stephen does so remain highly charged with the 'soaring impalpable imperishable' rhetoric of the spiritual: the art he embraces seems partly interchangeable with religion rather than altogether separate from or opposed to it.

Some of his conclusions, and some of his conflicts, are shared both by the hero of Mackenzie's *Sinister Street* – a novel which also looks back strongly to the aestheticism, dandyism and decadence of the 1890s – and by May Sinclair's central figure in *Mary Olivier*. At various stages, each is divided between the demands of religion and of an art which seems to offer more or less equivalent consolations. Similar equations of art and religion figure in other contemporary novels. In Woolf's *The Waves* (1931), Bernard remarks that 'some people go to priests; others to poetry . . . I to seek among phrases and fragments something unbroken' (p. 229). In *To the*

*Lighthouse* Woolf also suggests something of this equation between the powers of priests and of poetry, of religion and art. When Mr Ramsay reaches the lighthouse and Lily Briscoe completes her painting in the last chapter, her repeated comment 'It is finished' (pp. 236–7) echoes Christ's 'consummatum est'. Some connection between the two is further suggested by Lily's age when she begins her painting in the first section – 33, the same as Christ's at the end of his life.

The ending of *To the Lighthouse* helps confirm a new sense in the early twentieth century of a power in art in some ways equal to religion's in escaping 'the sluggish matter of the earth' or in finding a pattern or meaning for life. Woolf's novel is worth considering further for its more general indications of how and why art came to figure so significantly in contemporary fiction. Rather like Proust, describing various artists and their work in *A la recherche du temps perdu*, Woolf uses her account of Lily Briscoe and her painting as a figuration of wider interest in the powers and possibilities of art. In *A la recherche du temps perdu*, Marcel describes a painting as a 'little square panel of beauty which Elstir had cut out of a marvellous afternoon' (II, p. 436): cutting panels out of life, asking how art is framed from reality, or permanence out of change, is also a frequent practice in *To the Lighthouse*. In a way it even extends into the novel's use of square brackets, often to frame its sadder or darker passages, such as the description in the third section of a character who

> [. . . took one of the fish and cut a square out of its side to bait his hook with. The mutilated body (it was alive still) was thrown back into the sea.] (p. 205)

Elsewhere, shapes are cut and framed less painfully from life, though frequently. The novel's first section, 'The Window', opens with Mrs Ramsay helping her little boy to cut out pictures from an illustrated catalogue, while remembering that she must remain carefully framed herself, sitting in the window in the place Lily has chosen for her in her painting. Mrs Ramsay not only remains aware of her place in Lily's picture, she sometimes shows an ability to share in other ways – part of a general affinity with Lily – something of her painterly preoccupation with 'the relations of masses, of lights and shadows' (p. 62). During the latter stages of her triumphal dinner party, Mrs Ramsay mentally assembles a kind of still life out of the contents of the fruit bowl:

> her eyes had been going in and out among the curves and shadows of the fruit
> . . . putting a yellow against a purple, a curved shape against a round shape . . .
> until, oh, what a pity that they should do it – a hand reached out, took a pear,
> and spoilt the whole thing. (p. 125)

After the dinner party is over, she performs a kind of framing of
her own, turning and pausing in the doorway as she leaves to look
back over the happy scene in the hope that she can find a way to
make 'Life stand still here . . . making of the moment something
permanent' (p. 183).

For all her artistic uses of door-frame or fruit bowl, however,
Mrs Ramsay's ambitions to still life and somehow make it permanent depend upon people, not paint. She is a shaper of society,
of individuals and their relations, and not – except in occasional
moments of reflection – of Lily's abstract masses, lights and
shadows. Mrs Ramsay still believes order and pattern can be found
in the social world, and that marriage and stable relationships
create sufficient security and coherence for individual or social life.
The first part of *To the Lighthouse* concludes with order and stability established in these terms – with the news Mrs Ramsay has
hoped for about Paul and Minta's engagement; with the elegant
social integration of the dinner party; with the Ramsays' own marriage drawn together into one of its moments of wonderful con-
cord after their numerous bright, promising children have been
soothed to sleep upstairs.

But *To the Lighthouse* does not end there. In some ways, it is two
novels in one, the vision of its third part 'The Lighthouse', differing
from the first for reasons which appear in the middle section, 'Time
Passes'. This shows how war and the lapse of time intervene to
destroy the coherence, even the principles of coherence, which Mrs
Ramsay sustains with temporary success in the first part. In 'Time
Passes', death – Andrew Ramsay's death in the war, Prue's in child-
birth – carries away the brightest and best of Mrs Ramsay's children,
and also Mrs Ramsay herself. The novel comments on

> Mrs Ramsay making of the moment something permanent . . . as in another
> sphere Lily herself tried to make of the moment something permanent. (p. 183)

Death and decay in 'Time Passes' show the failure of Mrs
Ramsay's strategies for securing order, permanence or stability.

Her own death leaves the third part of the novel as Lily's sphere, one from which she often looks back critically on Mrs Ramsay and her priorities in the first. Lily seeks stability and permanence just as much as Mrs Ramsay, but her medium and methods differ: Lily's commitment to art highlights some of the limitations of Mrs Ramsay's allegiance to life, and the inevitability of eventual failure in her attempts to shape it. Mrs Ramsay even knows herself that the wish to make 'life stand still' at her dinner party is unrealizable:

> the scene . . . was vanishing even as she looked . . . it changed, it shaped itself differently, it had become, she knew, giving one last look at it over her shoulder, already the past. (p. 128)

The marriage she believes in establishes nothing more durable than her dinner party. As Lily reflects in 'The Lighthouse', Paul and Minta's union, which Mrs Ramsay so hoped for and encouraged, turns out indifferently, declining into dreary adulteries. Looking back on Mrs Ramsay's efforts, Lily concludes that her principles – such as 'Marry, marry!' – were 'limited, old-fashioned ideas' and that 'life has changed completely' in ways which have left them 'dusty and out of date' (p. 198). Lily's views confirm the conclusion reached in Chapter 3 – that the violence of the war and the cynicism of the years which followed made apparently 'old-fashioned' both marriage and other points of finality or stability which once provided a fitting sense of an ending in life, or in fiction. As Lily further suggests, after the scale and arbitrariness with which it had occurred in the war, even death hardly retained much more decisive significance than marriage. 'Oh the dead!' Lily reflects, 'one pitied them, one brushed them aside, one even had a little contempt for them. They are at our mercy' (p. 198).

Such changes in outlook and experience leave coherence or permanence available to Lily only in art, rather than in life. Life will not stand still: art does. '"You" and "I" and "she" pass and vanish; nothing stays; all changes; but not words, not paint', she concludes, finding 'a brush, the one dependable thing in a world of strife, ruin, chaos' (pp. 204, 170). Only in art is it possible to find 'in the midst of chaos . . . shape; this eternal passing and flowing . . . struck into stability' (p. 183). The ending of *To the Lighthouse* further endorses her views. The penultimate chapter shows the lighthouse finally reached, and the expectation set up by the novel's title and much of its first section at last fulfilled. Yet this actual achievement in the lives of its characters does not provide a firm or sufficient conclusion for the novel, fading into haziness and the impalpable: for Lily, 'the Lighthouse had become almost invisible, had melted away into a blue haze' (p. 236). Instead, it is Lily's decisive artistic gesture – the final line 'there, in the centre' which completes her painting, allowing her to lay down her brush and conclude 'I have had my vision' (p. 237) – which actually brings *To the Lighthouse* to a close.

It is only art or vision, this ending suggests, that make it possible to transcend 'eternal passing and flowing' or to endow an action – however complete in itself – with significance. This suggestion and the general interest in art throughout the third section make *To the Lighthouse* paradigmatic of some of the differences between Victorian and modernist fiction. Still believing in the possibility of finding shape within life and society – of arranging dinner guests and not only fruit into meaningful patterns – Mrs Ramsay rather resembles a Victorian novelist, and the first part of *To the Lighthouse*, with its apparently stable, happy ending, is not unlike a Victorian novel. The second and third parts show how twentieth-century life, especially after the First World War, seemed 'changed completely', and the sense of coherence in individual or social life too far diminished to serve the novel in conventional ways. Without much faith remaining in religion or in the stability of society, history, family life or the world in general, art offered a last possibility of finding 'in the midst of chaos, shape'. Art and artists begin to figure centrally in modernist fiction because apparently they, almost alone, offer a possibility of dealing with or escaping from a world characterized by 'strife, ruin and chaos', in Lily's view, or 'futility and anarchy' in T.S. Eliot's.

Art and artists in modernist fiction, however, represent not only this possibility of order, but sometimes also – as in Lily's case – the difficulties of realizing it. Art may have seemed more than ever desirable as a surviving domain of coherence in the early twentieth century, but at the same time the order it promised seemed more than ever difficult to create out of an increasingly fragmentary reality. Modernism's principal initiatives – the general, radical re-shapings of style and structure considered in Chapters 2 and 3 – can be seen to result from the need to find new, subtler strategies to contain new, radical challenges in the life of the times. Stephen

Spender sums up this view of modernism when he talks of the need to 'invent a new literature' for an age 'in many respects unprecedented and outside all the conventions of past literature and art': Katherine Mansfield likewise suggested after the war that 'in all this division and confusion' the novel 'must accept the fact of a new world' if it was to survive.[3] Modernist writers were obliged, in other words, not only to reject the novel as 'pudding', in James's terms, but to establish a whole new cuisine. This obligation made technique and style not only the tools of creation, but pressing enough matters also to force their way into the novel as themes or subjects in themselves.

Sometimes the artist likewise became the subject rather than only the agent of artistic creativity. This kind of self-consciousness appears in modernist fiction in a number of ways – first, in the number of novels concerned with art which are also autobiographies. The movement towards the *Künstlerroman* discussed above is also a move towards self-examination: portraits of an artist in the novel are most often self-portraits of the author who wrote it. In *A la recherche du temps perdu*, as his name implies Marcel is a figure close to Marcel Proust himself. Many of his long speculations on how to construct a fiction which 'suppresses the mighty dimension of Time' (III, p. 1087) reflect his author's problems in constructing the novel in which he appears – Proust chases his own tale in showing Marcel pursuing his. Joyce's title implies a similarly autobiographical aspect in *A Portrait of the Artist as a Young Man*. Joyce draws on details of his own early life and uses Stephen's lengthy speculations about art to work out a 'theory of esthetic' also partly his own. Other modernist works are still more explicitly self-portraits. *Mary Olivier* was described by May Sinclair as being 'as autobiographically accurate as I can make it'. In a letter written at the time *Tarr* was being serialized in *The Egoist* – immediately following its publication of *A Portrait of the Artist as a Young Man* – Wyndham Lewis acknowledges that 'I make Tarr too much my mouthpiece . . . Tarr has just a trifle too many of my ideas to be wholly himself'.[4] Most of Tarr's ideas could indeed be taken from *Time and Western Man*, and as Chapter 3 pointed out Lewis uses them – rather as Proust uses Marcel's thinking – to discuss or draw attention to the tactics of his fiction itself.

In this way, *Tarr* is typical of another aspect of modernist fiction's artistic self-consciousness: opinions about art not only reflect the views of the author, but relate directly to the novel in which they are expressed. Self-consciousness and a habit of self-portraiture extend into a kind of self-reflexiveness in which texts talk about their own methods, or artist-characters discuss or demonstrate problems and priorities which also figure in the construction of the novel in which they appear. A clear example of this is offered by the ending of *To the Lighthouse*, described above. Lily's comment 'It was done; it was finished. Yes, she thought . . . I have had my vision' (p. 237) could also be spoken by the novelist, who in this last sentence concludes *her* vision – the novel itself – at the same moment Lily completes her painting. Simultaneous conclusions are appropriate for phases of creativity, in paint and fiction, significantly correlated throughout *To the Lighthouse*. Several of the problems confronting Lily as an artist, and some of the solutions she finds for them, are closely analogous to decisions and strategies which shape Woolf's construction of the novel. Lily wonders, for example,

> how to connect this mass on the right hand with that on the left . . . the danger was that . . . the unity of the whole might be broken. (pp. 62–3)

Her doubts are ones Woolf herself might have confronted in the course of constructing a novel unusually split into parts reflecting single days, separated by a lapse of ten whole years. The device Lily uses to complete her painting – 'a line there, in the centre' (p. 237) – looks very much like the structural solution Woolf finds for the novel, placing the short, bleak middle section between the more expansive human visions of the first and third parts.

Woolf uses Lily's painting, Wyndham Lewis finds a 'mouthpiece' in Tarr, and Lawrence follows some of the ideas of Gudrun and Loerke in *Women in Love* as a means of reflecting on the nature and construction of their own art. Modernist fiction often turns in this way to visual art and painting as a figural context for self-examination of its own techniques. Nevertheless, such self-reflexiveness also, inevitably, finds a specifically literary focus. Chapter 2 showed modernist fiction holding up the mirror of art not so much to nature but to the mind, or at least to nature reflected in the mind. This chapter has so far outlined ways in which modernism also tends to examine the mirror of art itself; to represent the nature and processes of representation. Within the novel this naturally, ultimately, requires attention not only to visual art but to words and language, since the medium of fiction, obviously, is words and not paint. Awareness of words and language, of how they 'paint' reality, inevitably forms a part of the increasing artistic self-consciousness of modernism. This general modernist concern is first clearly apparent in two novels which consider literary rather than only visual art, *A la recherche du temps perdu* and *A Portrait of the Artist as a Young Man*.

## THE REVOLUTION OF LANGUAGE

In *A Portrait of the Artist as a Young Man*, Stephen Dedalus reflects at length on the nature and rewards of words and language:

> He drew forth a phrase from his treasure and spoke it softly to himself:
> – A day of dappled seaborne clouds.
> The phrase and the day and the scene harmonized in a chord. Words. Was it their colours? He allowed them to glow and fade, hue after hue: sunrise gold, the russet and green of apple orchards, azure of waves, the grey-fringed fleece of clouds. No, it was not their colours: it was the poise and balance of the period itself. Did he then love the rhythmic rise and fall of words better than their associations of legend and colour? Or was it that, being as weak of sight as he was shy of mind, he drew less pleasure from the reflection of the glowing sensible world through the prism of a language many-coloured and richly storied than from the contemplation of an inner world of individual emotions mirrored perfectly in a lucid supple periodic prose? (pp. 166–7)

Similar feelings are expressed by Marcel in *A la recherche du temps perdu*, his particular pleasure in prose itself dominating description of a journey past the spires of Martinville and Vieuxvicq:

> presently their outlines and their sunlit surfaces, as though they had been a sort of rind, peeled away: something of what they had concealed from me became apparent; a thought came into my mind which had not existed for me a moment earlier, framing itself in words in my head; and the pleasure which the first sight of them had given me was so greatly enhanced that, overpowered by a sort of intoxication, I could no longer think of anything else . . . it was . . . the form of words which gave me pleasure. (I, p. 197)

Marcel's pleasure in words themselves helps account for his conclusion that 'real life, life at last laid bare and illuminated . . . is literature'. What would normally be thought of as reality is for Marcel only 'a sort of rind' – a 'sunlit surface' to be peeled away in order not to engage more deeply with the world, nor even with thoughts about it, but with the forms and pleasures of language. Rather as Lily Briscoe discovers in *To the Lighthouse*, art makes reality 'melt away' or effectively 'become invisible': for Marcel, the mirror of art most rewardingly reflects not upon nature but upon itself. The most fascinating aspect of experience lies not in what is represented, but in the means of its representation; not in the world envisaged, but in the art and language which set out to record it yet somehow form a separate, sufficient domain of their own.

Stephen Dedalus's reflections point to a similar conclusion. In one way, his thoughts affirm the modernist preference discussed in Chapter 2, for an 'inner world of individual emotions' rather than an outer world 'open to the senses' – the kind of 'sensible world' usually favoured by realistic fiction. Yet both worlds, inner and outer, are in Stephen's view somehow separate from 'the poise and balance of the period itself . . . [the] supple periodic prose' used to record them. Words may be loved independently of their usual functions or associations: for Stephen, as for Marcel, language offers at least as much in itself as in what it signifies. In both Proust's vision and Joyce's, language edges away from the world it might represent, and from the consciousnesses which envisage it, towards a detached, autonomous existence of its own.

Later in this chapter, this sense of language in separate, independent existence is considered in relation to wider patterns of thought and culture in the early twentieth century. It is worth tracing first the various ways in which it appears in modernist fiction, both as a problem and an opportunity. The nature, problems and pleasures of language are issues which continue to figure especially prominently in Joyce's writing after *A Portrait of the Artist as a Young Man*, in the sustained parody of *Ulysses* first of all. In one way this parody operates at the level of character and story, Joyce's reworking of Homer casting Bloom as an unlikely modern Odysseus, heroically journeying not through the aftermath of the Trojan war but through a single Dublin day. But the parody of *Ulysses* concentrates principally on language, with some style of literature, journalism, ordinary speech, or officialdom appropriated, mocked and exaggerated in many of its chapters.

Constant parody, exaggeration and radical stylistic variation between individual chapters make the nature of language impossible
to ignore: throughout *Ulysses*, Joyce's mode of representation
competes for attention with what is actually represented.

*Ulysses* in this way departs decisively from the habits of the
nineteenth-century novel, whose language rarely varies greatly in
style from start to finish, and usually provides, as far as possible, a
transparent medium through which the world of the fiction is
observed by the reader. Henry James is sometimes criticized for a
language whose complexity borders on the opaque, yet in his
famous metaphor of looking out through various windows in 'the
house of fiction', even he assumes transparent glass for each.[5]
What interested James was the different points of view and angles
of observation each window offered for surveying the fictional
scene: it did not immediately concern him that the glass itself
might refract or colour the scene observed. For Joyce, language is
never straightforwardly a window on the world, but more often as
Stephen suggests a 'prism', colouring, shaping, or even obscuring it
– Hugh Kenner talks of Joyce's 'screens of language, through or
past which it is not easy to see' (p. 41). Readers of Joyce no longer
simply look through the window, but must also examine the glass:
as the critic Malcolm Bradbury puts it in *The Modern British Novel*
(1993)

> we must read this writing as writing, not, as with so many novels, simply looking
> through the word to the world it seems to stand for. (p. 158)

Or as Joyce himself explained, 'it is the material that conveys the
image . . . that interests you' – however fascinating the image itself.[6]

Of course, as Chapter 2 suggested, an interest in the material
that conveys the image, a foregrounding of the language of fiction,
can be seen as an enhancement of its capacity to represent the
world rather than a distraction from it. Even Joyce's more eccen-
tric uses of language can be explained as what Kenner calls 'gravitational fields' – spheres of speech and style shaped by influences
certain characters or locations exert. Nevertheless, though Kenner's
theory helps account for the striking, heterogeneous styles Joyce
uses, it does not really make them any less obtrusive when they
appear in the novel. The newspaper headlines which figure in
Chapter 7, 'Aeolus', may be explained as a consequence of its

setting in a newspaper office, but this does not diminish the unusual impact of their appearance in the text, nor the extent to which they draw attention to themselves and the language of journalism in general. Moreover, in a number of ways Kenner's idea of the 'gravitational field' provides a less thorough or satisfactory explanation for some of the later stages of *Ulysses*. Joyce's linguistic extravagance and virtuosity increase fairly steadily as the novel progresses, challenging more and more radically any attempt to account for them. At least by comparison with what follows, the early chapters of *Ulysses* seem relatively uncomplicated. Much of the novel's early stages is in the form of the 'duet for two narrators' discussed in Chapter 2, in which a supple prose slips subtly between the inner voice of Bloom (or of Stephen) and a more objective register describing them and the Dublin world they inhabit. As the novel goes on, however, phrase and day and scene harmonize less. Joyce's language offers a cloudier view of what Stephen calls the 'inner world' or the 'glowing sensible world'. If not before, by the time Chapter 12, 'Cyclops', is reached language draws attention to itself inescapably.

In this chapter Joyce's duet breaks up into two thoroughly unharmonious voices, competing instead of co-operating in presenting the scene. Highly colloquial Dublin street-speech conflicts with a grander, inflated rhetoric throughout 'Cyclops', concluding with this description of Bloom's barely dignified exit from Barney Kiernan's pub:

> And the last we saw was the bloody car rounding the corner and old sheepsface on it gesticulating and the bloody mongrel after it with his lugs back for all he was bloody well worth to tear him limb from limb. Hundred to five! Jesus, he took the value of it out of him, I promise you.
>
> When, lo, there came about them all a great brightness and they beheld the chariot wherein He stood ascend to heaven . . . And they beheld Him even Him, ben Bloom Elijah, amid clouds of angels ascend to the glory of the brightness at an angle of fortyfive degrees over Donohoe's in Little Green Street like a shot off a shovel. (pp. 448-9)

Such absurdly disparate styles do arise, in one way, from the 'gravitational field' in Kiernan's pub and the attitudes which compete within it. The grandiloquence mockingly corresponds to the Citizen's heroic, romantic but phoney vision of a noble Ireland, while the other styles belong to the drab, street-wise cynicism of his listeners. But the juxtaposition of styles also draws particular attention to the nature and limitations of each, making the chapter's subject not just the pub and what is seen in it, but *ways* of seeing and the effect of style in conditioning meaning. Named after the race of menacing one-eyed giants described by Homer, the subject of 'Cyclops' is narrowness of vision, and it shows how speech habits and registers contribute to this constraint. While seeming to represent the world to the mind, any single language or style actually defines, dictates and often limits what it is possible to see.

This is a limitation which *Ulysses* continues to demonstrate in the chapters that follow, and – through parody and its own repeated variations of style – also to resist. The next chapter, 'Nausicaa', goes on to mock the deadening, sentimental, namby-pamby-marmalady-drawersy style of popular magazine fiction. The one after, Chapter 14, 'Oxen of the Sun', is a final, extravagantly extended 'gravitational field', deriving not from character – Bloom's voice and consciousness fade from the novel after Chapter 13 – but once again from place. Setting the chapter in a maternity hospital creates a kind of appropriateness – as an imitation of the nine months of foetal growth from conception to birth – for Joyce's writing in nine sections, each of whose styles represents a phase in the historical development of the English language. The chapter thus moves from the archaic, alliterative style of 'Before born babe bliss had. Within womb won he worship' (p. 502) to the functional, prosaic modernity of

> Science, it cannot be too often repeated, deals with tangible phenomena. The man of science like the man in the street has to face hardheaded facts that cannot be blinked and explain them as best he can. (p. 547)

The diversity of the chapter as a whole allows – as in 'Cyclops' – languages to conflict with, criticize or clarify by contrast each other's nature and limitations. No single voice or style is left dominant overall: like the child eventually born in the hospital, language develops towards an independent life of its own, detached from any specific narrator, character, or inner consciousness. In the next chapter it leaves almost altogether the body of reality to which it is normally sustainingly connected, moving into the drunken hallucination and fantasy of 'Nighttown' before falling back exhausted into the monotonous clichés of Chapter 16.

Chapter 17, 'Ithaca', sobers up into what appears to be rigorous objectivity. In the form of what Joyce called 'mathematical catechism',[7] factual questions are often answered with long lists of apparently exact, detailed scientific data about Bloom's life and his day in Dublin. The questions and answers sound rather like a science examination, and the voices which provide them appear for the most part neutral, disembodied, independent of any character or 'gravitational field'. The end of the chapter, however, does offer what seems to be a clue to its speakers' identities. When Molly hears her husband coming to bed and stirs awake to talk to him, she is described as engaging in 'catechetical interrogation . . . reiterated feminine interrogation' (pp. 868–9). Perhaps Molly is in some way a source of the questions, with Bloom – always inclined to a scientific mentality – providing the answers? Molly, however, is awake only during the last few pages of 'Ithaca'. A better clue to the chapter's nature throughout is provided by the description of the couple lying in bed as 'listener and narrator' (p. 870). Narrator and listener in 'Ithaca' are not just Bloom and Molly, but in another sense the text and its reader. Joyce described the chapter as intended to allow 'the reader to know everything and know it in the baldest coldest way'.[8] In one way, the questions and answers of 'Ithaca' look like an opportunity for readers to get from the text 'hardheaded facts' and 'tangible phenomena', Joyce at last providing a firm reality independent of the screens and prisms of consciousness or stylized language through which almost everything in the novel has hitherto been refracted.

The kind of factual, precise questions asked, however, do not so much elicit absolute knowledge as parody the wish for it to exist, and the assumption that it can. Pretended scientific objectivity is often undermined, partly by Joyce's ineradicable lyricism. This continues to colour descriptions of Bloom and Stephen, for example, alone on 'the heavenborn earth', looking up from 'the penumbra of the garden' to observe 'the heaventree of stars hung with humid nightblue fruit' (pp. 819, 827). Set against this cosmic context,

Alone, what did Bloom feel?
The cold of interstellar space, thousands of degrees below freezing point or the absolute zero of Fahrenheit, Centigrade or Réaumur: the incipient intimations of proximate dawn. (p. 827)

Even at such moments, when 'Ithaca' moves from 'the heaventree of stars' to the exactness of temperature scales, seeming after all to present things in 'the baldest, coldest way', the chilliness of the language does not eradicate emotion, but actually highlights it, emphasizing by contrast Bloom's lonely human warmth. Scientific objectivity is further challenged by the absurdity of some of the knowledge presented – Stephen and Bloom's views, for example, are 'equal and negative' on 'the influence of gaslight or electric light on the growth of adjoining paraheliotropic trees' (p. 778). Moreover, the text's pretence to exactness and objectivity is often undermined by obvious omissions, speculations and inaccuracies – its falsification of Bloom's spending for the day, for example; or its implausible and unverifiable list of Molly's twenty-five lovers; or its erroneous suggestion that temperatures anywhere, even in interstellar space, ever fall below absolute zero. The question 'was the narration . . . unaltered by modifications' is answered 'absolutely' (p. 868), but the evidence of Ithaca suggests the impossibility of presenting an absolutely faithful, 'unmodified' version of anything. Supposedly the most precise, objective section of *Ulysses*, 'Ithaca' is actually its final demonstration that no language can be wholly transparent. Even the baldest, coldest, apparently most objective language modifies and mediates the world, refracting, colouring and recreating it through screens and prisms of structure and style. *Ulysses* constantly exposes the gap which results between language and reality, word and 'the world it seems to stand for' – a gap which generally grows wider as the novel goes on.

This gap widens further, and is much further explored and exploited in Joyce's writing after *Ulysses*. This first appeared as sections of 'Work In Progress' in the Paris-based journal *transition* in the late 1920s: it was eventually published in its entirety as *Finnegans Wake* in 1939. Joyce writes in its early stages that 'Here English might be seen' (p. 13), but if it can be, it is only fragmentarily and dimly. In 'the waters of babalong' (p. 103) which express the dreams of H.C. Earwicker – the sleeping Dublin publican in whose mind the material of the novel supposedly unfolds – language's familiar functions largely dissolve. For example, one of the many minor stories in *Finnegans Wake* begins

The Mookse and The Gripes.
Gentes and laitymen, fullstoppers and semicolonials, hybreds and lubberds!

Eins within a space and a wearywide space it wast ere wohned a Mookse. The onsesomeness wast alltolonely, archunsitslike, broady oval, and a Mookse he would a walking go. (My hood! cries Antony Romeo), so one grandsumer evening, after a great morning and his good supper of gammon and spittish, having flabelled his eyes, pilleoled his nostrils, vacticanated his ears and palliumed his throats, he put on his impermeable, seized his impugnable, harped on his crown and stepped out of his immobile *De Rure Albo*. (p. 152)

'If you are abcedminded' the text comments earlier, 'what curios of signs . . . in this allaphbed! Can you rede . . . its world?' (p. 18). If there is a world to be read in *Finnegans Wake*, it is obviously in unconventional ways. Rather than meaninglessness, as some early critics complained, the problem with reading *Finnegans Wake* is that it is actually overfraught with wayward, ever-expanding significances. These, however, do less to communicate a story – though this remains at least dimly visible, especially towards the end of the above extract – than to direct attention self-referentially at Joyce's means of expression and the curiosity of his signs. 'Eins within a space', for example, parodies the traditional opening 'once upon a time', emphasizing Joyce's distance from narrative convention and incidentally establishing the sort of equation of space and time typical of 1920s thinking. It reinforces this idea with the use of the German for once, 'Eins', with its half-suggestion of Einstein, who has also turned up as 'Winestain' a few pages earlier.

Almost every other word in the extract likewise functions obliquely; doubly or sometimes multiply in terms of pun or hidden suggestion. Does 'wast', for example, mean 'vast' or work as an archaic form of the verb to be, or in both senses? Is 'wearywide' very wide or wearisomely wide, or both? Constantly raising such questions, always shifting its vocabulary away from single determinate meanings, *Finnegans Wake* directs attention to the nature and relationships of words – to linguistic issues such as phonetics, etymology, or the semantics of English and sometimes of other languages – rather than to the traditional subjects of the novel. Gents and ladies, for instance – the characters conventionally of principal interest in fiction – are converted in the above extract to 'Gentes and laitymen, fullstoppers and semicolonials', becoming punctuation marks, features of language.

This kind of conversion and the strategies of *Finnegans Wake* in general are more or less defined by one of the novel's own phrases

– 'say mangraphique, may say nay por daguerre!' (p. 339). Among the multilingual puns of this statement can be found the suggestion that Joyce's work is primarily 'graphique', not 'por daguerre': it is writing, writing for itself, not as daguerreotype or any other quasi-photographic attempt to represent character or reality. In his essay 'The Revolution of Language and James Joyce', one of the editors of *transition*, Eugene Jolas, likewise remarks that 'Work in Progress' showed that

> The real metaphysical problem today is the word. The epoch when the writer photographed the life about him with the mechanics of words redolent of the daguerreotype, is happily drawing to its close. The new artist of the word has recognised the autonomy of language.[9]

Jolas's comment appears in *Our Exagmination Round his Factification for Incamination of Work in Progress* (1929), a volume of essays defending Joyce's work against contemporary puzzlement and criticism. In another of its essays, Samuel Beckett remarks that in 'Work in Progress' Joyce ensures that 'form *is* content, content *is* form . . . His writing is not *about* something; *it is that something itself*' (p. 14). Beckett's conclusions help to clarify the progress or change in orientation of Joyce's writing in the 1920s. In *Ulysses*, 'form' and 'content' share attention: Bloom, Molly, and Stephen mostly remain quite visible, even through thickening screens of language which inevitably also draw attention to themselves. In *Finnegans Wake*, the balance shifts firmly away from 'Gentes and laitymen': screens of language thicken towards an opacity no photography or daguerreotype can wholly penetrate, and the only way to 'rede' the world is to concentrate upon its language itself. The real problem – or the real interest – of *Finnegans Wake* is not in the real but the word, a word freely fleeing its denotative function, establishing 'the autonomy of language' and a 'new art of the word'. Representation and its literary medium are what *Finnegans Wake* principally represents: its language is more an 'exagmination' and celebration of itself than a communication of the world, inner or outer.

*Finnegans Wake* thus extends to extremes the separation of words and their associations, language and meaning, which interests Stephen in *A Portrait of the Artist as a Young Man*. Though

Joyce may have felt this separation more acutely than many of his contemporaries, and eventually explored it further than any of them, there were other modernist authors who shared his interests. One of Gertrude Stein's longest and most influential works, *The Making of Americans*, was published in 1925, more or less coinciding with the appearance of Joyce's 'Work in Progress' in *transition*, but she had begun it long before, as early as 1906. In this and much of her other early writing, Stein's punning, unpunctuated, highly repetitive prose forms a kind of verbal collage, undermining language's conventional constructions and semantic functions, and focusing attention on the texture of the writing itself, in ways which partly anticipate *Finnegans Wake*.

Like Joyce in *Finnegans Wake*, Stein generally finds – or creates – in language's potential autonomy a sense of freedom and an incentive to experiment. For other modernist authors, gaps between words and the world often seem fuller of problems than possibilities, and 'the limitations of language' (p. 133), in Rebecca West's terms, a subject of uneasiness or concern. In *To the Lighthouse*, Woolf shows Lily Briscoe doubting in her own way words' attachment to objects or associations, and questioning language's capacity to mean or represent anything:

> Little words that broke up the thought and dismembered it said nothing. 'About life, about death; about Mrs Ramsay' – no, she thought, one could say nothing to nobody. The urgency of the moment always missed its mark. Words fluttered sideways and struck the object inches too low. Then one gave it up; then the idea sunk back again . . . For how could one express in words these emotions of the body? (p. 202)

Ideas and conclusions in *To the Lighthouse* are often dramatized by the form of the text itself: in this case, something of Lily's scepticism about language reappears in the novel's own attempt to express things 'about death; about Mrs Ramsay'. Mrs Ramsay's death is framed in an odd, barely intelligible sentence, as if the ordinary shape of language could hardly contain the weight of emotion involved:

> [Mr Ramsay stumbling along a passage stretched his arms out one dark morning, but, Mrs Ramsay having died rather suddenly the night before, he stretched his arms out. They remained empty.] (pp. 146–7)

Further reservations about words and their capacity to express or contain reality appear in *The Waves*. Throughout, Bernard uses phrase-making and storytelling as a necessary refuge from the difficulties of life, explaining, for example,

> I must make phrases and phrases and so interpose something hard between myself and the stare of housemaids, the stare of clocks, staring faces, indifferent faces, or I shall cry. (p. 25)

Bernard feels compelled to seek in this way 'among phrases and fragments something unbroken', believing that life can be 'netted . . . with a sudden phrase . . . retrieved . . . from formlessness with words' (pp. 229, 232). Yet he is also sceptical about the very process in which he finds it so necessary to engage, worrying that 'life is not susceptible perhaps to the treatment we give it' (p. 229). As Woolf also considers in *Jacob's Room*, life may slip through the nets framed to catch it by novelists or, if they do catch it and succeed in imposing a consoling order upon parts of it, this is achieved at the expense of falsifying or excluding some of its raw reality. In the end Bernard tries to find words which can retain some immediacy in themselves, or to move beyond conventional language altogether. He remarks that instead of

> Stories . . . phrases . . . neat designs of life . . . I begin to long for some little language such as lovers use, broken words, inarticulate words . . .
>
> words of one syllable such as childrenspeak . . . I need a howl; a cry . . . I need no words. Nothing neat . . . I have done with phrases. How much better is silence . . . let me sit on and on, silent, alone. (pp. 204, 254)

Partly as a result of his particular concern with 'emotions of the body' and 'language lovers use', D.H. Lawrence also experienced uneasiness with the ordinary function of words. As Chapter 2 pointed out, his interest in profound emotions, love and passion – and the urge to follow these into his characters' unconscious as well as conscious minds – often severely strains ordinary language in his novels. Words are of little use in dealing with what *Women in Love* calls 'unspeakable communication' (p. 361) – experience 'beyond thought' (p. 221), beyond what can be reflected in ordinary consciousness. Birkin highlights this problem when he remarks of a passionate vision of Ursula that it 'could never be netted, it must fly by itself to the heart' and asks 'What was the good of talking, anyway? It must happen beyond the sound of words' (p. 282). Ursula shares his feelings:

> She knew, as well as he knew, that words themselves do not convey meaning, that they are but a gesture we make, a dumb show like any other. (p. 209)

In *Lady Chatterley's Lover* (1928), Constance Chatterley resents language in a more general way, not only for its failure to reach certain deep, crucial feelings, but for a deadening obstruction of *all* real intercourse with life. Significantly, like many of Lawrence's scenes of intense emotion, her relationship with the gamekeeper Mellors unfolds in terms somewhat apart from conventional language – or at any rate, in this case, outwith standard English. Full of 'thees' and 'thous', his broad Derbyshire dialect helps establish a private language 'such as lovers use'; one able to generate terms for physicality and more inventive and alert to love and the body. Constance's disdain for her husband, on the other hand, focuses on 'his consciousness, his words': she despises the lifelessness and obstruction of his

> turning everything into words ... How she hated words, always coming between her and life: they did the ravishing, if anything did: ready-made words and phrases, sucking all the life-sap out of living things ...
> How ravished one could be without ever being touched. Ravished by dead words become obscene, and dead ideas become obsessions. (pp. 96–7)

The idea of words ravishing or sucking the life out of things echoes Lily Briscoe's view of language dismembering thought and saying nothing about life. Constance's feeling that words come between her and life likewise resembles Bernard's sense of phrases interposing something hard between himself and the world. Such attitudes show both Woolf and Lawrence in one way following Joyce – in finding language definitely not a transparent medium, but instead something autonomous, a screen between the individual and the world surveyed. While Joyce finds this an incentive for experiment, play and even 'revolution of language', however, for Lawrence in particular it mostly offers a sense of blockage and constraint. The kind of limitations which Joyce freely mocks and parodies – in languages turned clichéd, dead or stale – Lawrence sees as inherent, ineradicable properties of *all* language. In *Psychoanalysis and the Unconscious* he remarks

> The idea is another static entity, another unit of the mechanical-active and materio-static universe . . . Ideas are the dry, unliving, insentient plumage which intervenes between us and the circumnambient universe, forming at once an insulator and an instrument for the subduing of the universe . . .
> 'In the beginning was the Word'. This is the presumptuous masquerading of the mind. The Word cannot be the beginning of life. It is the *end* of life . . . the mind is the dead end of life. (p. 246)

For Lawrence, language is not a prism through which reality can be refracted into new shapes and colours, but rather a kind of prison, a trapping of vital, open, or profound experience into narrowing categories the mind sets up for it: static forms; ready-made words and phrases; dead or deadening ideas. A similar view of language as trap or prison underlies Bernard's scepticism, in *The Waves*, about 'netting' experience into neat designs, or about relying on 'phrases laid like Roman roads across the tumult of our lives' (p. 223). This idea of language as a grid imposed on a vital 'tumult' extends the general modernist inclination (discussed earlier) to see life and reality as fluid, continuous, perpetually creative, but falsely apprehended by the divisive, dissecting apparatus of the intellect – clocks, calendars, concepts categories, or whatever. Chapter 3 explained that modernism looked resentfully at ways in which one set of such concepts and categories had been institutionalized, shaped into the huge net spread across the world from Greenwich, formalizing space and time into narrowing, defining orders. Some of the modernists resented language as another such net, another unit of the 'mechanical- . . . materio-static' forces restricting or ravishing rather than truly representing life. In this way, words and language – the very medium of their art – became for some of the modernists, as Eugene Jolas suggests, a real problem.

Significantly, Jolas suggests language not only as a real literary problem, but as 'the real metaphysical problem today'. Like the features of modernist writing discussed in the last two chapters, its new concern with language is apparent elsewhere in the culture of the early twentieth century, its philosophy or metaphysics included. Like the suspicion of the clock discussed in Chapter 3, modernist uneasiness with language is expressed particularly clearly in the philosophy of Henri Bergson. Like Lawrence, Bergson saw words as essentially fixed and static, and therefore only too likely to 'impose . . . their own stability' on the true fluidity of life and consciousness, 'dismembering' thought much as Lily Briscoe suggests. The intellect, with 'its insatiable desire to separate' seizes on language as a tool to arrest and define: as a result,

> the word with well-defined outlines overwhelms or at least covers over the delicate and fugitive impressions of our individual consciousness. (*Time and Free Will*, pp. 128, 132)

In Bergson's view, this leaves 'no common measure between mind and language' (p. 165). Worse, because it is so 'ill-suited to render the subtleties of psychological analysis' (p. 13), language helps establish 'finally two different selves' (p. 231). One is the self which can be made to belong in language: defined, solidified, made visible, but falsified; the other running on deeply, continuously, but almost inaccessibly, beyond the reach of words.

This suggestion that language splits the self points towards some of the later writing – Samuel Beckett's particularly – that followed from modernism. It also anticipates some later twentieth-century thinking, such as the diagnosis in Jacques Lacan's psychoanalysis that language induces a continuous and permanent division of the subject. Bergson's scepticism about language was also shared by several other philosophers in his own age. William James follows him in finding words isolating single, separate features from the continuity of experience, dismembering or dividing it into limiting categories. Such artificial limits ensure that 'language works against our perception of the truth' (I, p. 241). Nietzsche similarly criticizes language's imposition of stasis upon fluidity, category upon continuity. He remarks that

> Through words and concepts we are still continually misled into imagining things as being simpler than they are, separate from one another, indivisible, each existing in and for itself.

Nietzsche also goes further, questioning the possibility of any valid contact between language and reality:

mankind set up in language a separate world beside the other world, a place it took to be so firmly set that, standing upon it, it could lift the rest of the world off its hinges and make itself master of it . . . A great deal later – only now – it dawns on men that in their belief in language they have propagated a tremendous error.[10]

Such remarks suggest that Nietzsche's views, like those of James and Bergson, were a natural extension of the wider shift in contemporary epistemology discussed in Chapter 2 – one which was bound to question the nature and function of language. If authentic contacts between mind and world ceased to seem wholly possible, then language's confident provision of terms representing reality for the mind came to seem a pretence, even a delusion – an invitation to step securely onto a bridge over a gulf now considered unbridgeable. Language's innocence seemed to have been lost. Discussing this loss, Michel Foucault suggests that 'in its original form, when it was given to men by God himself, language was an absolutely certain and transparent sign for things' (p. 36). Since, however, 'the profound kinship of language with the world was . . . dissolved . . . things and words were to be separated from one another' (p. 43).

This is a separation further reflected and formalized in the linguistics of the period – in particular, by Ferdinand de Saussure's highly influential *Cours de linguistique générale*, first published in 1916. Saussure suggests that, rather than being connected absolutely or naturally, words and concepts, signifiers and signifieds, relate to one another only arbitrarily, as a result of habit and convention – a denial of the innocence, certainty or transparence of language which has become a foundation for much twentieth-century thought. Contemporary science also undermined secure contact between language and reality. Describing the astonishing session of the Royal Society at which confirmation of Einstein's theories was announced in 1919, *The Times* reported the President of the Society's claim that the meeting had just listened to 'one of the most momentous, if not the most momentous, pronouncements of human thought', but also mentioned his admission that 'no-one had yet succeeded in stating in clear language what the theory of Einstein really was'.[11] A relativistic reality eluded description other than in the language of mathematics: the most 'momentous' thoughts of humanity, as well as the profoundest of its passions, were now generally conceived as taking place beyond the certain reach of words.

Many thinkers, then, in the early twentieth century, contributed to a sense of language detached on the one hand from a reality it could no longer pretend wholly to master, and on the other from a mind whose fluid movements tended to be misrepresented by its static, defining aspects. As Nietzsche suggests, language came to seem a separate domain of its own, with no common measure securely existing either between words and mind or words and the world. The 'autonomy of language' was thus not simply an invention of James Joyce and modernist authors, but a 'real metaphysical problem' of much more far-reaching concern at the time – and also since. Modernism's investigation of how representation operates, of how art shapes itself in language, participates in an uneasy fascination with how reality can be signified, the world given form in words, which runs throughout the twentieth century, a recurrent stress in its thought. Miriam Henderson sums up doubts wider than her own, wider even than those of modernist fiction in general, when she remarks in *Pilgrimage*

> *All* that has been said and known in the world is in *language*, in words . . . then no one *knows* anything for certain. Everything depends upon the way a thing is put, and that is a question of some particular civilisation . . . Language is the only way of expressing anything and it dims everything . . . words . . . get more and more wrong. (II, p. 99)

Other factors in addition to contemporary philosophy contribute to the stresses on language modernism reflects. Psychoanalysis was obviously one of these. Freud may have encouraged the deeper attention to consciousness which appears in modernism, but he also, like D.H. Lawrence, shows how such attention exposes limits in the powers of language. In *The Interpretation of Dreams* (1899), Freud asks

> what representation can 'if' 'because' 'as though' 'although' 'either-or' and all the other conjunctions without which we cannot understand a phrase or sentence, receive in the dream? (p. 290)

He answers by suggesting that the dream can only 'reproduce logical connections in the form of simultaneous' (p. 292), leaving language – if it exists in the dream at all – fractured, unstructured, without ordinary sense. In *Ulysses*, Joyce clearly shows movement towards such a language accompanying movement towards unconsciousness and dream. As Bloom's thoughts revolve darkly towards sleep at the end of 'Ithaca', the 'baldest, coldest' scientific language dissolves and collapses completely:

> Going to bed there was a square round Sinbad the Sailor's roc's auk's egg in the night of the bed of all the auks of the rocs of Darkinbad the Brightdayler.
>     Where?
> . (p. 871)

Drifting towards unconsciousness, Bloom's language first expands into apparent nonsense, then shrinks to a final, silent point. Each movement indicates a different terminus of modernism's urge to 'look within' and 'examine the mind'. In one direction, this urge leads to a full stop on the edge of unconsciousness, of the blankness and silence which follows that final period – '.' – to Bloom's thoughts in *Ulysses*.[12] This is also close to the position Bernard reaches in *The Waves* when he decides how much better it is to sit on, silent and alone, rather than engage even in howls, cries, or the broken language of love. It is the logic Lawrence admits when he talks in *Women in Love* of an

> unspeakable communication . . . the reality of that which can never be known, vital, sensual reality that can never be transmuted into mind content, but remains outside, living body of darkness and silence. (p. 360)

Language, in this view, can reach only so far into the mind: the rest is silence.

Or – the other terminus – what rests outside the realm of consciousness or ordinary sense may still be approximated by a language that seeks, as best as it can, verbal equivalents for the unconscious and unspeakable. This is the direction Joyce briefly establishes in his very last attention to Bloom in *Ulysses*, in the passage above, and which he follows much further in *Finnegans Wake*. 'All the auks of the rocs of Darkinbad the Brightdayler' show his language moving from the bright day of *Ulysses* and the streams of consciousness which run through it towards the great night language, the stream of unconsciousness, which he considered *Finnegans Wake* and its burden of dreams. If as Proust suggests dreams leave language 'void of content' (II, p. 1014) – or in Freud's view, devoid of ordinary logic or conjunction – then a promising approximation to the language of dream is offered by the style of *Finnegans Wake*. Its self-referential 'curios of signs', denying ordinary meaning, ensure as Beckett suggests that 'form *is* content, content *is* form'. Considered in this way, however nonsensical it seems – in fact, *because* it seems nonsensical, or at least beyond ordinary sense – *Finnegans Wake* can be seen as the ultimate extension of modernism's urge to examine the mind.

The two movements, however – towards silence or the floods of 'babalong' in *Finnegans Wake* – expose what comes close to a contradiction in this modernist urge. If pursued far enough and deeply enough, the determination to look within may simply lead beyond what can be realized in the linguistic medium of fiction, requiring the complete reforging of language which appears in *Finnegans Wake*. The new modernist wish to 'examine the mind' not only revealed that at times 'little words . . . broke up the thought and dismembered it', but also that in certain areas they might be able to say nothing at all. Inevitably, given its interests, modernist fiction grew self-conscious and sometimes sceptical about its own medium, its use of language. If they moved deeply into the workings of the mind in their fiction, modernist authors were likely to experience a version of the feelings of Samuel Beckett's Unnamable, paradoxically concluding 'in the silence you don't know, you must go on, I can't go on, I'll go on' (p. 382). Silence tells readers nothing: the novel must go on in language, yet knowing that language cannot go on very far in recording that 'living body of darkness' within the self.

An 'unspeakable' experience of another sort, the First World War, had its own effects in placing stresses on language and in opening up gaps between reality and representation. In one way these resulted simply from ruin and desolation on a scale so far beyond anything known before that they just eluded description in familiar words or conventional literary forms. Some of Ernest Hemingway's early fiction dramatizes the impossibility of rendering war experience authentically within conventions quite inadequate for such monstrous events. In his short story 'Soldier's Home' (1926), for example, Hemingway's hero is forced to fabricate and lie in order to interest his audience, or even to seem to be telling the truth. The critic and historian Paul Fussell discusses in *The Great War and Modern Memory* (1979) ways that familiar forms of expression failed to match the reality of the war, or were used inappropriately and misleadingly – even by participants in the action who had every intention of remaining as truthful to it as possible.

The lasting effects of the war on language, however, were the work not of participants overwhelmed by the indescribable, but of governments and propagandists who quite deliberately over-whelmed the actual in words, in order to screen terrible truths from the public and turn carnage into patriotic glory. Talking about the start of the war, Richard Aldington remarks in *Death of a Hero*

> The long, unendurable nightmare had begun. And the reign of Cant, Delusion and Delirium . . .
>
> If the War had been an honest affair for any participant, it would not have needed the preposterous bolstering up of Cant . . .
>
> One human brain cannot hold, one memory retain, one pen portray the limitless Cant, Delusion, and Delirium let loose on the world during those four years . . . this sort of criminal rant was called Pisgah-Heights of Patriotism. (pp. 221–3)

Like his fellow German war-novelist Erich Maria Remarque, in his ironically entitled *All Quiet on the Western Front* (*Im Westen nichts Neues*, 1929), Aldington shows at several points in *Death of a Hero* the gap between actual experience and official report:

> Four or five times they passed corpses being carried down the trenches as they went up. There was, of course, nothing to report on the Western front. (p. 279)

Aldington's example is innocuous compared to some of the actual delusions practised by wartime propaganda and journalism during the war. Describing the first day's action in the battle of the Somme, for example, *The Times* reported

> Sir Douglas Haig telegraphed last night that the general situation was favour-able . . .
>
> The great offensive in the West has made a good beginning and promises exceedingly well . . .
>
> The day goes well for England and France . . . as far as can be ascertained our casualties have not been heavy.[13]

That was the report. In reality, the first morning of the Somme, 1 July 1916, saw the heaviest casualties ever sustained by the British army, devastating in the space of a few hours the 60,000 British soldiers involved in the first assault: 420,000 were killed or wounded before the battle eventually ended, months later.

Such gaps between reality and report multiplied far enough during the war to induce permanent scepticism about the agencies responsible for them. As Paul Fussell suggests,

> there is a sense in which public euphemism as the special rhetorical sound of life in the latter third of the twentieth century can be said to originate in the years 1914–18. It was perhaps the first time in history that official policy produced events so shocking, bizarre, and stomach-turning that the events had to be tidied up for presentation to a highly literate mass population . . .
>
> A lifelong suspicion of the press was one lasting result of the ordinary man's experience of the war. It might even be said that the current devaluation of letterpress and even of language itself dates from the Great War. (pp. 178, 316)

As Fussell indicates, scepticism about government, the Press and official reports has persisted and expanded throughout the twentieth century. The ubiquitous lies of governments and official institutions – as well as advertisers – have steadily added to language's potential for distortion rather than representation; to a capacity for rhetorical manipulation almost independently of meaning or truth. This capacity has sometimes been directly examined and exploited in literature – by Ernest Hemingway, for example, likely to be more conscious than other modernist writers of the war's effects on language since he was a journalist himself. Early short stories such as 'The Killers' (1928) or 'Hills Like White Elephants' (1928) explore the use of language, almost independently of the usual meaning of words, as a means of manipulating interlocutors or exerting power over them. Much the same dissembling and manipulation appears in the work of Harold Pinter – an admirer of Hemingway as well as of Joyce and Beckett – who continues in the later twentieth century to dramatize the potential and peculiarities of what he calls a language 'where under what is said, another thing is being said'.[14] For Hemingway and Pinter at least, the distortion and corruption of the twentieth century's language by its agencies of power are a source of fascination and literary opportunity as well as uneasiness.

For many of the modernists in the early part of the century, however, the principal effect of the war was not in opening up new layers, capacities or opportunities in language. Rather, the war's unspeakable experience and the cant which flowed around it generally added to doubts about language's reliability, exercising a particularly corrosive effect on certain words. In *The Good Soldier* (1915), written before the full impact of the war was felt, Ford Madox Ford's narrator still talks of the way 'good soldiers' find their profession 'full of the big words, courage, loyalty, honour, constancy' (p. 31). By contrast, in *Ulysses* Stephen Dedalus remarks 'I fear those big words . . . which make us so unhappy', with 'glorious' as one of his examples (p. 38), while in *A Farewell to Arms* (1929), written from Hemingway's own experience of the Italian campaign, the narrator finds that 'abstract words such as glory, honour, courage or hallow were obscene'. He adds that

> I was always embarrassed by the words sacred, glorious, and sacrifice and the expression in vain . . . I had seen nothing sacred, and the things that were glorious had no glory and the sacrifices were like the stockyards at Chicago if nothing was done with the meat except to bury it. There were many words that you could not stand to hear. (p. 202)

Living after 'the cataclysm . . . among the ruins', Constance Chatterley likewise regrets a kind of devaluation in the currency of certain words:

> 'Home!' . . . it was a word that had had its day. It was somehow cancelled. All the great words, it seemed to Connie, were cancelled for her generation: love, joy, happiness, home, mother, father, husband, all these great, dynamic words were half dead now, and dying from day to day. (p. 64)

For good soldiers and civilians alike, the terrible disillusion of the war and the ruins that followed it disallowed great words, big words, or abstract words. Yet of course these 'cancelled' words did not simply disappear. They continued in everyday usage, but hollowed out, emptied of meaning, a rhetoric disjunct from reality. Like other contemporary influences, the war in this way helped detach signifiers from signifieds – helped ensure, in Foucault's terms, that 'the profound kinship of language with the world was dissolved' and that 'things and words were . . . separated from one another'. For the hollow men and women of the 1920s, only a hollow language was left.

Gaps between word and world were also widened by the experience of exile, one shared in various ways by what critics have often considered a surprising number of modernist authors. Joseph

Conrad was a Pole who travelled the world before settling in Britain; Ford Madox Hueffer – who changed his name to Ford during the First World War – was of German extraction; Henry James was originally American before becoming a country gentleman in Sussex and eventually seeking British citizenship. Though D.H. Lawrence was native-born in Nottinghamshire, much of his life was passed abroad, eventually in Italy and Mexico, fleeing Britain in ways some of his characters contemplate in *Women in Love*. Born in Nova Scotia, Wyndham Lewis spent several of his formative years, early in the century, wandering on the continent. Dorothy Richardson grew up in London, but left by the age of 17 to work, like her heroine Miriam Henderson, as an English language teacher in a school in Germany.

Miriam's experience of this polyglot school community with its babble of conflicting languages – French, German, strange versions of English – provides one basis for her conclusion, quoted earlier, that 'language is the only way of expressing anything and it dims everything'. Another basis for this conclusion, however, was available to Richardson, or to any woman writer, even without leaving Britain. Unusually among modernist authors, Virginia Woolf was British both by origin and domicile: her Bloomsbury literary circle, and the London setting for *Mrs Dalloway*, seem to place her at the heart of metropolitan culture. Yet Woolf points to an inescapable form of exile, for all women writers, when she talks (in the passage from *A Room of One's Own* quoted in Chapter 2) about feeling 'outside . . . alien and critical' even when walking through Whitehall in central London. This sense of exile, of partial exclusion from a male-dominated culture and society, Woolf sees as having particular consequences for the language of women's writing. She explains in *A Room of One's Own* that for a woman novelist

> it is useless to go to the great men writers for help . . . the first thing she would find, setting pen to paper, was that there was no common sentence ready for her use . . . a man's sentence . . . was unsuited for a woman's use. (p. 76)

Dorothy Richardson likewise asks for a 'feminine prose' to escape the constraints of a male language unsuited to her purposes. Miriam Henderson discusses some of these restrictions and points to the disparities between the language of men and women when she remarks that

> In speech with a man a woman is at a disadvantage – because they speak
> different languages. She may understand his. Hers he will never speak nor
> understand . . . she must therefore, stammeringly, speak his. (II, p. 210)

Yet no woman, Miriam adds, can ever reveal 'her mental measure
. . . even the fringe of her consciousness' by speaking the language
of men (II, p. 210). Since culture is constructed in what Miriam
sees as effectively a foreign language, she finds 'there was nothing
to turn to. Books were poisoned. Art. All the achievements of men
were poisoned at the root' (II, p. 222).

Miriam's comments – like those of Richardson herself, or
Virginia Woolf – highlight a specific, aggravated, lack of 'common
measure' between women's consciousness and the conventional
language and forms available to express it. This lack contributed to
a certain state of exile, metaphorically at least, for women at the
time, though in a way a fruitful one. Uneasiness with ordinary
language and consequent readiness to reject conventional forms of
representation almost forced women writers, in the early twentieth
century, to take on the role outlined in Chapter 2 – as prime
movers of modernist innovation and stylistic experiment. Being
partly outside a culture, alien and critical, is not likely to be a
comfortable position, but may be a productive one, provoking re-
examination and reconstruction of that culture's conventional
forms and styles.

Exile in reality – geographic rather than only metaphoric –
affected modernist authors and their work in a variety of ways.
Some of Conrad and James's personal experience as foreigners
may be reflected in the regular interest of their novels in a 'first-
person singular' – one who is often a lonely stranger, gradually
puzzling out the demands of a complex new environment. Sea-life
and experience of empire, with all their conflicting diversities of
race and culture, also challenged Conrad in particular with a sense
of the relativity and provisionality of all world-views. For Conrad,
who spoke French as well as Polish before he learned English,
language was a crucial component of such diversity and relativity,
one often examined in his fiction. The speech of some of the minor
narrators who add to Marlow's story in *Lord Jim*, for example, and
of several of the other characters, shows strong traces of syntax or
vocabulary retained from languages more familiar to them than
English. Thus when he provides Marlow with the account of how

he helped rescue the *Patna*, the French Lieutenant describes as follows his first encounter with the ship's frightened passengers:

> '*Impossible de comprendre – vous concevez* . . . They crowded upon us. There was a circle round that dead man (*autour de ce mort*) . . . One had to attend to the most pressing. These people were beginning to agitate themselves – *Parbleu!*' (p. 108)

Malay vocabulary and speech patterns figure in the language of several characters, and the wise old German merchant, Stein, draws his conclusions about Jim and about life in general in a manner as bilingual as the French Lieutenant's:

> Because you not always can keep your eyes shut there comes the real trouble – the heart pain – the world pain . . . You not strong enough are, or not clever enough. Ja! (p. 163)

When recording the language of the Captain who takes Jim to Patusan – whose 'flowing English seemed to be derived from a dictionary compiled by a lunatic' (p. 182), and who talks of 'laughable hyaenas' and the 'weapons of a crocodile' – Conrad's polylingual speech forms move towards the absurd.

Throughout *Lord Jim*, however, alternation between languages principally emphasizes the absurdity of what one character calls the attempt to 'see a thing as it is' (p. 130), and affirms in its own way the kind of conclusion Miriam Henderson reaches when she remarks that 'everything depends upon the way a thing is put, and that is a question of some particular civilization'. Conrad's careful particularization of points of view, for each of the multiple narrators of *Lord Jim*, highlights the way any account of reality is coloured by the nature and outlook of individual observers. The novel also shows how any such individual outlook is further particularized by the qualities of the language in which it is framed. Like *Ulysses*, *Lord Jim* shows that nothing can be known absolutely 'as it is': nothing can be seen independently of ways of seeing it which are specific to individuals, the civilizations to which they belong, and ultimately the languages that they speak. Throughout, Conrad's polyglot colonial context contributes to a sense of exile not only from individual nations or civilizations, but from reality itself. Juxtaposition of different languages emphasizes the arbitrariness of each, and the incompleteness of their contact with a world that exists across 'a broad gulf that neither eye nor voice could span' (p. 256). Many of the novel's crucial moments take place in a silence which mocks the powers of the word. While Jim is soundlessly agonizing about missed chances of glory, Marlow occupies himself with writing endless, purposeless letters. When Jim makes his final, suicidal decision to present himself to Doramin's fury, his journal records 'I must now at once ... ' – followed by nothing except a blot in the shape of the head of an arrow (p. 256), as if disaster could be drawn but not described. As Marlow reflects, language can never achieve fullness, or final consummation of the desires of its speakers, or a true encapsulation of their world:

> the last word is not said . . . Are not our lives too short for that full utterance which through all our stammerings is of course our only and abiding intention? I have given up expecting those last words, whose ring, if they could only be pronounced, would shake both heaven and earth . . . The heaven and the earth must not be shaken. (pp. 171–2)

Joyce was as thorough an exile as Conrad, and as thoroughly immersed in foreign languages. Like his hero Stephen Dedalus, Joyce left Ireland in order to 'forge . . . the uncreated conscience' of his race, working as an English teacher in Trieste and elsewhere in Italy before moving on to Zurich in 1915 and then settling in Paris after the war. Lengthy foreign domicile and work – like Dorothy Richardson's – as a teacher of English placed Joyce permanently in a context of linguistic contrasts and conflicts after he left Ireland in 1904. Yet in some ways this experience began even earlier, as an inevitable part of Joyce's Irishness, and of Ireland's position within the British Empire during his early years there. This is suggested in *A Portrait of the Artist as a Young Man* when Stephen encounters an English priest and reflects that

> The language in which we are speaking is his before it is mine. How different are the words *home, Christ, ale, master*, on his lips and on mine! I cannot speak or write these words without unrest of spirit. His language, so familiar and so foreign, will always be for me an acquired speech. I have not made or accepted its words. My voice holds them at bay. My soul frets in the shadow of his language. (p. 189)

Stephen's 'fretting' against standard English, and its status for him as 'acquired speech', help account for his fascination with words and for his sense of their existence partly independently of meaning or 'associations' – perhaps even for his expertise with the language, which he turns out to know better, in some ways, than his English interlocutor. For Joyce himself, a lifetime among the shadows of many languages added to the critical, objective distance from standard English – familiar enough, yet the language of a foreign, imperial power – established in his Dublin youth. Such critical distance can be seen to underlie the parody, verbal play and lack of easy transparency in the language of *Ulysses*, and the eventual creation in *Finnegans Wake* of a polyglot, autonomous language in which English can sometimes only barely be seen.

The last line of *Ulysses* – not Molly's 'yes', but the record of where the novel was written, in 'Trieste-Zurich-Paris' – therefore provides an insight into the nature of Joyce's writing as a whole. It is also relevant to other contemporary authors, and in some ways to the development of modernism generally. Fretting against foreign languages – unfamiliar yet obviously functional systems of words – confirms a sense of arbitrariness in the relation of signifier and signified, and a need for language and representation to become subjects of enquiry. Awareness of foreign cultures and literatures – of their different habits of mind and ways of envisaging the world – may also have heightened some modernist authors' critical awareness of conventions of language and culture in which they worked themselves, adding to their readiness to reshape or abandon these conventions in favour of new techniques. In this way, not only women writers, but all modernist exiles may have found the experience of being 'outside . . . alien and critical' a provocative, shaping influence in the evolution of their art. It should not be thought surprising, or only an intriguing coincidence, that so many modernists were exiles. Exile encouraged concentration on a lonely self, partly independent of a surrounding society. More generally, it provided a strong incentive to reconsider and reconstruct literary forms – to engage in the stylistic and structural innovation which became the defining characteristic of modernism.

Mikhail Bakhtin's theories of narrative and language further clarify why this was so. Chapter 2 mentioned Bakhtin's view of the language of the novel as essentially 'a *system* of languages that mutually and ideologically interanimate each other' (p. 47). In this polyphonic or (in Bakhtin's terminology) 'polyglossic' system, simultaneous allegiances to more than one language – or form of

language – fret, compete and interfuse. Such tension and fretting
between languages Bakhtin shows to be fundamental to the origins
as well as to the continuing existence of the novel. Historically, the
novel genre first developed at a time when the autonomy of
national languages was being challenged – when

> the period of national languages, coexisting but closed and deaf to each other,
> comes to an end. Languages throw light on each other: one language can, after
> all, see itself only in the light of another language . . . In this actively polyglot
> world, completely new relationships are established between language and its
> object (that is, the real world) . . . the novel emerged and matured precisely
> when intense activization of external and internal polyglossia was at the peak of
> its activity; this is its native element . . .
>
> Thus did the interanimation of languages occur in the very epoch that saw the
> creation of the European novel. Laughter and polyglossia had paved the way for
> the novelistic discourse of modern times. (pp. 12, 82)

If, as Bakhtin shows, 'interanimation of languages' is fundamental
to the creation and development of the novel, *re*creation and *re*-
development of the genre – the business of modernism – may also
be likeliest to occur at historical points at which 'intense peaks' of
polyglossia recur. The opening years of the twentieth century con-
stitute such a point, a point when contacts between foreign and
native elements of speech and culture were once again a regular,
everyday experience of many people, and many authors. For the
complex of historical and cultural reasons examined above, new
relations were once again established between language and its
object. The new 'autonomy of language', bereft of the absolute
certainty or transparency which Foucault sees characterizing its
earlier relations with reality, created at the time a linguistic shift as
profound as the epistemological shift earlier discussed. A 'new
artist of the word', in Eugene Jolas's description, reshaped the
novel around new perceptions of the nature of language, as well as
new outlooks on the world in general.

This peculiar position of language in the early twentieth century,
and the general stress on means of representation, can therefore
be seen not only as an anxiety for the literature of the time but as
among the conditions and challenges which brought modernism
into being. Lack of 'common measure' between mind and word,
word and world, may be disturbing, but it demands new creativity

and new forms. It encouraged modernist authors – the greatest of them, James Joyce, in particular – to draw upon and recreate for the modernist period some of what Bakhtin defines as the novel's deepest powers. Laughter, celebration, mockery and parody Bakhtin sees as fundamental conditions of the novel's origins, with many continuing echoes throughout the subsequent history of the genre. Bakhtin traces the novel's polyglossic nature, its competing 'system of languages', back to the bawdy, irreverent, radical, liberating, energies of popular carnival in the middle ages. In these celebrations, 'parodic and travestying forms . . . kept alive the memory of . . . linguistic struggle' (p. 67), and through mockery and satire resisted the narrowing, deadening effects of official, institutionalized culture and language. Surviving echoes or re-animations of these conditions of origin Bakhtin defines as a continuing 'carnivalesque' aspect of the novel. Wit, humour and play make *Ulysses* a thoroughly carnivalesque text. Joyce mocks and parodies the styles of institutions and officialdom; of science; of journalism and of advertising – as well as of literary language and everyday speech. *Ulysses* is thoroughly heterogeneous and inventive in its use of words, constantly shifting and reorienting its language around the various speech patterns of its characters and avoiding any single, narrowing, register of its own. It is hugely, sometimes grotesquely, affirmative of the body, life and sex. 'Linguistic struggle' and the fretting of language figure in *Ulysses* not as difficulty but as excitement; not as painful necessities for the novel to deal with, but as sources of energy and interest for the text to exploit – above all, as a context for the display of Joyce's own extraordinary virtuosity with words.

Not every reader or critic finds this virtuosity happily or even accessibly extended in *Finnegans Wake*. Yet the inaccessibility of ordinary meaning is a necessary condition – in a way a virtue – of a text which goes much further even than *Ulysses* in exploiting and celebrating aspects of language other than the semantic. An admirer of Bakhtin, Julia Kristeva, suggests in discussing Joyce and other authors that 'resistance against modernist literature' (p. 142) often results from what she calls 'an obsession of meaning' – a failure to appreciate the full range of language's joys and powers. Her warning is particularly relevant to *Finnegans Wake*. Locating Joyce firmly in Bakhtin's category of the carnivalesque, Kristeva suggests that readers should understand that the aim of [his] practice, which reaches us as a language, is . . . not only to impose a music, a rhythm – that is, a polyphony – but also to wipe out sense through nonsense and laughter. This is a difficult operation that obliges the reader not so much to combine significations as to shatter his own judging consciousness. (p. 142)

Kristeva's approval of 'nonsense and laughter' wiping out sense offers a way to 'rede the world' Joyce constructs, independently of too much anxiety about its ordinary intelligibility. Obsession with meaning, as she points out, obscures the capacity of words to approximate to the condition of music as well as to convey ordinary sense; to create a rhythm and polyphony able to draw on powers deeper than those of intellect and meaning. In *A la recherche du temps perdu*, Proust considers music a 'means of communication between souls' which 'might have been – if the invention of language, the formation of words, the analysis of ideas had not intervened' (III, p. 260). Fascinated by sounds and their qualities throughout his fiction, Joyce, on the other hand, considers the possibilities offered by music always available – sometimes even more fully available – in language itself. In *A Portrait of the Artist as a Young Man*, Stephen finds 'the soft beauty of the . . . word' possessed of 'a touch fainter and more persuading than the touch of music' (p. 244). Chapter 11 of *Ulysses*, 'Sirens', opens with two pages of fragmentary, syncopated, onomatopoeic phrases, barely communicative of sense but resonant with the random sounds of the city – a kind of urban word-jazz, typical of modernism's invention of new styles in response to the jarring rhythms of city life; and of a verbal music to be heard in various ways and at many stages of *Ulysses*.

Such verbal music is audible throughout *Finnegans Wake*, which Samuel Beckett suggests 'is not to be read – or rather it is not only to be read. It is to be looked at and listened to'.[15] While Lily Briscoe complains in *To the Lighthouse* of 'little words that broke up the thought and dismembered it', the language of *Finnegans Wake* partly gives up thought and the compromised, doubtful relations of word and world, re-membering instead other powers of language – rhythmic, musical, close to Bernard's demand in *The Waves* for the spontaneous 'howl and cry'; remote from the corruption of meaning in public language wrought by the rhetoric of the First World War; resistant to the intellect's narrowing 'analysis of ideas' which made language, not only for Lily Briscoe but for so many writers and thinkers in the early twentieth century, not a reliable means of representation but a kind of prison for imagination and emotion. More than any other text in the history of fiction, *Finnegans Wake* achieves the condition of 'words-in-freedom' which one of F.T. Marinetti's Futurist Manifestos identified in 1913 as the likely way ahead for literature.

It is another question whether the joys of such a free, polyphonic, multi-layered language are best appreciated at the lengths to which Joyce extends them in *Finnegans Wake*, or whether they may offer a way ahead for poetry as much as fiction. At any rate, however fully or finally the methods of *Finnegans Wake* can be justified, they can be seen as full – perhaps final – extensions of modernism's concern and experimentation with language and its new, autonomous role in the modern age. Since it is difficult in some ways to see how Joyce's experimentation could be taken much further, and since *Finnegans Wake* was eventually published in the conveniently epochal year of 1939, it is often held to mark a kind of final terminus for modernism itself.

## MODERNISM AND POSTMODERNISM

Finnegans, however, never end but always begin again, and *Finnegans Wake* marks in twentieth-century writing a point of transition or new beginning and not only conclusion. Though in one way it is a final extension of modernist self-consciousness about art, representation and language, as such *Finnegans Wake* is also an antecedent for a self-referential, self-conscious writing – what Fredric Jameson defines as a 'language-centred postmodernism' – which has followed.[16] Several other critics have seen Joyce's 'autonomy of language' and 'new art of the word' helping instigate a phase of writing which extends – though into distinctly new areas – some of the initiatives of modernism. Christopher Butler uses *After the Wake* (1980) as the title of his 'Essay on the Contemporary Avant-Garde', and Ihab Hassan talks of *Finnegans Wake* as 'a "monstrous prophecy of our postmodernity"' . . . both augur and theory of a certain kind of literature' (pp. xiii–xiv).

The progress of Joyce's writing towards *Finnegans Wake* also helps confirm distinctions between modernism and postmodernism established in Brian McHale's study *Postmodernist Fiction* (1987).

McHale considers modernism dominated by epistemological questions and postmodernism by ontological ones. The epistemological shift and general changes in outlook at the end of the nineteenth century led modernism to question and experiment with ways reality can be known or assimilated – however uncertainly – by mind or text. Postmodernism extends such uncertainty radically, often assuming reality – if it exists at all – to be quite unknowable; no longer accessible through forms of representation, language in particular, which have become detached from it. Postmodernism investigates instead what separate worlds can be projected or constructed by language and text themselves, and how they interrelate. In terms of this argument, *A Portrait of the Artist as a Young Man*, for example, can be seen still to share in the generally epistemological interests of modernism. On that day of dappled seaborne clouds, words still seem more or less able to harmonize with or reflect 'the glowing sensible world', though Stephen thoroughly questions this relation and whether the primary pleasure or purpose of language is to be found in it. In *Finnegans Wake*, on the other hand, a fractured relation between word and world is no longer a matter of question but of assumption. Contact with a recognizable world is overwhelmed, in McHale's view, by 'the competing reality of language' (p. 234), which establishes *Finnegans Wake* as an ontologically separate, autonomous domain.

If this kind of development helped to make *Finnegans Wake* an augur and a prophecy, as Ihab Hassan suggests, what did it prophesy, and what literature did it inaugurate? Fulfilment of some of its 'prophecy' is apparent in the fiction of Samuel Beckett. Aware of Joyce's work throughout its progress, and occasionally a critical defender of it, Beckett was one of the first to respond to its 'autonomy of language'. In his outstanding work of fiction, the trilogy *Molloy, Malone Dies, The Unnamable* (1950–2), the Unnamable remarks, 'it all boils down to a question of words . . . all words, there's nothing else' (pp. 308, 381). Each of the trilogy's ageing narrators compensates for his failing life by spinning out distracting stories – endless, evasive artifices in words. Yet each constantly demonstrates and comments upon the inadequacies of the linguistic medium he employs. Language and the nature of narrative imagination are thus continually the subject of the trilogy. Contact with extra-textual reality is further overwhelmed by the eventual exposure of each narrator as only an imaginative figment or device of a subsequent one – a means whereby he has sought to distract himself from the 'black void' around him (p. 278). Typically of postmodernism, fictional worlds are unstable, revealing – even flaunting – their constructed, artificial qualities. Progressive revelation in Beckett's trilogy that all its storytellers and the worlds they create are no more than narrative devices and verbal constructs establishes a kind of autonomy of fiction or imagination, extending the autonomy of language and its continuously self-questioning discourse. Beckett's novels reveal themselves as fictions about the creation of fiction, demonstrating yet undermining the potentials of language and narrative as consolations for the black emptiness of life.

Flann O'Brien's *At Swim-Two-Birds* (1939) follows more cheerfully in the wake of Joyce. It is another fantasy, like *Finnegans Wake*, about a Dublin publican, though one whose sleep is troubled by more than dreams. O'Brien's publican is also an author, one who tries to control his characters by locking them up at night to limit their incessant drinking. Unfortunately, they escape while he sleeps, taking over his narrative themselves and filling it with bizarre tortures for their creator. Like Beckett's trilogy, *At Swim-Two-Birds* is thus a story about telling a story about storytelling, with much reflection about the nature of storytelling, the novel's own methods not least, also included. Each work extends in this way the autonomy, the ontological separateness and self-reflexiveness, of *Finnegans Wake*. Each is also a postmodernist paradigm, a prophecy of the self-reflexive foregrounding of language and fiction-making which has expanded in later writing and grown into a distinguishing characteristic of postmodernism. The French experimental novelist Alain Robbe-Grillet remarked in the 1960s that 'after Joyce' and other modernists

> it seems that we are more and more moving towards an age of fiction in which the problems of writing will be lucidly envisaged by the novelist, and in which his concern with critical matters, far from sterilising his creative faculties, will on the contrary supply him with motive power . . .
>
> Invention and imagination may finally become the subject of the book. (pp. 46–7, 63)

Especially since the 1960s, invention and imagination have indeed become more and more frequently the subject of the novel. A great many authors in recent decades have expanded on the self-consciousness of modernist art; writing stories about storytelling, or intruding into the fiction to comment on their own practice and proceedings, or to discuss other problems in relating language, fiction and reality. Among many others, Lawrence Durrell, Doris Lessing, John Fowles, Christine Brooke-Rose, Rayner Heppenstall, John Berger, B.S. Johnson and Alasdair Gray all engage in such ways in a postmodernist experimentation continuing at the present day.

Their work can also be related to a postmodern idiom much more widely apparent in a range of contemporary cultural forms and thinking. 'Postmodern' is a term still variously defined, but most commentators would agree that the increasing examination of language and representation within recent fiction can be seen as part of a wider postmodern challenge to all theories, explanations or versions of life – part of a widespread contemporary scepticism of all constructions of reality. Such scepticism is in one way appropriate to an era more than ever enthralled by its media, and by the commercial interests of Press and advertisers – an era in which it is more than ever essential to see language and image not as innocent means of representing a world, but as inevitably bound up with intentions to control it. Though more powerful and sinister in the latter half of the twentieth century, such intentions have of course been in evidence from the beginning – part of the modern industrial and financial world's determination to control imagination and desire as firmly as it had come to rule time and space by the end of the nineteenth century; part of the new conditions of modern life to which the modernists were forced, in ways further considered in the next chapter, to react.

As it differs at least in emphasis from its modernist predecessor, however, further discussion of postmodernism lies outwith the scope of this study. Its consequential relation to modernism is nevertheless worth stressing for at least two reasons. First, it can help to define the term 'postmodernism', which sometimes seems to grow vaguer as it is more and more fashionably and frequently employed. What McHale calls the 'element of logical and historical *consequence*' with which 'postmodernism follows *from* modernism' (p. 5) helps place recent writing within a clear critical and historical perspective. Secondly, looking at recent postmodernist writing in terms of its antecedents shows that – despite changing historical stresses, discussed in the next chapter, which moved the novel substantially away from modernism, even during the early 1930s – modernist initiatives distinctly survived and went on to shape a whole phase of the fiction that followed. Despite general changes of interest at the time, these modernist initiatives were in some instances carried forward into later writing by authors whose work actually began in the 1930s: not only Samuel Beckett and Flann O'Brien, but also Lawrence Durrell, Malcolm Lowry and Jean Rhys.

Postmodernism is in any case only the most obvious and thoroughgoing of later beneficiaries of modernism. Greatly enlarging what Ezra Pound once called 'the international store of literary technique',[17] modernism's innovative styles have continued to influence later authors much more generally. Without necessarily engaging in the radical self-questioning of postmodernism, writers since the 1930s have often simply borrowed or adopted techniques – for entering individual consciousness, or reshaping the chronology of the novel, or generally re-examining the resources of language and imagination – which modernism spectacularly established in the early decades of the century. Modernism's influence on writing, as the century ends, continues to be felt as the major new initiative to have appeared during it.

## ───── 5 ─────

# *VALUE*

## THE END OF MODERNISM

> In 1930 it was impossible – if you were young, sensitive, imaginative –
> not to be interested in politics; not to find public causes of much more
> pressing interest than philosophy. In 1930 young men . . . were forced
> to be aware of what was happening in Russia; in Germany; in Italy; in
> Spain. They could not go on discussing aesthetic emotions and per-
> sonal relations . . . they had to read the politicians. They read Marx.
> They became communists; they became anti-fascists.
>
> (Virginia Woolf, 'The Leaning Tower', 1940)[1]

Not all the 'young men' Woolf refers to conformed immediately to
the pattern she outlines in 'The Leaning Tower'. At least one member of 'the group which began to write about 1925' (p. 170) whom
she considers in her essay, Christopher Isherwood, went on discussing 'aesthetic emotions and personal relations' in his early fiction in
ways similar to those of the modernists. Isherwood later acknowledged that he had 'learned a few lessons from these masters and put
them into practice':[2] clear 'echoes', as he calls them, of the work of
James Joyce and Virgina Woolf appear in his first two novels, *All the
Conspirators* (1928) and *The Memorial* (1932). In each, interior
monologue often predominates over conversation or action, much
as it does in Woolf's fiction. In *All the Conspirators*, there are also
sections of randomly associating thoughts closer to the stream-of-
consciousness method of Joyce, and the novel's concern with art and
writing – sometimes apparently autobiographical – resembles
Joyce's interests in *A Portrait of the Artist as a Young Man* (1916), or
Woolf's use of the artist Lily Briscoe in *To the Lighthouse* (1927).
The structure and temporality of *The Memorial* also profit from
some of the 'lessons' of modernism. Its sections are headed '1928',
'1920', '1925' and '1929': conventional chronology is further

renounced, in favour of 'time in the mind', by the intense memories and recollections which break into the characters' interior monologues. Repeated flashbacks and deferred explanations show Isherwood apparently acting on Ford Madox Ford's explanation that 'to get . . . a man in fiction you could not begin at his beginning . . . you must . . . work backwards and forwards over his past'. Isherwood later explained that in *The Memorial* he tried 'to start in the middle and go backwards, then forwards again . . . time is circular, which sounds Einstein-ish and brilliantly modern'.[3]

Such 'brilliantly modern' techniques make *The Memorial* an outstanding late modernist novel. A significant aspect of Isherwood's modernist technique, however, is how quickly it disappears from his fiction later in the 1930s. His next novel, *Mr Norris Changes Trains* (1935), has little of the structural complexity or inward registration of thought which mark *The Memorial* and *All the Conspirators*. Instead, it is largely straightforward in chronology, and visual and descriptive in recording its characters' behaviour and details of their lives in the city of Berlin. *Goodbye to Berlin* (1939) is similar. Preference for direct, uncomplicated contact with observed reality is emphasized by Isherwood's narrator describing himself as 'a camera with its shutter open, quite passive, recording, not thinking' (p. 11). In a way, of course, a genuinely 'passive recording' is unrealizable: just as a camera has to be pointed somewhere, any recording in language is 'pointed' by its point of view and style. Nevertheless, Isherwood's idea of the narrator as a camera shows how far he had moved away from modernism by the end of the 1930s. Discussing Joyce's work in 1929, Eugene Jolas suggests that 'the epoch when the writer photographed the life about him with the mechanics of words . . . is happily drawing to its close'. Writing ten years later, Isherwood apparently wanted to open up this epoch once again. Though *All the Conspirators* and *The Memorial* so clearly 'echo' modernist determination to 'illumine the mind within rather than the world without', in the 1930s Isherwood's priorities reversed – 'the world without', rather than inward attention to mind and consciousness, becoming the principal focus of his attention.

Isherwood's career is exemplary in this way, indicating the shape and strength of modernist influences at the end of the 1920s, but also how these seemed to fade in the decade which followed. Modernist fiction continued to appear during it, of course –

Woolf's *The Waves* in 1931; Joyce's *Finnegans Wake* in 1939; the early novels of some of the writers mentioned at the end of Chapter 4 – but in general the 1930s are considered a period of decline or redirection of modernism's innovative energies. Many of the generation of novelists Woolf discusses, emerging in the late 1920s, followed the same pattern of development as Isherwood, or more or less began from the conclusion – in favour of realist rather than modernist methods – which he eventually reached. Both George Orwell and Graham Greene, for example, sometimes echo the modernists. Orwell's third chapter in *A Clergyman's Daughter* (1935) resembles the 'Nighttown' section (Chapter 15) of *Ulysses*, and the interior monologues and occasional stream of consciousness of Greene's *England Made Me* (1935) also suggest a debt to Joyce. Such echoes, however, are occasional and fragmentary in work which is on the whole much more conventional in style. Greene talks of favouring 'straight sentences, no involutions' in order to 'present the outside world economically and exactly'[4] and Orwell deliberately looks back to model his strategies on the work of writers modernism rejected, such as H.G. Wells.

In 'The Leaning Tower', Woolf indicates several factors – some obvious, some more complex – which help account for this general movement away from modernist methods in the 1930s. As the passage already quoted suggests, novelists were inevitably subject to the intensifying pressure of the decade's politics and 'public causes'. By the mid-1930s British writers – and to some extent the general public – were uneasily aware of the rise of Hitler in Germany; of the continuing menace of Mussolini in Italy; perhaps above all, of the Spanish Civil War. Though Woolf remarks that there was 'neither war nor revolution in England itself', there was nevertheless 'the influence of change . . . the threat of war' (II, p. 170). In fact, the economic depression which followed the collapse of the Wall Street stock market late in 1929 – as well as facilitating Hitler's rise to power in Germany – thoroughly changed and dominated British affairs throughout the 1930s. Even by 1931, the pound had been devalued, the Labour Party ousted by a National Government brought in to deal with the emergency, and unemployment had reached a scale which provoked hunger marches and riots.

Such crises, domestic as well as international, were likely to have discouraged 1930s novelists – as Woolf suggests – from continuing to write about the kind of 'aesthetic emotions', profound relations, or subjective states which had occupied the attention of the modernists. Young men or young women writing in 1930 might have been drawn back to realist style – to presenting the outside world economically and exactly – simply by the urgency of what was happening in that world, in reality itself. A major factor in Christopher Isherwood's change of tactics between *The Memorial* and *Mr Norris Changes Trains*, for example, might have been the need to represent to the British public as clearly and immediately as possible the threat of Adolf Hitler, one which Isherwood had discovered for himself on visits to Berlin in the early 1930s. A lucid, documentary style, with the supposed exactness and objectivity of a camera, 'recording, not thinking', might have seemed the best possible means of communicating the threatening political problems of the time.

Background and education also disposed members of Isherwood's generation to concentrate on these problems. Woolf points out in 'The Leaning Tower' that for her own generation, the modernist generation,

> when the crash came in 1914 all those . . . who were to be the representative writers of their time, had their past, their education, safe behind them, safe within them. They had known security; they had the memory of a peaceful boyhood, the knowledge of a settled civilisation. (pp. 169–70)

Far from having 'their education safe within them' by 1914, Isherwood's generation found the First World War a significant background in their schooling. As Woolf points out, many of the new writers emerging in the 1930s had been educated at public school, a conservative environment likely to have forced them into reacting against establishment values that seemed thoroughly complicit with the conduct of the war. This common educational background may have contributed to a later readiness to 'become communists or anti-fascists'; to adopt anti-establishment political commitments heightening their attentiveness to the 'public causes' of their time. As W.W. Robson remarks, for many writers in the 1930s 'the red flag was intertwined with the old school tie' (p. 127).

Immediate events and 'public causes' in any case had a different and in some ways more inescapable importance for writers in the 1930s than for the modernists. Modernist writers were of course thoroughly challenged themselves by public causes and events: these could hardly have been more disturbing than they were

during the First World War. The difference, however, as Woolf
indicates, is that the modernists were able to look back to a more
stable pre-war period – to return in memory, as Woolf suggests, to
'a settled civilisation'. As Chapter 3 explained, memories of
security lost in the past encouraged the modernists to reshape time
and history in their fiction; to re-establish connections with a vanished epoch. In *A la recherche du temps perdu* (1913–27) and in *To
the Lighthouse* (1927), Proust and Woolf indicate the recovery of
the past through art and memory as one of few consolations available to a generation living on in a desolate post-war world. Such
consolation was difficult enough for the modernists to establish: it
was still less accessible to the generation which succeeded them.

This is reflected in the dates Isherwood chooses for the four
sections of *The Memorial* – 1920, 1928, 1925, 1929. However much
the younger generation of writers wished to follow the modernists
in reshaping time and history in their fiction – in working 'backwards and forwards over the past' – there were difficulties for them
in extending this process back into the more peaceful years before
the war. For Christopher Isherwood, born in 1904, and his contemporaries, these years and the 'knowledge of a settled civilisation'
which they offered existed at most as recollections of early childhood – the kind of youthful memory which fails in the end to
provide much real escape from the approaching Second World
War in George Orwell's *Coming up for Air* (1939). Perhaps as a
result, Orwell and Isherwood's generation was readier than the
modernists to deal with contemporary history not through imaginative strategies which transformed or sought to escape its processes, but through direct, political commitment to transforming
reality and historical process themselves. Lacking a settled civilization in adult memory, writers in the 1930s were more disposed to
commit themselves to the creation of one in actuality; to espouse
the political ideologies – communism or socialism – likeliest to
assist in this process; and to direct their fiction at the immediate
'public causes' and political problems of their world.

## THE EVASIONS OF MODERNISM

A disposition to deal directly with political issues led not only to
the shift away from modernist styles and structures exemplified by

Isherwood's writing, but at times to hostile criticism of modernism, often on the grounds of its supposed evasiveness and self-indulgence. Looking back on the modernist inclination of his early novels, Isherwood comments ruefully on the 'excessive reverence for Mrs Woolf' which had marked this stage of his writing. Other contemporary novelists rejected modernism more vehemently. In his essay 'Inside the Whale' (1940), George Orwell suggests of the modernists that

> what is noticeable about all these writers is that what 'purpose' they have is very much up in the air. There is no attention to the urgent problems of the moment, above all no politics in the narrower sense . . . when one looks back at the 1920s . . . in 'cultured' circles art-for-art's sake extended practically to a worship of the meaningless. Literature was supposed to consist solely in the manipulation of words.[5]

Factors which turned novelists against styles which had dominated the previous decade also affected 1930s critics, some of whom denounced modernism in terms similar to Orwell's, or stronger. Commitment to communism and anti-fascism encouraged interest in what was happening in Russia at the time: some British critics were therefore quickly aware of Karl Radek's famous denunciation of modernism at the Soviet Writers Congress of 1934, and inclined to extend its implications in their own work.[6] Philip Henderson, for example, incorporates a reference to Radek's attack on Joyce into his highly critical assessment of modernism in *The Novel Today: Studies in Contemporary Attitudes* (1936). Henderson considers that

> it is the duty of writers, as those who express the creative needs of the race, not only to hope for the establishment of a reasonable society, but actively to assist, as writers, towards bringing such a society into being. (p. 52)

He therefore regrets that 'many modern writers dare not look too closely at social reality' (p. 14) but choose instead to remain 'emmeshed in the chaos of subjectivism' (p. 81). Reacting to 'a sense of the collapse of their world', modernist writers, in Henderson's view,

> retired further and further into private worlds detached from social reality, their characters attempting to lead lives either entirely on an intense emotional, passional plane as with Lawrence, or on a plane of aesthetic abstraction and contemplative withdrawal from all significant activity whatsoever, as in the case of Joyce and Virginia Woolf. (p. 103)

Henderson's criticism of modernism's 'detachment from social reality' was echoed by other commentators at the time, such as Alick West, in *Crisis and Criticism* (1937), or Ralph Fox, who complains in *The Novel and the People* (1937) of a 'false outlook on life . . . in Proust and Joyce' and of their apparent reluctance to see 'the individual as a whole, as a social individual' (p. 105).

Adverse criticism of modernist writers was not new in the 1930s: many of the first reactions to their work, to Joyce's *Ulysses* in particular, express a more complete – sometimes shocked – rejection than anything which came later. Criticism from the 1930s, however, remains particularly significant in two ways. First, its preference for 'social reality' – rather than anything 'emmeshed in the subjective' – helps define the climate of opinion in which modernism slipped away from the more central position it had occupied in the literary imagination of the previous decade. Secondly, views expressed by Henderson and others in the 1930s indicate directions followed by some later critics and expanded into more thoroughgoing, substantial rejections of modernism. Thus in 'The Ideology of Modernism' (1957) Georg Lukács develops more fully and influentially much the same sort of thinking as Henderson follows in the passages quoted above. For Lukács, as for Henderson, modernism is limited by its characters' existence in 'private worlds, detached from social reality'. Lukács considers that 'attenuation of reality underlies Joyce's stream of consciousness': this 'rejection of narrative objectivity, the surrender to subjectivity' contributes to 'reduction of reality to a nightmare' – to a vision of 'ghostly un-reality, of a nightmare world'. In this nightmare modernist world, both social relationships and their historical context seem to Lukács to disappear:

> in the work of leading modernist writers . . . Man . . . is by nature solitary, asocial, unable to enter into relationships with other human beings . . . Man, thus conceived, is an ahistorical being.

By directing attention away from social reality, and through what Lukács calls 'the denial of history, of development, and thus, of perspective', modernist writing establishes an 'assumption that the objective world is inherently inexplicable' and therefore beyond improvement or change. For Lukács,

the ideology of most modernist writers asserts the unalterability of outward reality
. . . human activity is, *a priori*, rendered impotent and robbed of meaning.[7]

Lukács is worth quoting at length, as he provides what is probably still the most reasoned and influential negative view of modernism, one necessary to consider in any assessment of this phase
of writing. Moreover, Lukács's thinking is typical of a wider range
of negative reactions. Though not all criticism of modernism is
based on its supposed lack of political or social relevance, most
hostile views do take something of the same form as Lukács's.
Hugh Walpole, for example, found faults in modernism additional
to those identified by other commentators in the 1930s – complaining of what he calls the 'modern' phase of recent fiction that 'there
*is* a moral world, and . . . the novelists of [this] generation are
losing a great deal by disregarding it' (p. 29). Though emphasizing
different priorities, Walpole's reasoning remains fundamentally
comparable to Lukács's. For each, modernism ignores conventional fiction's capacity to contribute wisdom or ideas to the organization of ordinary life and the social sphere. This 'attenuation of
reality' leaves modernism out of touch with the world and the most
significant aspects of its experience – political, in Lukács's view;
moral in Walpole's. A reply to Lukács's criticisms, therefore, can
also help answer other commentators and critics, contributing to a
concluding evaluation of modernist writing in general.

It might be supposed that such a reply could be based easily on
the fiction of D.H. Lawrence, shown throughout this study to be
thoroughly concerned with new social pressures in what he calls 'the
modern industrial and financial world'. 'The Industrial Magnate'
chapter of *Women in Love* probably gives as full an account as any
twentieth-century novel of the restructuring of industry around Taylorist imperatives, and of the reifying consequences of this process
for a particular workforce and ultimately for the whole of modern
industrialized society. Lawrence covers very much the same ground
as Lukács in this chapter, and even uses some of the same vocabulary as Lukács employs – not in 'The Ideology of Modernism', but in
the passage quoted in Chapter 3 from *History and Class Consciousness*, published two years after *Women in Love* in 1923. Generally,
*The Rainbow* (1915) and *Women in Love* offer a very wide-ranging
history of social change in Britain between the Industrial Revolution
and the time of the First World War, with *Lady Chatterley's Lover*

(1928) extending this picture into the years after the war. An actual social historian could hardly offer anything more thorough or compelling, at least in tracing the effects of social and economic change within the modern psyche.

And yet even in the course of presenting what seems such thorough social awareness, Lawrence's fiction reveals something of the evasiveness, the assumption of 'the unalterability of outward reality', which Lukács complains of. In *Lady Chatterley's Lover*, for example, Lawrence records that

> when Connie saw the great lorries full of steel-workers from Sheffield, weird, distorted smallish beings like men, off for an excursion to Matlock, her bowels fainted and she thought: Ah God, what has man done to man? What have the leaders of men been doing to their fellow-men? They have reduced them to less than humanness; and now there can be no fellowship any more! It is just a nightmare. (p. 159)

Lawrence raises a genuine question about social organization: 'what have the leaders of men been doing to their fellow-men?' He even offers a genuine answer, 'they have reduced them to less than humanness' – an answer confirmed by many pages at this point in the novel showing 'apartness and hopelessness [in] . . . this terrifying new and gruesome England' (pp. 159, 163). But although these conditions of modern industrial reality are firmly established, and clear questions raised about them, Lawrence's treatment of a 'new and gruesome England' does not go on to a point where it could suggest means of progress, or even the possibility of change. Instead, just as this point seems to be reached, the issue of industrialism's dehumanizing effect on modern life is consigned instead to the domain of 'nightmare'. Since no answers or alternatives can be further pursued rationally in this domain, the clear vision of terrible and gruesome processes in *Lady Chatterley's Lover* remains one which accepts them as inevitable. Connie's reflections in the passages which follow extend this view of a terrible yet unalterable modern existence. She considers industrial development in the past, and surveys the dreary, wasted landscape which is its result in the present, but adds 'God alone knows where the future lies' (p. 161). Any possibility of purposeful movement towards a better future is further negated when, thinking of the colliers – reduced like the steel-workers to a less than human existence –

Connie comments 'Supposing the dead in them ever rose up! But no, it was too terrible to think of' (p. 166).

There are other indications in Lawrence's fiction that he finds – like Connie – that however nightmarish contemporary reality may be, any attempt to alter its inhuman structuring may be worse still, too difficult or too terrible to contemplate. It is only at the end of *The Rainbow* that he suggests the possibility of 'a new architecture' for society as a whole, with 'the old, brittle corruption of houses and factories swept away' (p. 496). Yet even here, the forces which might sweep the world clean, changing 'the face of the world's corruption' (pp. 495–6), are as Chapter 3 suggested vague and visionary, mystical rather than practical – a 'new germination' (p. 496), rather than a new set of economic or social structures. Such an ending is consistent with much of Lawrence's fiction. In *The Plumed Serpent* (1926), for example, redemption for 'the mechanical cog-wheel people' and 'automatism' of modern Mexico comes not from 'wrong contacts like agitators and socialism' (pp. 104–5), but from a rediscovery of the gods Quetzalcoatl and Huitzilopochtli and their ancient religion – as if Connie's claim that 'God alone knows where the future lies' were somehow to be taken literally. Elsewhere in Lawrence's work, when alternatives to the rigours of 'the modern industrial and financial world' are not mystic or religious, they are nevertheless presented in emotional rather than rational terms – most often shown to arise from the redeeming power of individual relationships and the dark energies of sexuality which they contain. *The Rainbow* differs from Lawrence's other fiction only in being more than usually optimistic in envisaging this redeeming potential somehow extending over a whole society, rather than just two elect members of it, such as Birkin and Ursula in *Women in Love*.

Such faith in relationships and their redeeming psychic energies is consoling but limiting. Part of Lawrence's complaint about modern industrialism, repeated in Connie's reflections quoted above, is that its Taylorist rationalization of labour left workers effectively more like machines than human beings. Lawrence's own rejection of the rational, however, simply concedes as an inevitable adjunct of the nightmare modern world one of the faculties which most urgently needed to be contested and repossessed. The economic rationalization draining 'humanness' out of modern life might reasonably have been resisted – analyzed and challenged on its own terms. Instead, by relying on the dark, mystic and intuitional, Lawrence leaves little solid ground for purposeful change in society, but at best only for the construction of personal refuges more or less outside it – for the creation of 'private worlds, detached from social reality', in fact. Views of modern reality as nightmare, and the projection principally of visionary or emotional solutions to its problems, is in the end, as Lukács suggests, a kind of evasiveness, even of escapism. Lawrence's own flight from an irredeemable, industrialized Britain is anticipated by his fiction some time before his actual departure with his wife Frieda in the 1920s. Ironically, *The Plumed Serpent* suggests conditions they found in Mexico often reduplicated those they had tried to leave behind.

Lawrence's ultimate evasion of questions of political or historical change is particularly disappointing, given the extent of social awareness his fiction also shows, but otherwise not unusual among modernist writers. In *Ulysses* (1922), Joyce seems similarly convinced that the course of history is something to be ignored or escaped from rather than confronted or altered – a view summed up in one of the novel's most quoted lines: 'History, Stephen said, is a nightmare from which I am trying to awake' (p. 42). This, of course, is not necessarily Joyce's own opinion. Stephen may be closer to expressing Joyce's views in *A Portrait of the Artist as a Young Man* (1916) than he is in *Ulysses*, which on the whole presents Leopold Bloom in a more favourable light. Yet in his own way Bloom denies history almost as firmly as Stephen, remarking in Chapter 12, 'Cyclops', that

> it's no use . . . Force, hatred, history, all that. That's not life for men and women, insult and hatred. And everybody knows that it's the very opposite of that that is really life . . .
> – Love, says Bloom. I mean the opposite of hatred. (p. 432)

Bloom's alternative to the pangs of history sounds rather like D.H. Lawrence's – love providing a way out of the depredations of force and hatred, and the integrity of individual relationships compensating for wider social disintegration. These possibilities are in a way further endorsed by the novel's conclusion – Molly's sleepy recollections of love and passion accumulating, as Chapter 3 explained, into an affirmation of humanity which transcends particular time, place or history and soothes her back into unconsciousness again. It is a conclusion emblematic of wider tactics of modernism in making reality and history dream-like or impalpable; transformed or escaped through vision. Such tactics in a way confirm Fredric Jameson's conclusion that modernist narrative possesses a 'political unconscious'. Contemporary society and history are assigned a 'nightmare' character often enough by modernist novelists to suggest that the unconscious – the domain of dream and nightmare, beyond rational control – is where they most wish politics to be placed. Such thinking curiously inverts other new strategies in the modernist age. Freud suggests that dream and nightmare are worth bringing to light and analyzing to see what they contribute to understanding of the real psychic condition of the patient. Modernist fiction, on the other hand, consigns the real conditions of history to the realm of nightmare apparently in order to avoid analyzing them, or at any rate to avoid taking such analysis far enough to demand more than a release of sexual or emotional energy as an antidote to force and hatred in the modern industrial and financial world.

When history and contemporary politics are not suppressed into nightmare in this way, they are often escaped or transcended through myth – or art, as Chapter 4 discussed. The sense of timeless, transcendental order in myth particularly appealed to modernist poets, and most famously to T.S. Eliot in *The Waste Land* (1922). In discussing *Ulysses*, however, Eliot talks of myth and Joyce's pattern of references to Homer also offering the contemporary novel

> a way of controlling, of ordering, of giving a shape and a significance to the immense panorama of futility and anarchy which is contemporary history.[8]

In *To the Lighthouse*, Lily Briscoe similarly refers to an artist's brush as 'the one dependable thing in a world of strife, ruin, chaos' (p. 170). While Woolf and Eliot seek a transcendence of strife, ruin, futility and anarchy by means of myth, or art, neither much considers how the problems of contemporary life might be addressed in fact. Instead, as Lukács suggests, historical reality is held to be nightmarish but unalterable, and if shape and significance are to survive in art, it has to remain partly aloof from the anarchic historical reality it surveys. As Chapter 4 explained, art therefore sometimes seemed to the modernists a self-contained alternative to reality – almost the art-for-art's sake which George Orwell criticizes – rather than a means through which life could be more clearly envisaged, regulated or understood. In this way, the modernists can indeed be seen to have renounced some of art's traditional responsibility as – in Hugh Walpole's terms – a moral agent in the world, or – in Georg Lukács's – a political one.

## The Value of Modernism

Art will live on only as long as it has the power to resist society.
(Theodor Adorno, *Aesthetic Theory* (1970), p. 321)

How should modernist fiction be valued, and what place assigned it in the history of twentieth-century literature? How far can Lukács's and other criticisms of modernism be answered? From one point of view, of course, such criticisms might not much need to be answered at all. Despite the seriousness of Lukács's accusations, confirmed in the discussion above, they might be considered to highlight only one or two negative aspects of a literature usually held, on the whole, to offer far more in the way of admirable features. Modernism has not only continued, as the last chapter explained, as a major influence on subsequent generations of writers – more or less recovering from its loss of influence in the 1930s – it has for the most part steadily gained in critical interest and esteem in the latter half of the century. Lukács's voice is one of fairly few raised against a phase of writing analyzed in many shelves of mostly favourable criticism, and firmly installed in the teaching of most universities.

This kind of esteem, however, raises as many difficulties as it solves – in particular, the problem that modernism has often been seen as an intellectual, élitist form of art, more certain of critical and academic approval than genuine popularity. In the nineteenth century, critical success and popularity in the novel form were largely synonymous. Since the turn of the century they have often moved apart, partly as a result of changes in the finances of publishing and in the size of the reading public mentioned in the last chapter. Since the time of Henry James and Joseph Conrad, critics and academics have often reserved their highest praise for novels which sold relatively few copies at the time of their first publication, and in some cases also thereafter. Conrad's habit of incorporating a narrator and a circle of listeners into his fiction might even be seen as a figuration of anxiety about finding readers for his work – as an attempt to create within the fiction an audience which he suspected might not exist in fact, or exist only on a limited scale. In later modernist writing, interior monologues, unusual chronologies, self-conscious concerns with language and with art create complex, challenging novels – perhaps more exciting, but generally more difficult and demanding to read than most fiction in the nineteenth century.

To the charges raised by Lukács, in other words, there might be added the suggestion that modernist fiction lost touch with the everyday world not only by ceasing to write about it, but by ceasing to write about anything in ways easily accessible to the majority of its inhabitants. Opponents of modernism have often extended this charge, suggesting that at a time when culture was becoming more and more the possession of the masses – through the general spread of literacy and of new media such as the cinema – modernist writers quite deliberately chose to create a difficult, challenging art which only an intellectual élite could fully appreciate or understand. John Carey, for example, claims in his study *The Intellectuals and the Masses* (1992) that

> Realism of the sort that it was assumed the masses appreciated was abandoned ... The principle around which modernist literature and culture fashioned themselves was the exclusion of the masses. (pp. 17, 21)

Carey and other critics see such élitism as consistent with the anti-democratic politics which, notoriously, many of the modernists professed. But at least where modernist novelists are concerned – rather than the poets, Ezra Pound, T.S. Eliot or W.B. Yeats – any such notoriety is neither uniform nor universal. Only Wyndham Lewis was a sustained supporter of fascism – a position in some ways consistent with an artistic preference for hard outlines and rigid control which made him as often an enemy as an exemplar of modernism. D.H. Lawrence sometimes seems more contradictory or confused than reactionary – able in *The Plumed Serpent*, for example, to claim 'Bolshevism is one sort of bullying, capitalism another' and to alternate 'ghastly fear of the rabble' with a sense of 'the pathos of the victims of modern industry and capitalism' (pp. 73, 136, 52). And there is little to be said against the politics of James Joyce; or of Virginia Woolf, who was a firm supporter of Suffragism – indeed, in the latter case, Carey limits himself to the accusation of 'snobbery' (p. 178).

Critics preoccupied with modernist authors' professed politics in any case overlook Lawrence's advice to trust the tale and not the teller. As the cultural theorist Theodor Adorno concludes, the 'substance of major art works frequently diverges from the political orientation of their producers' (p. 364), and it is the politics of novels themselves, rather than their authors, which probably have the widest and most significant impact on readers. It is at any rate the politics of texts which are examined in the discussion which follows, addressing accusations of élitism after first outlining one response to the charge of irresponsibility to contemporary society and history. This latter issue can be clarified by further considering some of the fiction which followed modernism in the 1930s. Not all novels at the time, not even those most firmly committed politically, turned against modernist styles. For example, in one of the most accomplished of novels published in the 1930s, *A Scots Quair* (1932–4), Lewis Grassic Gibbon uses a range of interior monologues not only to communicate the thoughts and feelings of a few principal characters, but to gain access to the consciousness of many members of a working, rural community. The kind of Free Indirect Discourse characteristic of D.H. Lawrence's fiction – very flexibly employed – allows Gibbon to alternate the novel's attention freely between many individuals, and to develop a kind of choric voice for the community as a whole. The novel's structure is equally sophisticated. Rather in the manner of Ford Madox Ford's *Parade's End*, chapters are circular, beginning at a moment later than the events they go back to describe, ending with the story advanced again to the time from which the chapter began. This pattern allows immediate events to be held alongside wider vision of their significance; actuality to be juxtaposed with the ideal. Rather than denying history or politics, such patterning remains completely engaged with contemporary conflicts and injustices, while also showing the possibility of a more worthwhile life beyond them, and the kind of political organization which could move towards it. In these ways, the structure and the communism of speech in *A Scots Quair* establish an exact formal reflex for the left-wing commitments of the 1930s.

Like Lewis Grassic Gibbon, Malcolm Lowry remains in touch with contemporary history and politics while also adopting modernist methods. Begun in the late 1930s, Lowry's *Under the Volcano* (1947) resembles *Ulysses* fairly closely in construction and technique. Its chapters occupy hours in a single day, and its narrative is principally focused within the minds of three characters, transcribed in a complex mixture of stream of consciousness, Free Indirect Discourse and interior monologue. This transcription is further complicated by the nearly permanent drunkenness of Lowry's central figure, the Consul Geoffrey Firmin. His thoughts at times tumble almost indecipherably among distorted fragments of conversation, perception and hallucination: the result is a 'whirling cerebral chaos' (p. 309) sometimes resembling the 'Nighttown' section of *Ulysses* (Chapter 15) more than any other. Yet even such a highly private, nightmare world is neither wholly 'detached from social reality' nor a 'denial of history'. Instead, much of what impinges upon characters' internal consciousness – newsreels of the civil war in Spain, the growth of fascism in Mexico – troublingly reflects the origin and nature of political conflicts darkening the late 1930s. Firmin's drunkenness is itself related to contemporary history both consequentially and metaphorically – as a response to, and a reminder of, its unendurable quality. In Lowry's own view,

> The drunkenness of the Consul is used on one plane to symbolise the universal drunkenness of mankind during the war, or during the period immediately preceding it . . . his fate should be seen also in its universal relationship to the ultimate fate of mankind.[9]

Though at an especially drunken moment the Consul talks of history and 'its worthless stupid course' (p. 311) as being unalterable, this is an idea contested throughout *Under the Volcano* – in particular, in this drunken scene, by the Consul's half-brother Hugh, committed to the Republican cause in Spain. In general, as Lowry suggests, confinement within the Consul's consciousness is not a refuge from the course of history, but a highlighting of its threats, focused unusually immediately through the experience of a character whose pain and stupidity is emblematic of the wider uneasiness of his time.

Both Malcolm Lowry and Lewis Grassic Gibbon thus demonstrate that modernist techniques are neither invariably nor necessarily ahistoric or apolitical. This, of course, is not much of a defence against Lukács's charge that such techniques *were* employed evasively and irresponsibly by earlier modernist authors. Yet there is also evidence that their use of these techniques was less negative and limiting than Lukács claims. As suggested earlier, modernism continues to provide a major influence on writing in the twentieth century: its effect on reading has in some ways been equally decisive. This is not – or not only – a matter of the difficulty and complexity with which modernist texts confront their readers, denying them the relative straightforwardness of construction and realism of style characteristic of the Victorian novel and indeed much fiction written since. Modernist novels *are* genuinely difficult and challenging, but this can also be considered – if not by Georg Lukács, at least by another thinker on the left, Roland Barthes – as a way of establishing for readers a freedom and responsibility which more conventional fiction denies them. Barthes clarifies this modernist potential in distinguishing what he calls 'readerly' ('*lisible*') and 'writerly' ('*scriptible*') texts. 'Readerly' texts are closer to the conventions of the nineteenth-century novel, whose readers generally enter a straightforwardly constructed world in which the nature and motives of characters are clearly, objectively explained, allowing their lives and actions to be understood with a minimum of effort. Modernist fiction, on the other hand, challenges its readers to reconsider the nature of fiction and its relation to reality, and to reconstruct for themselves fictional worlds complexly envisaged through the consciousness of characters, often transcribed in diverse styles and unusual structures. Modernist fiction approximates in such ways to the writerly text. In Barthes's view, this kind of text almost forces readers to become writers themselves – or at any rate to enter into active collaboration with an author who obliges them to construe meanings and develop the text's significances for themselves. Barthes draws an analogy between the challenges of this writerly text and those created by the kind of musical composition which followed from the work of Schoenberg:

> we know that today post-serial music has radically altered the role of the 'interpreter', who is called on to be in some sort the co-author of the score, completing it rather than giving it 'expression'. The Text is very much a score of this new kind: it asks of the reader a practical collaboration.

Collaboration of this kind, Barthes suggests, leaves the reader 'no longer a consumer, but the producer of the text'.[10]

Like several of the differences which separate modernist fiction from its predecessors, Barthes's distinction may be one mostly of degree or extent – quantitative rather than entirely qualitative. Every novel – nineteenth-century, modernist, or otherwise – requires some practical, imaginative collaboration from its readers. Yet what modernism demands in this way is certainly greater, quantitatively, and more challenging than almost anything in nineteenth-century fiction. Contributing to a more active involvement or 'collaboration' in the novel, this also establishes a more decisive, responsible attitude towards its values. The realism of nineteenth-century literature can seduce readers into accepting uncritically – as similar or even identical to reality – fictional worlds which are actually thoroughly conditioned by the politics and values of their authors. Since readers of a writerly or modernist text are more involved in producing its meanings and values for themselves, they are more likely to avoid passive acceptance of those of the author.

At certain levels they may also be more disposed, by such texts, to look beyond social reality in its current shape. Even when it happens to offer explicit proposals about how society might be reorganized, nineteenth-century fiction's realism retains a degree of implicit commitment to the world as it exists; to reality as it is conventionally structured and represented. Moreover, the fictional worlds of nineteenth-century writing most often offer a reassuring sense of completeness which may be a disincentive to look at the possibilities or need for change in social reality, beyond the novel. Adorno dismisses the attempt of this kind of art

> to offer to the existing world a kind of solace . . . Claiming to be able to posit a well-rounded totality . . . creates the false impression that the world outside is such a well-rounded whole, too. (p. 2)

Adorno argues instead that 'formal radicalism has a social moment' (p. 73). The social or political implications of modernist fiction's radicalism, and its difference from the 'well-rounded' conventions of the nineteenth-century, can be illustrated by returning to the contrast of Lawrence's *The Rainbow* and *Women in Love* which concluded Chapter 3. Consecutive construction and a firm conclusion, even one on the level of vision and Lawrentian mysticism, leave *The Rainbow* closer to nineteenth-century conventions than is *Women in Love*. The latter is denied a consoling sense of order or completeness by its fragmentary structure and an apparent scepticism about the very possibility of satisfactory endings. Birkin's refusal in the very last lines of the novel to acknowledge the stability or wholeness of his relationship with Ursula leaves *Women in Love* without a secure, final sense of order in the society and relationships portrayed. Readers close the novel in uncertainty, returning from fiction to life with a raw sense of incompleteness and – possibly – a particular readiness to question what denies order and coherence to modern society in general.

Some such questioning is invited throughout *Women in Love*, as well as at its end. The need to reconstruct meaning and coherence from a fragmentary fiction may leave readers, at every stage, more disposed to question forces which leave modern life incoherent and fragmented in fact. Though in *Lady Chatterley's Lover* and elsewhere Lawrence stops short of providing satisfactory answers of his own to such questions – and even hesitates to pursue them very far in directions his fiction logically suggests he might – this does not prevent readers from doing so for themselves. In fact, it might provide a compelling incentive to investigate areas which the author leaves open or incompletely resolved. Such openness may be morally as much as politically enabling. Though Hugh Walpole complains of the absence of a moral dimension from modernist fiction, it may be that the most moral sort of text is one which leaves readers free to determine morality for themselves. Modernism is closer to doing so than is nineteenth-century fiction, often ready to draw general conclusions on behalf of its readers and to point out regularly what they might be thinking about individual characters and actions.

Other worthwhile consequences follow from this writerly aspect of modernist fiction. Involving readers in producing rather than passively consuming texts can help to alert them to devices – and motives – through which meaning is produced and reality made consumable in other media as well as in literature. As the last chapter concluded, this is a crucial concern in a century more than ever dominated by the media, and it is highlighted by attention to language and means of representation throughout modernist fiction, in *Ulysses* particularly. Joyce's constant alternations of style make readers recognize how 'outward reality', far from being un-alterable, is inescapably altered and particularized by styles, forms and words chosen to frame it. By demonstrating so thoroughly its capacity to warp and shape the world, Joyce's narrative also en-ables readers to recognize how easily language can be used as a tool of commercial, political or other forms of manipulation. The manipulative powers of journalism and advertising are given par-ticular attention. Bloom himself is after all an advertising man of a kind, and his zany reflections on improved slogans for Plumtree's Potted Meat, or his headline-ridden visit to the newspaper office in the 'Aeolus' chapter (7), vividly demonstrate some of the new powers – and peculiarities – of language in shaping and controlling the outlook of the modern age.

As Chapter 4 also explained, modernist fiction goes some way towards redressing – as well as just indicating – difficulties and distortions inherent in the use of language in the modern age. Stylistic diversity and linguistic inventiveness help to make mod-ernism a carnivalized literature, one which resists language's servi-tude to established social orders and systems of power, keeping it open instead as a domain of contention, play and change. Like other difficult, challenging aspects of modernist fiction, its self-reflexive, complex language may therefore be seen as neither wilfully élitist nor an arid intellectual exercise, however much it may be a source of difficulty for readers accustomed to the relative straightforwardness and stylistic homogeneity of nineteenth-century fiction. Rather than seeking primarily to *exclude* the masses, modernist fiction challenges some of the forces which seek to reduce individuals *to* a mere mass – forces of government, com-merce or advertising which treat the population as a conveniently inert, homogeneous body, to be manipulated independently of individual will or imagination.

Roland Barthes's views provide one answer to Georg Lukács and other critics of modernism: Fredric Jameson offers material for another, based more on modernism's relations with its society and history than its effect on readers. Jameson's ideas have already been discussed in Chapters 2 and 3 – in particular, his view that modernism offers

Utopian compensation for increasing dehumanization on the level of daily life . . .

> A Utopian compensation for everything reification brings with it . . . for every-
> thing lost in the process of the development of capitalism. (pp. 42, 236)

This thinking reappears in Jameson's attempts to modify some of Lukács's arguments. Discussing visual art, Jameson suggests

> Lukács is not wrong to associate the emergence of . . . modernism with the
> reification which is its precondition; but he oversimplifies and deproblematizes a
> complicated and interesting situation by ignoring the Utopian vocation . . . the
> mission to return at least a symbolic experience of libidinal gratification to a
> world drained of it, a world of extension, gray and merely quantifiable. (p. 63)

Thinking of modernism in general, Jameson adds

> In short, it is evidently wrong to imagine, as Lukács sometimes seems to do, that
> modernism is some mere ideological distraction, a way of systematically displac-
> ing the reader's attention from history and society to pure form, metaphysics,
> and experiences of the individual monad; it is all those things, but . . . the
> modernist project is more adequately understood as the intent . . . to 'manage'
> historical and social, deeply political impulses, that is to say, to defuse them, to
> prepare substitute gratifications for them. (p. 266)

Jameson's argument in *The Political Unconscious* clearly justifies his claim that modernism is more complex and interesting than Lukács allows. This does not of itself, of course, demonstrate that modernism is any more responsible to its age and its history than Lukács believes. In fact, what claims to be an alternative or modi-fied form of Lukács's argument is at times differentiated from it only rather precariously. Jameson's idea of symbolic or 'substitute gratification' does not seem very different from the 'ideological distraction' and 'displacement of attention' which, in his assess-ment, is all that Lukács considers modernism to offer.

Acknowledging that Lukács is 'not wrong' – even in the course of proposing modifications to his ideas – Jameson confirms that his criticisms of modernism cannot be entirely denied or dismissed. Yet it is worth taking Jameson's own idea of 'substitute gratifica-tion' further – perhaps slightly further than he takes it himself. Much of the present study has followed his thinking, showing mod-ernism's formal innovations opening up dimensions – spatial, tem-poral or linguistic – in which individual life can still be considered integral and whole despite the reifying, fragmenting processes of the modern, industrialized, capitalist world. As Jameson explains, these innovations can indeed be seen as ways of defusing, in imagination, this world's real tensions; of providing gratifying or 'Utopian' consolations which might in the end function principally as distractions from actual history and society, much as Lukács considers. It is also possible, however, that at the symbolic or imaginative level Jameson discusses, modernist fiction not only offers consolation but also implies critique. It keeps open at least in imagination alternative possibilities, substitute visions, which function not only as gratification or distraction from contemporary social reality, but potentially or implicitly as criticism of it.

For example, as Chapter 3 discussed, time in the modernist age had not been lost – as Proust's title suggests – so much as stolen. By the early twentieth century, a Taylorized industry had established more and more rigorous methods of converting time into money; placing modern life more and more exclusively in the hands of the 'commercial clock'. Modernist fiction resists this appropriation of the dimension of time not only by its explicit hostility to the clock, but by means of unconventional, non-chronologic narratives which emphasize alternative ways of conceiving life and experience. The writerly task of reconstructing a fictional world and its temporality out of the unconventional material of a modernist text ensures that *any* ordering of temporality is recognized as a construct, an artifice and not an absolute. The clock can therefore be construed as only one of several possible means of shaping the dimension of time, rather than the agent of a primary, universal order which many interests, commercial or otherwise, had sought to make it by the early twentieth century. Much the same sort of critique of the way modern reality had come to be habitually – but often dehumanizingly – conceived and organized is made available by other aspects of modernist innovation, in ways discussed earlier in relation to language and to the internalization of narrative perspective. Modernism may not have done much directly, of course, in any of these ways, to re-shape the modern world or alter its politics. Yet in this respect it is not really more limited than the art of any other period. In general, as Jameson admits, 'it is clear that the work of art cannot itself be asked to change the world or to transform itself into political praxis' (p. 234). More reasonably, it can be asked to shape and facilitate imagination of how the world *might* be ordered differently – a demand which, in many ways, modernist fiction fulfils. Regardless of the politics of its authors, modernist writing contributes to what one commentator calls 'an adversary culture'; a source of alternative vision variously resistant to the deadening pressures of modern life.[11] This adversarial role is perhaps so often overlooked because it is rarely a matter of direct, explicit statement – such as appears in much Victorian or Edwardian fiction – but rather of an implied social criticism discernible in modernist texts principally in the areas of style, structure and form.

Jameson's explanation of how narrative creates its 'substitute gratifications' also opens up another possibility, if not necessarily for a defence of modernist fiction, at least for a reading which defines for it a lasting significance and interest as evidence, or symptom, of the stresses of its age. Jameson remarks that

> the production of aesthetic or narrative form is to be seen as an ideological act in its own right, with the function of inventing imaginary or formal 'solutions' to unresolvable social contradictions. (p. 79)

Whether in the sublime form of myths, or the ridiculous one of jokes, or in many variously respectable manifestations between, all narratives work at one level, as Jameson suggests, as an imaginative resolution of problems or 'contradictions' in contemporary actuality. Seen in this way, however much or little modernist authors reflected social reality deliberately, it inevitably remained an influential presence in their work, their narrative forms conditioned or 'produced' by the challenges of their age. So even if modernism's unusual, innovative narratives seem a 'denial of history', they can still be seen as a denial of history which – like any other choice of narrative forms – is itself historically conditioned. Moreover, the nature of the denial may have much to reveal about the nature of what is denied, about the pressures of history within the contemporary imagination. As Jameson suggests, there is in any reading of fiction the possibility of finding history inscribed in the structure and texture of the narrative; of 'construing purely formal patterns as a symbolic enactment of the social within the formal and the aesthetic' (p. 78). Analysis of the narrative forms which were developed by the modernists need not, therefore, be distracted from forces of contemporary history, politics or social reality. On the contrary, in tracing ways narrative comes to terms with these forces, criticism can also illumine something of the nature and operation of these forces themselves.

This potential can be summed up through a metaphor about the aim2s of art, artists and criticism which Joseph Conrad includes in his Preface to *The Nigger of the 'Narcissus'* (1897):

> Sometimes, stretched at ease in the shade of a roadside tree, we watch the motions of a labourer in a distant field, and after a time, begin to wonder languidly as to what the fellow may be at. We watch the movements of his body, the waving of his arms, we see him bend down, stand up, hesitate, begin again. It may add to the charm of an idle hour to be told the purpose of his exertions. If we know he is trying to lift a stone, to dig a ditch, to uproot a stump, we look with a more real interest at his efforts; we are disposed to condone the jar of his agitation upon the restfulness of the landscape . . . we understood his object.
>
> And so it is with the workman of art . . . We talk a little about the aim – the aim of art which, like life itself, is inspiring, difficult – obscured by mists. (pp. 13–14)

Conrad's languid picture seems at first to offer the kind of vision, aloof from the hard world of labour, for which Lukács criticized modernist writers. But for Conrad the labourer is actually equated with the writer – 'the workman of art' – while it is the critic or reader who is the indolent observer. His metaphor suggests two main ways in which such observation, the business of reading or criticism, may be conducted. First, work in the field of modernism can simply be admired or described for itself. Criticism can applaud and detail the modernist novel's energy in breaking from the past; its exertions in creating new shapes and forms; the flexibility of its style; the ingenuity of its construction, and so on. The shelves of admiring criticism of modernism are mostly devoted, perhaps legitimately enough, to this sort of analysis.

Secondly, however, it can add to more than just 'the charm of an idle hour' to assess the work of modernist writers in terms not only of the nature but 'the purpose of . . . exertions'. Modernism does now belong to 'a distant field' – distant enough, as the Preface suggested, to make it a movement that can be seen clearly in relation to the historical terrain on which it operated, and in the context of contemporary forces and realities that resisted, challenged and shaped its labours. Wallace Stevens suggests that modern poetry can be described as 'the poem of the mind in the act of finding / What will suffice'.[12] Modernist fiction can be considered in similar terms. Writing which so thoroughly reoriented the conventions of the novel can still be admired and enjoyed as an outstanding act of the literary mind in the twentieth century. The 'real interest in [its] efforts', however, surrounds the question of why such exertions in reshaping time, space, language and art seemed to the modernists to be all that could suffice. Looking for answers to this question, making the aims and needs of modernist art less 'difficult – obscured', has been the main object of this study. There is still as much as ever to admire in the power and promise of modernist imagination, but also much to learn from the way this imagination reacts to the pressures of the 'modern industrial and financial world' in the twentieth century's first three decades. In its closing years, such pressures have certainly not diminished: looking back on the distant field of modernism offers some ways of understanding them; of seeing how they can be imagined.

# NOTES

1. The *Oxford English Dictionary* records Jonathan Swift remarking on 'abominable curtailings and quaint modernisms' in 1737; and another commentator talking of 'imperfections and modernisms' in 1897.

   For a discussion of the complex question of how – and with what degree of approval – terms such as 'modern', 'modernism' and 'modernity' continue to be employed, see Jürgen Habermas, *The Philosophical Discourse of Modernity* (Cambridge: Polity, 1987), especially Chapter 1.

   R.A. Scott-James borrows the term 'modernism' from Thomas Hardy and from contemporary theology, where it was used to refer to the liberalizing movements which attempted to update traditional beliefs and religious doctrines in the early years of the century.
2. Virginia Woolf, 'Mr. Bennett and Mrs. Brown' (1924), rpt. in *Collected Essays* (London: Hogarth Press, 1966), I, p. 326; and 'Modern Fiction' (1919), rpt. in *Collected Essays*, II, pp. 106–7.
3. Quoted in Virginia Woolf, *A Writer's Diary: Being Extracts from the Diary of Virginia Woolf*, ed. Leonard Woolf (1953; rpt. London: Triad, 1985), p. 97.
4. Quoted in Michael Levenson, *A Genealogy of Modernism* (Cambridge: Cambridge University Press, 1984), p. 217.
5. Robert P. Morgan, 'Secret Languages: The Roots of Musical Modernism' in Monique Chefdor, Ricardo Quinones and Albert Wachtel, eds, *Modernism: Challenges and Perspectives* (Chicago: University of Illinois Press, 1986), p. 41.
6. See Christopher Butler, *Early Modernism: Literature, Music and Painting in Europe, 1900–1916* (Oxford: Clarendon Press, 1994); and Peter Nicholls, *Modernisms: A Literary Guide* (London: Macmillan, 1995).
7. Virginia Woolf, letter of 6 May 1922, rpt. in *The Letters of Virginia Woolf*, ed. Nigel Nicholson and Joanne Trautmann (London: Chatto, 1975–80), II, p. 525; see also *A Writer's Diary* (note 3), p. 138, and discussion of Woolf in Chapter 3.

8. Virginia Woolf, *A Writer's Diary* (note 3), pp. 55–6; Woolf, letter of 25 June 1921, *Letters*, II, p. 476. In this letter Woolf does, however, add of Lawrence that 'he is honest, and therefore he is 100 times better than most of us'.

9. Friedrich Nietzsche, 'The Wanderer and his Shadow' (1880), rpt. in *Human, all too Human: A Book for Free Spirits*, trans. R.J. Hollingdale (Cambridge: Cambridge University Press, 1986), p. 378.

10. F.T. Marinetti, 'Destruction of Syntax – Imagination without Strings – Words-in-Freedom' (1913), rpt. in Umbro Apollonio, ed., *Futurist Manifestos* (London: Thames and Hudson, 1973), p. 96.

11. ibid., p. 97; 'The Founding and Manifesto of Futurism' (1909), p. 22.

12. Carola Giedion-Welcker, 'On Ulysses by James Joyce', *Neue Schweizer Rundschau* (1928), rpt. in Robert H. Deming, ed., *James Joyce: The Critical Heritage* (London: Routledge and Kegan Paul, 1970), II, p. 443.

## CHAPTER 2

1. Marcel Proust, *Remembrance of Things Past* (1913–27), trans. C.K. Scott Moncrieff and Terence Kilmartin (Harmondsworth: Penguin, 1983), III, pp. 585, 931, 950; Virginia Woolf, 'Phases of Fiction' (1929), rpt. in *Collected Essays* (London: Hogarth Press, 1966), II, p. 81.

2. C.H. Rickword, 'A Note on Fiction', *The Calendar of Modern Letters*, October 1926; rpt. in Peter Faulkner, ed., *A Modernist Reader: Modernism in England 1910–1930* (London: Batsford, 1986), p. 160.

3. Henry James, Prefaces to *The Spoils of Poynton, The Tragic Muse, The Princess Casamassima, The Portrait of a Lady*; rpt. in R.P. Blackmur, ed., *The Art of the Novel: Critical Prefaces* (London: Charles Scribner's Sons, 1934), pp. 120, 85, 70, 51.

4. ibid., Prefaces to *The Princess Casamassima* and *The Portrait of a Lady*, pp. 65, 46.

5. J. Hillis Miller, 'The Interpretation of *Lord Jim*' in Morton W. Bloomfield, ed., *The Interpretation of Narrative: Theory and Practice* (Cambridge, MA: Harvard University Press, 1970), p. 220.

6. Henry James, 'The New Novel' (1914), rpt. in *Notes on Novelists: with some other Notes* (London: Dent, 1914), p. 276.

7. *The Good Soldier* (1915; rpt. Harmondsworth: Penguin, 1977), p. 167. Conrad's views are recorded in his 'Author's Note' in *Lord Jim*.

8. Henry James, 'The Younger Generation' (1914), rpt. in Leon Edel and Gordon N. Ray, eds, *Henry James and H.G. Wells* (London: Rupert Hart-Davis, 1958), p. 200.

9. D.H. Lawrence, letter of 5 June 1914; *The Collected Letters of D.H. Lawrence*, ed. Harry T. Moore (London: Heinemann, 1962), I, p. 282.

10. In *The Dialogic Imagination*, ed. Michael Holquist, trans. Caryl Emerson and Michael Holquist (Austin: University of Texas Press, 1981), Bakhtin remarks that, in general, 'The novel can be defined as a diversity of social speech types (sometimes even diversity of languages) and a diversity of individual voices, artistically organized' (p. 262). For his particular idea of 'hybridization', see pp. 358–62. See also David Lodge, *After Bakhtin* (London: Routledge, 1990).
11. Dorothy Richardson, Foreword to *Pilgrimage* (1915–67; rpt. London: Virago, 1979), I, pp. 10, 11.
12. J.D. Beresford, Introduction to Dorothy Richardson, *Pointed Roofs: Pilgrimage* (London: Duckworth, 1915), p. vi.
13. May Sinclair, 'The Novels of Dorothy Richardson', *The Egoist*, April 1918, p. 58.
14. My translation of '. . . sa nouveauté, sa hardiesse, et les possibilités qu'elle offrait pour exprimer avec force et rapidité les pensées les plus intimes, les plus spontanées, celles qui paraissent se former à l'insu de la conscience et qui semblent antérieur au discours organisé . . . une forme qui permettait d'atteindre si profondément dans le Moi le jaillisement de la pensée et de la saisir si près de sa conception'. Valery Larbaud, 'Preface' to Edouard Dujardin, *Les lauriers sont coupés* (1888; rpt. Paris: Albert Messein, 1925), p. 6.
    Joyce picked up a copy of Dujardin's novel on a station bookstall in Paris in 1903. He was ready to acknowledge borrowing from it: see Richard Ellmann, *James Joyce* (Oxford: Oxford University Press, 1982), pp. 126, 519–20. Debate about the nature and extent of his debt continues among critics: see, for example, Anthony Burgess, 'French Pioneer in the Music of Language', review of Edouard Dujardin, *The Bays are Sere*, trans. Anthony Suter, *The Independent*, 1 March 1991, p. 23.
15. Henry James, 'The Future of the Novel' (1899), rpt. in Edel and Ray, op. cit. (note 8), p. 57.
16. D.H. Lawrence, letter of 22 April 1914, *Collected Letters* (note 9), I, p. 273; and *England, My England* (1924; rpt. Harmondsworth: Penguin, 1960), p. 20.
17. 'H.C.H', review of *The Trap*, *The Calendar of Modern Letters*, June 1925, pp. 328–9.
18. James Joyce, letter of 3 January 1920, in *Selected Letters of James Joyce*, ed. Richard Ellmann (London: Faber and Faber, 1975), p. 246.
19. Quoted in Frank Budgen, *James Joyce and the Making of Ulysses* (London: Grayson & Grayson, 1934), pp. 15, 17.
20. Virginia Woolf, 'Modern Fiction', *Collected Essays* (note 1), p. 107; Virginia Woolf, 'Modern Novels (Joyce)' (1918), rpt. in Bonnie Kime Scott, ed., *The Gender of Modernism: A Critical Anthology* (Bloomington and Indianapolis: Indiana University Press, 1990), p. 643.

21. Virginia Woolf, *A Writer's Diary: Being Extracts from the Diary of Virginia Woolf*, ed. Leonard Woolf (1953; rpt. London: Triad, 1985), p. 102; J. Hillis Miller, 'The Rhythm of Creativity in *To the Lighthouse*', in Robert Kiely, ed., *Modernism Reconsidered* (London: Harvard University Press, 1983), pp. 171, 173. Hillis Miller's use of the phrase '*style indirect libre*' (p. 173) confirms that he has Free Indirect Discourse in mind.

22. Ford Madox Ford, *The Critical Attitude* (London: Duckworth, 1911), p. 97; D.H. Lawrence, 'John Galsworthy' (1928), rpt. in Anthony Beal, ed., *Selected Literary Criticism* (London: Heinemann, 1955); Henry James, 'The Younger Generation', rpt. in Edel and Ray, op. cit. (note 8), pp. 187, 195.

23. H.G. Wells, letter to Henry James, 8 July 1915, rpt. in Edel and Ray, op. cit. (note 8), p. 264; H.G. Wells, *Kipps* (1905; rpt. London: Fontana, 1973), p. 241; H.G. Wells, 'The Contemporary Novel' in Edel and Ray, pp. 148, 141.

24. See Philip Henderson, *The Novel Today: A Study in Contemporary Attitudes* (London: John Lane, 1936), p. 27; J.B. Priestley, *Literature and Western Man* (London: Heinemann, 1960), pp. 425–6; Angus Wilson, 'Arnold Bennett's Novels', *London Magazine*, October 1954, p. 60.

25. A selection of Freud's papers was published in 1909; *Three Contributions to a Theory of Sex* in 1910; and *The Interpretation of Dreams* in 1913. Havelock Ellis's six-volume *Studies in the Psychology of Sex* (1897–1910) refers frequently to Freud. On Freud's early significance for modernism, see Christopher Butler, *Early Modernism: Literature, Music and Painting in Europe 1900–1916* (Oxford: Clarendon Press, 1994), pp. 89–95.

26. D.H. Lawrence, *St Mawr* in *St Mawr and The Virgin and the Gypsy* (1925, 1930; rpt. Harmondsworth: Penguin, 1988), p. 55. Throughout his story, Lawrence uses the horse St Mawr partly to represent 'terrible mystery' and physical or natural forces beyond what can be understood intellectually.

27. D.H. Lawrence, letter of 16 September 1916, *Collected Letters* (note 9), I, p. 475; D.H. Lawrence, *Fantasia of the Unconscious and Psychoanalysis and the Unconscious* (1923; rpt. London: Heinemann, 1961), pp. 11, 208, 246.

28. The opinion is expressed by Tommy Dukes in D.H. Lawrence, *Lady Chatterley's Lover* (1928; rpt. Harmondsworth: Penguin, 1982), p. 39. Lawrence himself puts forward similar views in, for example, *Fantasia of the Unconscious* (note 27), p. 170ff., or in his letter of 8 December 1915, in which he states 'I am convinced . . . that there is another seat of consciousness than the brain and the nerve system: there is a blood-consciousness which exists in us independently of ordinary mental consciousness', *Collected Letters* (note 9), I, p. 373.

29. Virginia Woolf, 'Character in Fiction', *The Essays of Virginia Woolf*, ed. Andrew McNeillie (London: Hogarth Press, 1988), III, p. 504.
30. 'The Contemporary Novel', in Edel and Ray, op. cit. (note 8), p. 147.
31. Friedrich Nietzsche, *Human, all too Human: A Book for Free Spirits* (1880), trans. R.J. Hollingdale (Cambridge: Cambridge University Press, 1986), p. 13; *The Gay Science* (1882), trans. Walter Kaufmann (New York: Vintage Books, 1974), p. 219.
32. Nietzsche quotes this view, approvingly, from Kant in *Human, all too Human* (note 31), p. 22; *The Will to Power* (1901), trans. Walter Kaufmann and R.J. Hollingdale (London: Weidenfeld and Nicholson, 1968), p. 265.
33. Quoted in Stanford Schwartz, *The Matrix of Modernism* (Princeton, NJ: Princeton University Press, 1985), p. 14.
34. Friedrich Nietzsche, *Beyond Good and Evil* (1886), trans. R.J. Hollingdale (Harmondsworth: Penguin, 1990), p. 44.
35. Virginia Woolf, 'The Narrow Bridge of Art' (1927), *Collected Essays* (note 1), II, p. 219.
36. T.S. Eliot, 'Rhapsody on a Windy Night' (1914), *Collected Poems: 1909–1962* (London: Faber and Faber, 1974), p. 27. I am grateful to Faber and Faber for permission to quote from T.S. Eliot's *Collected Poems*.
37. D.H. Lawrence, letter of 5 June 1914, *Collected Letters* (note 9), I, p. 282.
38. Andrew Marvell, 'The Garden' (1681), *Collected Poems*, ed. Elizabeth Story Donno (Harmondsworth: Penguin, 1972), p. 101.

## CHAPTER 3

1. D.H. Lawrence, *Apocalypse* (1931; rpt. Harmondsworth: Penguin, 1981), pp. 54, 93; Virginia Woolf, *A Writer's Diary: Being Extracts from the Diary of Virginia Woolf*, ed. Leonard Woolf (1953; rpt. London: Triad, 1985), p. 138.
2. These plans are reproduced in, for example, Richard Ellmann, *Ulysses on the Liffey* (London: Faber and Faber, 1974), p. 188ff.
3. Henri Bergson, *Mind Energy: Lectures and Essays* (1919), trans. H. Wildon Carr (London: Macmillan, 1920), p. 94.
4. D.H. Lawrence, letter of 5 June 1914; *The Collected Letters of D.H. Lawrence*, ed. Harry T. Moore (London: Heinemann, 1962), I, p. 282.
5. Quoted in Joseph Blotner, *Faulkner: A Biography* (New York: Random House, 1984), p. 563.
6. See Wyndham Lewis, *Time and Western Man* (London: Chatto and Windus, 1927), pp. 13–18, for Lewis's account of how Einstein might have derived his ideas from Bergson. Lewis suggests that 'In any

reasonable, and not romantic, account of the matter, we must suppose the mathematical physicist not entirely unaffected by neighbouring metaphysical thought.'

7. Alexander Moszkowski, *Einstein the Searcher: His Work Explained from Dialogues with Einstein*, trans. Henry L. Brose (London: Methuen, 1921), pp. 114, 117; My tranlsation of 'il n'ya qu'un temps psychologique, différent du temps du physicien', a remark attributed to Einstein in François Heidsieck, *Bergson et la notion de l'éspace* (Paris: Le Circle du Livre, 1957), p. 164.

8 Friedrich Nietzsche, *The Birth of Tragedy* in *The Birth of Tragedy and The Genealogy of Morals* (1871; 1887), trans. Francis Golffing (New York: Doubleday, 1956), p. 111; *The Gay Science* (1882), trans. Walter Kaufmann (New York: Vintage Books, 1974), pp. 172, 173; *Human, all too Human: A Book for Free Spirits* (1880), trans. R.J. Hollingdale (Cambridge: Cambridge University Press, 1986), p. 20.

9. Sigmund Freud, *The Interpretation of Dreams* (1899), trans. A.A. Brill (London: George Allen and Co., 1913), p. 15. Freud quotes 'toute impression, même la plus insignifiante, laisse une trace inaltérable, indéfiniment susceptible de reparaître au jour' from J. Delboeuf, *Le Sommeil et les rêves* (Paris, 1885). In the passage quoted below, he refers to Fr. Scholz, *Schlaf und Traum* (Leipzig, 1887), and J. Volkelt, *Die Traumphantasie* (Stuttgart, 1875).

10. See Lewis's short story, 'You Broke My Dream', which mentions 'R. Dunne, Esq.', in Wyndham Lewis, *The Wild Body* (London: Chatto and Windus, 1927), p. 295.

11. Wyndham Lewis, *Paleface* (London: Chatto and Windus, 1929), p. 255; *Time and Western Man* (London: Chatto and Windus, 1927), p. 129.

12. Wyndham Lewis, *The Art of Being Ruled* (London: Chatto and Windus, 1926), p. 389.

13. Fredric Jameson, *Fables of Aggression: Wyndham Lewis, the Modernist as Fascist* (London: University of California Press, 1979), pp. 124, 123.

14. Quoted in Shiv K. Kumar, *Bergson and the Stream of Consciousness Novel* (London: Blackie, 1962), pp. 36–7.

15. John Stevenson, *British Society 1914–45* (London: Allen Lane, 1984) records that 'A report on bad time-keeping in the ship-building, munitions and transport industries at the end of April 1915 blamed lost time on the ease with which highly paid workers could purchase beer and spirits' (p. 71). Even by the end of 1914, earlier closing times had been introduced by about half the local authorities in England.

16. Edward Said, 'Yeats and Decolonization', *Literature in the Modern World: Critical Essays and Documents*, ed. Dennis Walder (Oxford: Oxford University Press and Open University Press, 1990), p. 36.

17. Quoted in Stephen Kern, *The Culture of Time and Space 1880–1918* (Cambridge, MA: Harvard University Press, 1983), p. 18.

18. In Marcel Proust, *Remembrance of Things Past* (1913–27), trans. C.K. Scott Moncrieff and Terence Kilmartin (Harmondsworth: Penguin, 1983), II, p. 1029, Marcel records his lover Albertine's absolute wonder at finding that she is able to visit by car, in a single afternoon, several villages previously separated from each other by a day's journey.

19. As well as apparently misunderstanding Bergson's philosophy, Moszkowski gives the wrong date for Max Planck's Nobel Prize.

20. Anton Giulio Bragaglia, 'Futurist Photodynamism' (1911), rpt. in Umbro Apollonio, ed., *Futurist Manifestos* (London: Thames and Hudson, 1973), p. 39. See also pp. 14–15 and pp. 39–40 for an account of the work of Muybridge and Marey. *Futurist Manifestos* also reproduces 'Dynamism of a Dog on a Leash' and 'Little Girl Running on a Balcony', Figures 30 and 31.

21. The quotation is from the opening page (15) of the first United States edition of *Tarr* (New York: Alfred Knopf, 1918). Neither the serialization of the novel in *The Egoist*, nor the one-volume British edition of 1918 (from which other quotations in this study are taken), nor Lewis's revised edition of 1927 contains the strange form of punctuation '.='. But there is evidence that the edition published in the United States was closest to Lewis's original manuscript and reproduces the form of punctuation he chose for it.

22. Hugh Kenner, *The Stoic Comedians: Flaubert, Joyce and Beckett* (London: University of California Press, 1962), p. 59.

23. The phrase was coined by Herbert Spencer, but accepted by Darwin himself.

24. Virginia Woolf, 'The Leaning Tower' (1940), rpt. in *Collected Essays* (London: Hogarth, 1966), II, pp. 166–7.

25. Letters of 4/5 August 1914, 10 August 1914, 18 June 1915, 2 September 1914, in *The Letters of Henry James*, selected and edited by Percy Lubbock (London: Macmillan, 1920), pp. 398, 403, 493, 416–17; Wyndham Lewis quoted in Michael Levenson, *A Genealogy of Modernism* (Cambridge: Cambridge University Press, 1984), p. 9.

26. Virginia Woolf, 'The Leaning Tower' (note 24), pp. 167, 170.

27. Bakhtin, of course, refers to an earlier period of history than the one beginning around 1840 which Lawrence describes. Lawrence stresses, however, that the quality of life the Brangwens enjoyed at this time had lasted more or less unchanged for centuries. And Bakhtin suggests (pp. 217–18) that the 'ancient matrices' he discusses occasionally survive or leave 'traces' in the literature of later periods.

28. Quoted in Harry T. Moore, *The Priest of Love: A Life of D.H. Lawrence* (London: Heinemann, 1974), p. 73; Lawrence, letter of 5 June 1914, *Collected Letters* (note 4), I, p. 282.

29. Lawrence, letter of 5 June 1914 (note 28).

30. D.H. Lawrence, letter of 19 December 1916, in Aldous Huxley, ed., *The Letters of D.H. Lawrence* (London: Heinemann, 1932), p. 386.

31. The Kaiser's remark 'I never wanted this' is quoted in Alan Palmer, *The Kaiser: Warlord of the Second Reich* (London: Weidenfeld and Nicolson, 1978), p. 188. The remark grew famous in Britain after the war was over.

32. D.H. Lawrence, letter of 27 July 1917, *Collected Letters* (note 4), I, p. 519.

33. Italo Calvino, *If on a Winter's Night a Traveller*, trans. William Weaver (London: Picador, 1982), p. 13.

34. T.S. Eliot, 'Ulysses, Order, and Myth' (1923), rpt. in Frank Kermode, ed., *Selected Prose of T.S. Eliot* (London: Faber and Faber, 1975), p. 177.

CHAPTER 4

1. Henry James, 'The Younger Generation' (1914), rpt. in Leon Edel and Gordon N. Ray, eds, *Henry James and H.G. Wells* (London: Rupert Hart-Davis, 1958), p. 215; Henry James, 'The Art of Fiction' (1884), rpt. in Leon Edel, ed., *The House of Fiction: Essays on the Novel by Henry James* (London: Rupert Hart-Davis, 1957), pp. 23–4.

2. Virginia Woolf, *A Writer's Diary: Being Extracts from the Diary of Virginia Woolf*, ed. Leonard Woolf (1953; rpt. London: Triad, 1985), p. 178.

3. Stephen Spender, *The Struggle of the Modern* (London: Hamish Hamilton, 1963), p. x; Katherine Mansfield, 'A Ship Comes into Harbour' (1919), rpt. in Bonnie Kime Scott, ed., *The Gender of Modernism: A Critical Anthology* (Bloomington and Indianapolis: Indiana University Press, 1990), p. 313.

4. Quoted in Jean Radford, Introduction to May Sinclair, *Mary Olivier: A Life* (1919; rpt. London: Virago, 1980), p. [vii]; Wyndham Lewis, letter of March 1916, in W.K. Rose, ed., *The Letters of Wyndham Lewis* (London: Methuen, 1963), p. 76.

5. Preface to *The Portrait of a Lady*, rpt. in *The Art of the Novel: Critical Prefaces*, ed. R.P. Blackmur (London: Charles Scribner, 1934), p. 46ff.

6. Quoted in Frank Budgen, *James Joyce and the Making of Ulysses* (London: Grayson & Grayson, 1934), p. 180.

7. ibid., p. 263.

8. ibid., p. 263.

9. Eugene Jolas, 'The Revolution of Language and James Joyce' in Samuel Beckett et al., *Our Exagmination Round his Factification for Incamination of Work in Progress* (1929; rpt. London: Faber and Faber, 1972), p. 79.

10. Friedrich Nietzsche, 'The Wanderer and his Shadow' (1880), rpt. in *Human, all too Human: A Book for Free Spirits*, trans. R.J. Hollingdale (Cambridge: Cambridge University Press, 1986), p. 306; *Human, all too Human*, p. 16.
11. 'Revolution in Science: New Theory of the Universe: Newtonian Ideas Overthrown', *The Times*, 7 November 1919, p. 12.
12. Not all printed texts of *Ulysses* include that final full stop. It appears in Hans Walter Gebler's 'Corrected Text', published in 1984, though a good deal of doubt has since been cast on this edition's accuracy. The Penguin edition otherwise followed throughout this study does not have the dot, but evidence from other sources strongly suggests that it should be there. I am grateful to Fritz Senn of the James Joyce Institute, Zurich, for confirming this conclusion and for clarification of the issue in general.
13. 'Forward in the West', 'The Battle of the Somme', 'The Day Goes Well', *The Times*, 3 July 1916, pp. 8, 9, 10.
14. Harold Pinter, 'Writing for the Theatre': speech to the National Student Drama Festival, 1962, included as Introduction to Harold Pinter, *Plays: One* (London: Methuen, 1976), p. 14.
15. F.T. Marinetti, 'Destruction of Syntax – Imagination without Strings – Words-in-Freedom' (1913), rpt. in Umbro Apollonio, ed., *Futurist Manifestos* (London: Thames and Hudson, 1973), p. 95; Samuel Beckett, 'Dante . . . Bruno. Vico.. Joyce' in Samuel Beckett et al., *Our Exagmination Round his Factification for Incamination of Work in Progress* (1929; rpt. London: Faber and Faber, 1972), p. 14.
16. Fredric Jameson, *Fables of Aggression: Wyndham Lewis, the Modernist as Fascist* (London: University of California Press, 1979), p. 123.
17. Ezra Pound, 'Paris Letter', *The Dial*, June 1922, p. 625.

CHAPTER 5

1. *Collected Essays* (London: Hogarth Press, 1966), II, p. 172.
2. Christopher Isherwood, Foreword (1957) to *All the Conspirators* (1928; rpt. London: Methuen, 1984), p. 7.
3. Ford Madox Ford, *Joseph Conrad: A Personal Remembrance* (London: Duckworth, 1924), pp. 129–30; Christopher Isherwood, *Lions and Shadows* (1938; rpt. London: Methuen, 1982), p. 182.
4. Graham Greene, 'God and Literature and So Forth', interview with Anthony Burgess, *The Observer*, 16 March 1980, p. 33.
5. Christopher Isherwood, Foreword to *All the Conspirators* (note 2), p. 8; George Orwell, 'Inside the Whale' (1940), rpt. in Sonia Orwell and Ian Angus, eds, *The Collected Essays, Journalism and Letters of George Orwell* (1968; rpt. Harmondsworth: Penguin, 1970), I, p. 557.

6. See Karl Radek, 'James Joyce or Socialist Realism', a report delivered at the Congress of Soviet Writers, August 1934, rpt. in Robert H. Deming, *James Joyce: the Critical Heritage* (London: Routledge and Kegan Paul, 1970), II, pp. 624–6.

7. Georg Lukács, 'The Ideology of Modernism' (1957), rpt. in Terry Eagleton and Drew Milne, eds, *Marxist Literary Theory: A Reader* (Oxford: Blackwell, 1996), pp. 148, 147, 152, 148, 144, 154, 147, 155.

8. T.S. Eliot, 'Ulysses, Order, and Myth' (1923), rpt. in Frank Kermode, ed., *Selected Prose of T.S. Eliot* (London: Faber and Faber, 1975), p. 177.

9. Malcolm Lowry, letter of 2 January 1946, rpt. in Harvey Breit and Marjorie Bonner Lowry, eds, *Selected Letters of Malcolm Lowry* (1967; rpt. Harmondsworth: Penguin, 1985), p. 66.

10. Roland Barthes, *Image Music Text*, trans. Stephen Heath (London: Fontana, 1982), p. 163; Roland Barthes, *S/Z*, trans. Richard Miller (New York: Hill and Wang, 1974), p. 4.

11. In *The Concept of Modernism* (Ithaca and London: Cornell University Press, 1990) Astradur Eysteinsson argues that 'modernism contains the rudiments of an adversary culture . . . tends to negate the cultural experience most readily furthered by bourgeois society . . . problematizes and seeks to interrupt the predominant modes of communication in this society' (p. 222).

12. Wallace Stevens, 'Of Modern Poetry', *The Collected Poems of Wallace Stevens* (London: Faber and Faber, 1955), pp. 239–40.

# SELECT BIBLIOGRAPHY

FICTION

Alain-Fournier, *Le Grand Meaulnes*, 1913, trans. Frank Davidson, Harmondsworth: Penguin, 1974.

Aldington, Richard, *Death of a Hero*, 1929 (rpt. London: Hogarth, 1984).

Beckett, Samuel, *The Beckett Trilogy: Molloy, Malone Dies, The Unnamable*, 1950–2 (rpt. London: Picador, 1983).

Conrad, Joseph, *Chance*, 1913 (rpt. Harmondsworth: Penguin, 1984).

Conrad, Joseph, *Heart of Darkness*, 1902 (rpt. Harmondsworth: Penguin, 1995).

Conrad, Joseph, *Lord Jim*, 1900 (rpt. Harmondsworth: Penguin, 1968).

Conrad, Joseph, *Nostromo*, 1904 (rpt. Harmondsworth: Penguin, 1969).

Conrad, Joseph, *The Nigger of the 'Narcissus': Typhoon and Other Stories*, 1897, 1903 (rpt. Harmondsworth: Penguin, 1968).

Conrad, Joseph, *The Secret Agent*, 1907 (rpt. Harmondsworth: Penguin, 1967).

Conrad, Joseph, *Under Western Eyes*, 1911 (rpt. Harmondsworth: Penguin, 1975).

Conrad, Joseph, *Victory*, 1915 (rpt. Harmondsworth: Penguin, 1976).

Dickens, Charles, *David Copperfield*, 1849–50 (rpt. Harmondsworth: Penguin, 1977).

Dujardin, Edouard, *Les lauriers sont coupés*, 1888 (rpt. Paris: Albert Messein, 1925).

Faulkner, William, *The Sound and the Fury*, 1929 (rpt. Harmondsworth: Penguin, 1971).

Fitzgerald, F. Scott, *The Beautiful and Damned*, 1922 (rpt. Harmondsworth: Penguin, 1974).

Fitzgerald, F. Scott, *The Great Gatsby*, 1926 (rpt. Harmondsworth: Penguin, 1968).

Ford, Ford Madox, *The Good Soldier*, 1915 (rpt. Harmondsworth: Penguin, 1977).

Ford, Ford Madox, *Parade's End*, 1924–8 (rpt. Harmondsworth: Penguin, 1982).

Forster, E.M., *Howards End*, 1910 (rpt. Harmondsworth: Penguin, 1969).

Forster, E.M., *A Passage to India*, 1924 (rpt. Harmondsworth: Penguin, 1967).

Gibbon, Lewis Grassic (James Leslie Mitchell), *A Scots Quair*, 1932–4 (rpt. London: Pan, 1982).

Greene, Graham, *England Made Me*, 1935 (rpt. Harmondsworth: Penguin, 1982).

Hemingway, Ernest, *The Essential Hemingway*, London: Panther, 1977.

Huxley, Aldous, *Antic Hay*, 1923 (rpt. Harmondsworth: Penguin, 1976).

Huxley, Aldous, *Crome Yellow*, 1921 (rpt. London: Triad, 1977).

Huxley, Aldous, *Point Counter Point*, 1928 (rpt. Harmondsworth: Penguin, 1975).

Isherwood, Christopher, *All the Conspirators*, 1928 (rpt. London: Methuen, 1984).

Isherwood, Christopher, *Goodbye to Berlin*, 1939 (rpt. London: Panther, 1977).

Isherwood, Christopher, *Mr Norris Changes Trains*, 1935 (rpt. London: Panther, 1977).

Isherwood, Christopher, *The Memorial*, 1932 (rpt. London: Panther, 1978).

James, Henry, *The Ambassadors*, 1903 (rpt. Harmondsworth: Penguin, 1973).

James, Henry, *The Portrait of a Lady*, 1881 (rpt. Harmondsworth: Penguin, 1973).

James, Henry, *What Maisie Knew*, 1897 (rpt. Harmondsworth: Penguin, 1977).

Joyce, James, *A Portrait of the Artist as a Young Man*, 1916 (rpt. Harmondsworth: Penguin, 1973).

Joyce, James, *Dubliners*, 1914 (rpt. Harmondsworth: Penguin, 1971).

Joyce, James, *Finnegans Wake*, 1939 (rpt. London: Faber and Faber, 1971).

Joyce, James, *Stephen Hero*, 1944 (rpt. London: Panther, 1977).

Joyce, James, *Ulysses*, 1922 (rpt. Harmondsworth: Penguin, 1992).

Lawrence, D.H., *England My England*, 1924 (rpt. Harmondsworth: Penguin, 1960).

Lawrence, D.H., *Kangaroo*, 1923 (rpt. Harmondsworth: Penguin, 1976).

Lawrence, D.H., *Lady Chatterley's Lover*, 1928 (rpt. Harmondsworth: Penguin, 1982).

Lawrence, D.H., *Sons and Lovers*, 1913 (rpt. Harmondsworth: Penguin, 1968).

Lawrence, D.H., *St Mawr and the Virgin and the Gypsy*, 1925, 1930 (rpt. Harmondsworth: Penguin, 1988).

Lawrence, D.H., *The Lost Girl*, 1920 (rpt. Harmondsworth: Penguin, 1977).

Lawrence, D.H., *The Plumed Serpent*, 1926 (rpt. Harmondsworth: Penguin, 1995).

Lawrence, D.H., *The Rainbow*, 1915 (rpt. Harmondsworth: Penguin, 1971).

Lawrence, D.H., *Three Novellas: The Fox, The Ladybird, The Captain's Doll*, 1923 (rpt. Harmondsworth: Penguin, 1971).

Lawrence, D.H., *Women in Love*, 1921 (rpt. Harmondsworth: Penguin, 1971).

Lewis, Wyndham, *Tarr*, London: The Egoist Press, 1918.

Lewis, Wyndham, *The Apes of God*, 1930 (rpt. Santa Barbara, CA: Black Sparrow Press, 1981).

Lewis, Wyndham, *The Childermass*, London: Chatto and Windus, 1928.

Lewis, Wyndham, *The Wild Body*, London: Chatto and Windus, 1927.

Lowry, Malcolm, *Under the Volcano*, 1947 (rpt. Harmondsworth: Penguin, 1983).

Mackenzie, Compton, *Sinister Street*, 1913–14 (rpt. Harmondsworth: Penguin, 1983).

Mansfield, Katherine, *The Collected Short Stories of Katherine Mansfield*, Harmondsworth: Penguin, 1981.

O'Brien, Flann, *At Swim-Two-Birds*, 1939 (rpt. Harmondsworth: Penguin, 1975).

Orwell, George, *A Clergyman's Daughter*, 1935 (rpt. Harmondsworth: Penguin, 1982).

Orwell, George, *Coming up for Air*, 1939 (rpt. Harmondsworth: Penguin, 1962).

Proust, Marcel, *Remembrance of Things Past*, 1913–27, trans. C.K. Scott Moncrieff and Terence Kilmartin, 3 vols, Harmondsworth: Penguin, 1983.

Remarque, Erich Maria, *All Quiet on the Western Front*, 1929, trans. A.W. Wheen, London: Mayflower, 1968.

Richardson, Dorothy, *Pilgrimage*, 1915–67 (rpt. in 4 vols, London: Virago, 1979).

Sinclair, May, *Life and Death of Harriett Frean*, 1922 (rpt. London: Virago, 1980).

Sinclair, May, *Mary Olivier: A Life*, 1919 (rpt. London: Virago, 1980).

Stein, Gertrude, *Look at Me Now and Here I Am: Writings and Lectures 1909–45*, Harmondsworth: Penguin, 1971.

Stein, Gertrude, *The Making of Americans*, 1925 (rpt. London: Peter Owen, 1968).

Tomlinson, H.M., *All Our Yesterdays*, London: Heinemann, 1930.

Wells, H.G., *Tono-Bungay*, 1909 (rpt. London: Pan, 1972).

West, Rebecca, *The Return of the Soldier*, 1918 (rpt. London: Virago, 1980).

Woolf, Virginia, *Between the Acts*, 1941 (rpt. London: Panther, 1978).

Woolf, Virginia, *Jacob's Room*, 1922 (rpt. London: Panther, 1976).
Woolf, Virginia, *Mrs Dalloway*, 1926 (rpt. Harmondsworth: Penguin, 1976).
Woolf, Virginia, *Orlando*, 1928 (rpt. Harmondsworth: Penguin, 1975).
Woolf, Virginia, *To the Lighthouse*, 1927 (rpt. Harmondsworth: Penguin, 1973).
Woolf, Virginia, *The Waves*, 1931 (rpt. Harmondsworth: Penguin, 1973).

BACKGROUND AND CRITICAL

Adorno, Theodor, *Aesthetic Theory*, 1970, ed. Gretel Adorno and Rolf Tiedemann, trans. C. Lenhardt, London: Routledge and Kegan Paul, 1984.
Apollonio, Umbro (ed.), *Futurist Manifestos*, London: Thames and Hudson, 1973.
Bakhtin, Mikhail, *The Dialogic Imagination: Four Essays*, ed. Michael Holquist, trans. Caryl Emerson and Michael Holquist, Austin: University of Texas Press, 1981.
Barthes, Roland, *Image Music Text*, trans. Stephen Heath, London: Fontana, 1982.
Barthes, Roland, *S/Z*, trans. Richard Miller, New York: Hill and Wang, 1974.
Beckett, Samuel et al., *Our Exagmination Round his Factification for Incamination of Work in Progress*, 1929 (rpt. London: Faber and Faber, 1972).
Benjamin, Walter, *Illuminations*, 1955, ed. Hannah Arendt, trans. Harry Zohn, New York: Schocken Books, 1968.
Bergson, Henri, *Creative Evolution*, 1907, trans. Arthur Mitchell, London: Macmillan, 1911.
Bergson, Henri, *Durée et simultanéité: à propos de la théorie d'Einstein*, Paris: Librairie Felix Alcan, 1922.
Bergson, Henri, *Mind Energy: Lectures and Essays*, 1919, trans. H. Wildon Carr, London: Macmillan, 1920.
Bergson, Henri, *Time and Free Will: An Essay on the Immediate Data of Consciousness*, 1889, trans. F.L. Pogson, London: George Allen and Unwin, 1971.
Bloomfield, Morton W. (ed.), *The Interpretation of Narrative: Theory and Practice*, Cambridge, MA: Harvard University Press, 1970.
Bradbury, Malcolm, *The Modern British Novel*, London: Secker and Warburg, 1993.
Bradbury, Malcolm and James McFarlane (eds), *Modernism: 1890–1930*, Harmondsworth: Pelican, 1976.
Brooker, Peter (ed.), *Modernism/Postmodernism*, London: Longman, 1992.

Budgen, Frank, *James Joyce and the Making of Ulysses*, London: Grayson & Grayson, 1934.

Bullett, Gerald, *Modern English Fiction: A Personal View*, London: Herbert Jenkins, 1926.

Butler, Christopher, *After the Wake: Essays on the Contemporary Avant Garde*, Oxford: Oxford University Press, 1980.

Butler, Christopher, *Early Modernism: Literature, Music and Painting in Europe, 1900–1916*, Oxford: Clarendon Press, 1994.

Carey, John, *The Intellectuals and the Masses: Pride and Prejudice among the Literary Intelligentsia, 1880–1939*, London: Faber and Faber, 1992.

Carruthers, John, *Scheherazade: or the Future of the English Novel*, London: Kegan Paul, Trench, Trubner and Co., 1928.

Chefdor, Monique, Ricardo Quinones and Albert Wachtel (eds), *Modernism: Challenges and Perspectives*, Chicago: University of Illinois Press, 1986.

Cohn, Dorrit, *Transparent Minds: Narrative Modes for Presenting Consciousness in Fiction*, Princeton, NJ: Princeton University Press, 1978.

Daiches, David, *The Novel and the Modern World*, Cambridge: Cambridge University Press, 1960.

Deming, Robert H. (ed.), *James Joyce: The Critical Heritage*, 2 vols, London: Routledge and Kegan Paul, 1970.

Drew, Elizabeth, *The Modern Novel: Some Aspects of Contemporary Fiction*, London: Jonathan Cape, 1926.

Dunne, J.W., *An Experiment with Time*, London: A. and C. Black, 1927.

Eagleton, Terry, *Criticism and Ideology: A Study in Marxist Literary Theory*, London: Verso, 1976.

Eagleton, Terry and Drew Milne (eds), *Marxist Literary Theory: A Reader*, Oxford: Blackwell, 1996.

Edel, Leon, and Gordon N. Ray (eds), *Henry James and H.G. Wells*, London: Rupert Hart-Davis, 1958.

Eliot, T.S., *Selected Prose of T.S. Eliot*, ed. Frank Kermode, London: Faber and Faber, 1975.

Ellmann, Richard, *James Joyce*, Oxford: Oxford University Press, 1982.

Eysteinsson, Astradur, *The Concept of Modernism*, Ithaca, NY: Cornell University Press, 1990.

Faulkner, Peter, *Modernism*, London: Methuen, 1977.

Faulkner, Peter (ed.), *A Modernist Reader: Modernism in England 1910–1930*, London: Batsford, 1986.

Ford, Ford Madox, *Joseph Conrad: A Personal Remembrance*, London: Duckworth, 1924.

Ford, Ford Madox (as Ford Madox Hueffer), *The Critical Attitude*, London: Duckworth, 1911.

Forster, E.M., *Aspects of the Novel*, 1927 (rpt. Harmondsworth: Penguin, 1971).

Foucault, Michel, *The Order of Things: An Archaeology of the Human Sciences*, 1966, London: Tavistock, 1970.

Fox, Ralph, *The Novel and the People*, London: Lawrence and Wishart, 1937.

Freud, Sigmund, *The Interpretation of Dreams*, 1899, trans. A.A. Brill, London: George Allen and Co., 1913.

Friedman, Alan, *The Turn of the Novel*, New York: Oxford University Press, 1966.

Fussell, Paul, *The Great War and Modern Memory*, London: Oxford University Press, 1979.

Genette, Gérard, *Narrative Discourse*, 1972, trans. Jane E. Lewin, Oxford: Blackwell, 1986.

Gilbert, Sandra M. and Susan Gubar, *No Man's Land: The Place of the Woman Writer in the Twentieth Century*, 3 vols, London: Yale University Press, 1988–1994.

Gilbert, Sandra M. and Susan Gubar (eds) *The Female Imagination and the Modernist Aesthetic*, London: Gordon and Breach, 1986.

Habermas, Jürgen, *The Philosophical Discourse of Modernity*, Cambridge: Polity, 1987.

Hassan, Ihab, *The Postmodern Turn: Essays in Postmodern Theory and Culture*, Lincoln: Ohio State University Press, 1987.

Heidsieck, François, *Henri Bergson et la notion de l'éspace*, Paris: Le Circle du Livre, 1957.

Henderson, Philip, *The Novel Today: A Study in Contemporary Attitudes*, London: John Lane, 1936.

Isherwood, Christopher, *Lions and Shadows: An Education in the Twenties*, 1938 (rpt. London: Methuen, 1982).

James, Henry, *Notes on Novelists: with some other Notes*, London: Dent, 1914.

James, Henry, *The Art of Fiction and Other Essays*, New York: Oxford University Press, 1948.

James, Henry, *The Art of the Novel: Critical Prefaces*, ed. R.P. Blackmur, London: Charles Scribner's Sons, 1934.

James, Henry, *The House of Fiction: Essays on the Novel*, ed. Leon Edel, London: Rupert Hart-Davis, 1957.

James, Henry, *The Letters of Henry James*, 2 vols, selected and edited by Percy Lubbock, London: Macmillan, 1920.

James, William, *The Principles of Psychology*, 2 vols, London: Macmillan, 1890.

Jameson, Fredric, *The Political Unconscious: Narrative as a Socially Symbolic Act*, London: Methuen, 1981.

Joyce, James, *Selected Letters of James Joyce*, ed. Richard Ellmann, London: Faber and Faber, 1975.

Keating, Peter, *The Haunted Study: A Social History of the English Novel 1875–1914*, London: Secker and Warburg, 1989.

Kenner, Hugh, *Joyce's Voices*, London: Faber and Faber, 1978.

Kermode, Frank, *Lawrence*, London: Fontana, 1985.

Kern, Stephen, *The Culture of Time and Space 1880–1918*, Cambridge, MA: Harvard University Press, 1983.

Kiely, Robert (ed.), *Modernism Reconsidered*, London: Harvard University Press, 1983.

Kristeva, Julia, *Desire in Language: A Semiotic Approach to Literature and Art*, 1977, ed. Leon S. Roudiez, trans. Thomas Gora, Alice Jardine and Leon S. Roudiez, Oxford: Blackwell, 1981.

Kumar, Shiv K., *Bergson and the Stream of Consciousness Novel*, London: Blackie, 1962.

Lacan, Jacques, *The Four Fundamental Concepts of Psycho-Analysis*, 1973, ed. Jacques-Alain Miller, trans. Alan Sheridan, Harmondsworth: Penguin, 1977.

Lawrence, D.H., *Apocalypse*, 1931 (rpt. Harmondsworth: Penguin, 1981).

Lawrence, D.H., *Collected Letters*, ed. Harry T. Moore, 2 vols, London: Heinemann, 1962.

Lawrence, D.H., *Fantasia of the Unconscious and Psychoanalysis and the Unconscious*, 1923 (rpt. London: Heinemann, 1961).

Lawrence, D.H., *Selected Literary Criticism*, ed. Anthony Beal, London: Heinemann, 1955.

Leavis, F.R., *New Bearings in English Poetry*, London: Chatto and Windus, 1932.

Levenson, Michael H., *A Genealogy of Modernism: A Study of English Literary Doctrine 1908–1922*, Cambridge: Cambridge University Press, 1984.

Levenson, Michael H., *Modernism and the Fate of Individuality: Character and Novelistic Form from Conrad to Woolf*, Cambridge: Cambridge University Press, 1991.

Lewis, Wyndham (ed.), *Blast*, 2 vols, 1914 and 1915 (rpt. Santa Barbara, CA: Black Sparrow Press, 1981).

Lewis, Wyndham, *Men without Art*, 1934 (rpt. New York: Russell and Russell, 1964).

Lewis, Wyndham, *Paleface*, London: Chatto and Windus, 1929.

Lewis, Wyndham, *The Art of Being Ruled*, London: Chatto and Windus, 1926.

Lewis, Wyndham, *Time and Western Man*, London: Chatto and Windus, 1927.

Lodge, David, *After Bakhtin: Essays on Fiction and Criticism*, London: Routledge, 1990.

Lubbock, Percy, *The Craft of Fiction*, London: Jonathan Cape, 1921.

Lukács, Georg, *History and Class Consciousness: Studies in Marxist Dialectics*, 1923, trans. Rodney Livingstone, London: Merlin Press, 1990.

Lukács, Georg, 'The Ideology of Modernism', 1957, rpt. in Terry Eagleton and Drew Milne (eds), *Marxist Literary Theory: A Reader*, Oxford: Blackwell, 1996, pp. 141–62.

Marx, Karl, *Capital: A Critique of Political Economy*, 1867–94, trans. Ben Fowkes, 3 vols, Harmondsworth: Penguin, 1979.

McHale, Brian, *Postmodernist Fiction*, London: Methuen, 1987.

Miller, Jane Eldridge, *Rebel Women: Feminism, Modernism and the Edwardian Novel*, London: Virago, 1994.

Milton, Colin, *Lawrence and Nietzsche: A Study in Influence*, Aberdeen: Aberdeen University Press, 1987.

Moszkowski, Alexander, *Einstein the Searcher: His Work Explained from Dialogues with Einstein*, trans. Henry L. Brose, London: Methuen, 1921.

Nicholls, Peter, *Modernisms: A Literary Guide*, London: Macmillan, 1995.

Nietzsche, Friedrich, *Beyond Good and Evil: Prelude to a Philosophy of the Future*, 1886, trans. R.J. Hollingdale, Harmondsworth: Penguin, 1990.

Nietzsche, Friedrich, *Human, all too Human: A Book for Free Spirits*, 1880, trans. R.J. Hollingdale, Cambridge: Cambridge University Press, 1986.

Nietzsche, Friedrich, *The Birth Of Tragedy and the Genealogy of Morals*, 1871, 1887, trans. Francis Golffing, New York: Doubleday, 1956.

Nietzsche, Friedrich, *The Gay Science*, 1882, trans. Walter Kaufmann, New York: Vintage Books, 1974.

Nietzsche, Friedrich, *The Will to Power*, 1901, trans. Walter Kaufmann and R.J. Hollingdale. London: Weidenfeld and Nicolson, 1968.

Nietzsche, Friedrich, *Thus Spoke Zarathustra: A Book for Everyone and No One*, 1892, trans. R.J. Hollingdale, Harmondsworth: Penguin, 1971.

Orr, John, *The Making of the Twentieth-Century Novel: Lawrence, Joyce, Faulkner and Beyond*, London: Macmillan, 1987.

Orwell, George, *The Collected Essays, Journalism and Letters of George Orwell*, ed. Sonia Orwell and Ian Angus, 4 vols, 1968 (rpt. Harmondsworth: Penguin, 1970).

Pinkney, Tony, *D.H. Lawrence and Modernism*, Hemel Hempstead: Harvester Wheatsheaf, 1990.

Priestley, J.B., *Literature and Western Man*, London: Heinemann, 1960.

Quennell, Peter, *A Letter to Mrs. Virginia Woolf*, London: Hogarth Press, 1932.

Quinones, Ricardo, *Mapping Literary Modernism: Time and Development*, Princeton, NJ: Princeton University Press, 1985.

Read, Herbert, *Art Now: An Introduction to the Theory of Modern Painting and Sculpture*, London: Faber and Faber, 1933.

Richards, Jeffrey and John M. Mackenzie, *The Railway Station: A Social History*, Oxford: Oxford University Press, 1988.

Robbe-Grillet, Alain, *Snapshots and Towards a New Novel*, 1963, trans. Barbara Wright, London: Calder and Boyars, 1965.

Robson, W.W., *Modern English Literature*, Oxford: Oxford University Press, 1970.

Russell, Bertrand, *The ABC of Relativity*, London: Kegan Paul, Trench, Trubner and Co., 1926.

Schwartz, Stanford, *The Matrix of Modernism*, Princeton, NJ: Princeton University Press, 1985.

Scott, Bonnie Kime (ed.), *The Gender of Modernism: A Critical Anthology*, Bloomington and Indianapolis: Indiana University Press, 1990.

Scott-James, R.A., *Modernism and Romance*, London: John Lane, 1908.

Smyth, Edmund (ed.), *Postmodernism and Contemporary Fiction*, London: Batsford, 1991.

Spender, Stephen, *The Struggle of the Modern*, London: Hamish Hamilton, 1963.

Spengler, Oswald, *The Decline of the West*, 1918–22, trans. Charles Francis Atkinson, London: G. Allen and Unwin, 1934.

Stevenson, John, *British Society 1914–45*, London: Allen Lane, 1984.

Stevenson, Randall, *A Reader's Guide to the Twentieth-Century Novel in Britain*, Hemel Hempstead: Harvester Wheatsheaf, 1993.

Taylor, Frederick W., *The Principles of Scientific Management*, New York and London: Harper and Brothers, 1911.

Trilling, Lionel, *The Liberal Imagination*, London: Secker and Warburg, 1951.

Trotter, David, *The English Novel in History, 1895–1920*, London: Routledge, 1993.

Walder, Dennis (ed.), *Literature in the Modern World: Critical Essays and Documents*, Oxford: Oxford University Press and Open University Press, 1990.

Walpole, Hugh, *A Letter to a Modern Novelist*, London: Hogarth, 1932.

Waugh, Patricia (ed.), *Revolutions of the Word: Intellectual Contexts for the Study of Modern Literature*, London: Arnold, 1997.

West, Alick, *Crisis and Criticism*, London: Lawrence and Wishart, 1937.

Williams, Raymond, 'The Metropolis and the Emergence of Modernism', rpt. in Peter Brooker (ed.), *Modernism/Postmodernism*, London: Longman, 1992, pp. 82–93.

Woolf, Virginia, *A Room of One's Own*, 1928 (rpt. Harmondsworth: Penguin, 1975).

Woolf, Virginia, *A Writer's Diary: Being Extracts from the Diary of Virginia Woolf*, ed. Leonard Woolf, 1953 (rpt. London: Triad, 1985).

Woolf, Virginia, *Collected Essays*, 4 vols, London: Hogarth Press, 1966.

Woolf, Virginia, *The Letters of Virginia Woolf*, 6 vols, ed. Nigel Nicholson and Joanne Trautmann, London: Chatto, 1975–80.

Zegger, Hrisey Dimitrakis, *May Sinclair*, Boston: Twayne, 1976.

# INDEX